Law and American Literature

A Collection of Essays

BORZOI BOOKS IN LAW AND AMERICAN SOCIETY

Law and American Literature

A Collection of Essays

Carl S. Smith
Northwestern University

John P. McWilliams, Jr.
Middlebury College

Maxwell Bloomfield
Catholic University of America

ALFRED A. KNOPF   NEW YORK

This book was originally developed as part of an American Bar Association program on law and humanities with major funding from the National Endowment for the Humanities and additional support from the Exxon Education Foundation and Pew Memorial Trust. The ABA established this program to help foster improved understanding among undergraduates of the role of law in society through the creation of a series of volumes in law and humanities. The ABA selected a special advisory committee of scholars, lawyers, and jurists (Commission on Undergraduate Education in Law and the Humanities) to identify appropriate topics and select writers. This book is a revised version of the volume first published by the ABA. However, the writer, and not the American Bar Association, individual members and committees of the Commission, the National Endowment for the Humanities, Exxon Education Foundation, or Pew Memorial Trust, bears sole responsibility for the content, analysis, and conclusion contained herein.

THIS IS A BORZOI BOOK
PUBLISHED BY ALFRED A. KNOPF, INC.

First Edition
9 8 7 6 5 4 3 2 1
Copyright © 1983 by Alfred A. Knopf, Inc.

LIBRARY OF CONGRESS CATALOGING IN PUBLICATION DATA

Smith, Carl S.
Law and American literature.

(Borzoi books in law and American society)
Bibliography: p.
1. American literature—History and criticism—Addresses, essays, lectures. 2. Law and literature—Addresses, essays, lectures. 3. Law and literature—Addresses, essays, lectures. 4. Law and literature—History and criticism—Addresses, essays, lectures.
I. McWilliams, John P. II. Bloomfield, Maxwell H.
III. Title. IV. Series.
PS169.L37S64 1982   808'.06634021   82-21345
ISBN 0-394-33190-7 (paperbound)   0-394-33574-0 (hardbound)

Manufactured in the United States of America

Preface

This book seeks to develop further a recent trend in legal and literary scholarship. Students of literature have become increasingly interested in the broad literary questions of style, meaning, and interpretation that appear with special clarity and urgency in legal writing but that have wide application to all literature. Likewise, legal scholars, who have long acknowledged both the importance of style in legal writing and the insights of creative writers into legal issues, are examining how critical methods developed for the analysis of imaginative literature may apply to their own work. Literary and legal journals have begun to feature articles or even whole issues on law and literature, while sessions of the Modern Language Association and law school classes have been devoted to the same topic.

The three essays in this volume study the interrelationship of American law and literature from the point of view of the literary scholar and the cultural historian. Carl Smith's essay, "Law as Form and Theme in American Letters," considers two broad subject areas. In the first part of the essay, Smith explains how the ways in which the law uses language affect our sense of whether legal writing is or is not "literary." Smith finds that legal writing is a special language, but one that has many literary qualities important to its function. In the second part of the essay, he traces a central tradition of criticism of the law in the work of several of America's most distinguished writers.

Although John McWilliams's essay, "Innocent Criminal or Criminal Innocence: The Trial in American Fiction," seems the narrowest in scope of the three, it is in some ways the most broad-ranging in method because it demonstrates how legal study and the analysis of specific literary works can be fruitfully combined. McWilliams's purpose is to explore how the law functions as both a moral and institutional standard for conduct in four major American novels that climax in a criminal trial. The four novels are Cooper's *The Pioneers,* Melville's *Billy Budd,* Dreiser's *An American Tragedy,* and Wright's *Native Son.* He analyzes these books (and several others) in the larger contexts of the actual cases on which they were based, the political and social outlooks of the authors, and contemporary developments in legal thought. Thus, he speaks of *Billy Budd* in relation to the *Somers* mutiny and Holmes's *The Common Law,* and he explores the links between legal and literary realism in works by Dreiser, Darrow, and Roscoe Pound. All four novels, McWilliams points out, raise important moral, social, and legal questions about the meaning of the terms *guilt* and *innocence.* The four novels both contain and mirror changing legal ideas about the purposes of criminal justice.

Maxwell Bloomfield's "Law and Lawyers in American Popular Culture" surveys a rich and largely unexplored body of literary works aimed at a general audience, in order to reconstruct the image of legal figures in American life. He focuses on the early years of the Republic and on the Porgressive era, but his essay has broader application since it shows how popular literature helps us understand the public's opinions of lawyers, courts, and the general workings of the legal system. Bloomfield is concerned with how popular literature has reflected public opinion and shaped both the public's knowledge of the law and people's expectations of how the law serves society. In each period that he examines, he shows how popular literature defines models of legal figures to be admired or despised—such as the ideal republican lawyer and the rascally pettifogger. He then connects these models to the dominant social and political issues of their time.

Each essay can stand independently, though the three essays certainly overlap in important ways. Together they are meant to examine the crucial relationship between law and literature in the United States and to point out methods by which these relationships can be more fully clarified. Suggestive rather than exhaustive in approach, the essays are aimed at encouraging further study in this challenging and diverse field. The pronouncements of the law must always be, after all, a form of literature, just as literature must always shape cultural attitudes toward law. To aid others in exploring such interrelationships, questions for discussion and annotated bibliographies appear after each essay.

M. B.
J. P. M., Jr.
C. S. S.

Contents

LAW AS FORM AND THEME
IN AMERICAN LETTERS:
AN ESSAY IN LAW
AND AMERICAN LITERATURE

Carl S. Smith

Associate Professor of English and Urban Affairs
Northwestern University

The study of law and literature in the United States is of interest not only for what it reveals about legal and literary history and practice, but also because it leads to a larger consideration of the nature of both law and literature generally as intellectual, aesthetic, and social forms.* The American legal system and American letters each has its own traditions, but there are important links between law and literature as cultural institutions. This essay explores two major aspects of their interrelationship. The first section discusses how the law approaches language and uses words. This section also considers the differences and similarities between legal writing and conventional literature. The second section examines ways in which American writers have scrutinized the law in their work. It traces a major tradition of criticism of the legal system in the writings of many of America's most respected literary figures.

The two sections together reveal how law and literature encroach on each other. In many important respects legal writing and certain legal forms and practices are highly literary, and their literary qualities are fundamental to how the law works in society. The law relies on literary technique to express its authority as effectively as possible, and legal writing is a significant part of America's literary heritage. At the same time, the law has been a central subject in American literature. American writers concerned with issues of justice have been especially fascinated by the law, wary of its authority, and eager to capture some of its power in their own expression.

===== I =====

The Law as Literary Form

Legal writing here means the expression in words of the rules and principles of the law and the language through which legal institutions of government and those who work with and within them (including, most prominently, lawyers and judges) function. Legal language thus includes both the words legal writing uses and the ways it employs them collectively to communicate meaning. Legal writing encom-

* The author would like to thank several people for their advice and interest in the preparation of this essay. These people include the Literature Advisors of the Commission on Undergraduate Education in Law and the Humanities, and T.H. Breen, Gerald L. Fetner, Jerry Goldman, Edward H. Levi, Stephen Presser, Russell Reising, Jane S. Smith, and Alan Trachtenberg.

3

passes constitutions and charters, legislation, judicial decisions and court records, briefs and other types of arguments and statements used in legal proceedings, contracts and other binding agreements, and a multitude of licenses and other forms. It does not here include writings *about* the law by either the foolish or the wise, whether in speeches or other types of public address, histories and memoirs, essays and treatises, or poems, plays, and novels. This kind of legal writing is discussed later in this essay and, more fully, in the other two essays in this volume.

Even with the exclusions, legal writing is still a vast and motley text, for the law is obsessed with words, using language to shape a universe of deeds. Virtually every contact individuals have with the law appears to begin with a statute, contract, or printed form. If they are involved in a legal dispute, they and their lawyers proceed to a judgment through a carefully phrased presentation of the case. Words are critical at every turn. Establishing an effective case involves "getting it in writing" and persuasively "telling it to the judge." Statements made by an individual in a hearing or trial are taken down verbatim and carefully preserved. Judges' opinions are printed and consulted in deciding subsequent cases. Each important understanding between individuals and institutions must be made into an explicit document of public record to be sure that the understanding is binding. In all situations, every word of the text is subject to careful scrutiny and interpretation, on which enforcement depends.

Is this vast and motley text "literature"? Although *literature* can be defined so widely as to include any expression in words, the term usually applies to writing done with imagination and inventive intelligence. What distinguishes literature from any collection of words is not simply that it takes a certain shape (such as a novel or a poem), but that it aspires to have an aesthetic appeal that goes beyond its immediate meaning. The reader or listener appreciates a good poem, novel, play, or essay in large part because its tone is so apt, its figurative language so alive, its structure so carefully crafted, and its ideas so effectively expressed. These qualities can stir the emotions and arouse the intellect, so that the audience enters into the world that the work of literary art reflects or creates.

By these standards, most legal writing does not seem at first examination to be "literary." The problems begin with the basic vocabulary of the law. To the layperson and even to some lawyers, as well as to a literary sensibility, this vocabulary is a ponderous collection of verbal peculiarities, words and phrases too obscure and too dull to qualify even as intriguing curiosities. Legal writing is a forest of opaque terms, sometimes in Latin or another foreign tongue. To wander here is to encounter *writs of certiorari* and *misprisions of felony*, doctrines like *estoppel* (not to be confused with *estoppel by deed*), and individuals with names like *plaintiff* and *claimant*.

Words met with in this context are sometimes drained of their potential richness and do not quite mean what they seem. Words with a broad range of definitions in regular use, such as *action, appeal, seizure, conversion, conviction, assign, suit,* and *instrument*, become one-dimensional and technical. Terms like *guilty* describe the results of a complex procedure rather than the state of an individual's soul. Trying to pursue the precise meaning of some of these terms is frequently difficult, for they inhabit a closed world in which they are defined in terms of one another, and the neophyte in search of clarification in a law dictionary is led on an unmerry chase. The assumption that the legal and everyday definitions of certain terms are more or less the same is often misleading. As William Safire recently observed, "The trick is to remember that the language of law is not necessarily the language of life."[1] Some words have several different meanings in relation to different areas of law. The word *abandon*, for example, has separate definitions in insurance, patent, maritime, and family law. In addition, the figurative language of the law has in some cases lost its poetic qualities. Lon L. Fuller explains that the law speaks of the *merger* of estates, the *breaking* of contracts, and the *ripening* of obligations, but that such terms "have become naturalized in the language of the law" and "are usually not even felt as metaphors." Instead, "they have acquired a special legal significance which comes to the mind of the lawyer when they are used, so instinctively, indeed, that he is usually unaware that they have a more vivid sensual connotation."[2]

When words are gathered into sentences in legal documents, problems multiply. Much legal exposition as well as language seems to ignore the premises of literary art. Unlike imaginative literature,

---

[1] William Safire, "On Language: We Wuz Robbed," *New York Times Magazine*, January 31, 1982, p. 13.
[2] Lon L. Fuller, *Legal Fictions* (Stanford, Calif.: Stanford University Press, 1967), p. 12.

legal writing seems to be narrow in its purposes, trapped by mechanical conventions, and single-mindedly unreflective. Rather than being bold and inventive, the bearer of wisdom and delight, and the inspiration of profound insights, much legal writing strikes readers as tedious, cryptic, and unenlightening. One of the most important encounters individuals have with legal language is their confrontation with a will—either making their own or interpreting ones in which they are named (or *not* named) heirs, trustees, or executors. Here, as in many contracts and legal notices, are whole paragraphs of what attorneys call "boiler-plate" and which lay readers immediately recognize as the stupefying world of "legalese," full of phrases whose meaning and importance sometimes cannot be easily explained even to the highly literate, but which, one is assured by the attorney, must be there if the client is to get what he wishes.

Legal style often seems unnecessarily repetitive. It is hard sometimes to understand how succeeding paragraphs in a contract add much to what comes before, or why in making a will one must say "give, devise, and bequeath" when one word seems to do the work of all three. A lawyer might tell a client that all these terms are needed to make things "legal and proper," no doubt failing to explain why once one has said "legal," one has to add "proper"—and vice versa. "Here is the inevitable lawyer's writing—" the noted Supreme Court Justice Felix Frankfurter observed, "the dull qualifications and circumlocutions that sink any literary barque or even freighter, the lifeless tags and rags that preclude grace and stifle spontaneity." Quoting Judge Benjamin Cardozo, Frankfurter agreed that even the writings of most judges, which would seem to allow for the fullest creative freedom of expression, were characterized by "caution and reticence." As Frankfurter noted, these qualities "are indispensable to wisdom in law, certainly to wisdom in adjudication," but are not "the wellsprings of literature."[3]

To argue that much legal writing is not literary because it lacks the aesthetic dimensions of conventional literature is perhaps beside the point. Legal language has evolved to serve American society and legal institutions, not the muse, and to criticize it because it is not poetry is to attack it for not being what it was never intended to be

---

[3] Felix Frankfurter, "When Judge Cardozo Writes," in *Law and Politics: Occasional Papers of Felix Frankfurter, 1913–1938,* ed. Archibald MacLeish and E.F. Prichard, Jr. (New York: Harcourt, Brace & Company, 1939), p. 104.

and to ignore its historical development and social function. Legal expression may strike most people as overly formal, abstruse, archaic, redundant, and restrictive, but those who defend it contend that the words and forms the law uses are primarily functional, and that they conform to the special needs of legal reasoning and are clear to those to whom society entrusts the workings of justice. If contracts, statutes, judicial decisions, and trials are full of verbal peculiarities, it is commonly argued, they are so to make certain that the terms on which individuals and institutions proceed are consistent and clear, and that when there are conflicts in society, each case can be treated fairly and surely. The lawyer, legislator, or judge may be as concerned as is any novelist or poet with the larger humanistic questions of justice and truth, and drafting contracts, making laws, and explaining decisions require the skilled mastery of a special language. But legal writing does not have the same freedom of expression as poetry (nor the same restrictions, such as meter and rhyme), and it does have the obligation to serve more sharply defined social needs than does literature. While all literature works within a tradition of conventions, the retention of certain formulas and forms is especially important to the continuity of the law as a stable institution in society.

The differences between legal writing and literature should not obscure several important similarities, however. A novel or poem, of course, may speak quite directly to social needs. In addition, many would-be works of literary art fall far short of aesthetic distinction and make for anything but enjoyable and enlightening reading. And, despite the apparently unliterary (or even antiliterary) tendencies of the forms and formulas of legal language and expression, legal writing shares several of the characteristics of imaginative literature. These literary characteristics, furthermore, are not incidental but basic to the way the law functions. They figure most obviously in the language the law uses and the methods of exposition it commonly employs, but they are also inherent in the law as an evolving institution and in the legal system's proceedings and working assumptions.

Legal language has a highly figurative, especially symbolic, dimension. Like all specialized languages, legal language evokes the sphere of life to which it applies. Since this sphere is the law, the basis of secular authority in society, the very language of the law often has a resonance and an authority that are imaginatively arresting. Charles

A. Miller observes that this applies particularly to phrases associated with constitutional concepts, which "may acquire a life force of their own, demonstrating the power of words as symbols." Sometimes the rights and privileges claimed are not explicitly in the Constitution, but the phrases make it seem as if they are. Miller explains further, "Whether these symbols are unspecific and worshipped by all, such as 'freedom,' or specific 'code words' that may divide the country, such as 'freedom of choice,' the language conveys much more than it says and forms the tools for political and judicial combat."[4] "Freedom of contract" became an important phrase earlier this century during discussions of legislation regulating labor, as did "executive privilege" during the Watergate controversy. Today, opposing sides in the debate over legalized abortions speak in terms of "the right to life" and "the right to privacy."

Even isolated common legal turns of phrase can exercise imaginative power over those who speak, read, and hear them. Certain terms, like the plea of *nolo contendere*, possess charm as verbal antiques or esoteric catchwords, but, more importantly, they command attention beyond their immediate meaning because of their long association with legal institutions. When they are used, they instantly conjure up the whole legal system that orders society. Just the *sound* of certain words or aggregations of words in wills, deeds, contracts, and other legal documents excites feelings ranging from fear to respect, especially when those words involve the individual who reads them in some obligation or right he or she owes or is owed. The mere mention of a phrase like *habeas corpus*—even though and perhaps because most people do not know precisely what it means— elicits a sense of the complexity, thoroughness, and power of the law for good or ill in human affairs. The very obscurity of some terms and their ancient derivation remind those who encounter them of the pervasiveness and vigilance of the law—that it has been around a long time, that it knows human nature very well, and that it has thoroughly considered and made provision for situations of which most people have never dreamed.

Over the years there have been several attempts to demystify this language. "Plain-language" legal dictionaries have appeared for the benefit of the layperson, and recently several "plain-language"

---

[4] Charles A. Miller, "Constitutional Law and the Rhetoric of Race," in *Law in American History*, ed. Donald Fleming and Bernard Bailyn, *Perspectives in American History* 5 (1971):149.

statutes have been drafted prescribing that certain basic forms of legal agreements must be written in a language that is readily understandable. In New York, for example, leases must be printed in type of a minimum size or larger (thus "fine print" is effectively eliminated) and "written in a clear and coherent manner using words with common and everyday meanings." But those who have tried to accomplish this task have sometimes found it hard to reconcile the citizen's right to understand with an effective legal language.

Besides, people sometimes *want* the language of the law to be something separate and special, and they derive genuine aesthetic pleasure and personal reassurance from its mystery. The inaccessibility of legal language to the common reader is important to its symbolic power. If legal language were no different from any other, it might seem to lose its special force. Individuals may even be more pleased than puzzled when their attorney draws up a document for them that they, and, in their best estimate, other laypeople find unaccountably long, complicated, and incomprehensible, for they believe that in its difficulty resides its strength. (The more cynical might argue that these same people then feel more justified in going to a lawyer in the first place—and paying his professional fees— rather than trying to express their wishes or argue their cases themselves.) They appreciate all the repetition and the arcane words because they think that these make the document more "legal," and therefore more able to do what they want it to do.

Not just the words, but also the formal scrolls, seals, and type faces of many legal documents such as subpoenas and licenses work symbolically. If they look "legal," they demand to be taken seriously, especially by those who do not understand them very well but who instinctively believe in their force. Contemporary novelist Stanley Elkin discusses the symbolic power of such documents in his novella "The Bailbondsman," when his title character and narrator, Alexander Main, talks about the official papers of his profession. "I love a contract like the devil," Main admits, "admire the tall paper and the small print—I mean the *print*—the lawful shapes and stately content." He continues, "I'm talking the *look* of the instrument, texture, watermark, the silk flourish of the bright ribbon . . . the beautiful formulas simple as pie, old fashioned quid pro quo like a recipe in the family generations."[5] Individuals and organizations sometimes try to

[5] Stanley Elkin, "The Bailbondsman," in *Searches and Seizures* (New York: Random House, 1973), p. 5.

evoke symbolically the authority of legal forms to convince others of the power and trustworthiness of their words. The warranties that come with the cheapest appliances are printed on an imitation parchment and arranged in an official-looking manner to assure the purchaser that the manufacturer has put his promises of quality and performance into a binding contract, even if the warranty may in practical fact be virtually worthless.

Some of the phrases that appear in common legal documents and forms have other figurative, even poetic, qualities. Their aesthetic value, as well as their direct meaning, is very important to those who use them. When deciding how one's worldly goods will be divided among heirs, for example, one finds some assurance in the somber redundancy of "last will and testament" and "give, devise, and bequeath," as well as in the dignified alliteration of "rest, residue, and remainder." These phrases, one hopes, not only help express one's wishes but will also impress the world that one has acted responsibly and that one's life has been of sufficient consequence to require such formalities. Similarly, a man and a woman pledging their lives to each other with the traditional marriage vows appreciate the elegant balance of phrases like "to have and to hold," even if the legal distinctions between "having" and "holding" are not clear to them. An indictment for homicide makes the crime seem more heinous when it states that the defendant "did kill and murder" his victim and uses a special locution to say that he acted "with malice aforethought." And a witness is perhaps more inclined to veracity when he swears to tell "the truth, the whole truth, and nothing but the truth."

Like legal language, more elaborate forms of legal exposition have significant literary qualities, and some demand careful attention to style. A lawyer has considerable latitude in preparing his case and in speaking in court, and the reputations of many of America's best-known lawyers, such as Clarence Darrow, are heavily based in the persuasive eloquence of their arguments, apart from any special knowledge of the law. Daniel Webster at the bar became a figure of legend who, when he argued a case, "could turn on the harps of the blessed and the shaking of the earth underground," and who, with the evidence all against him as he pleaded for a man's soul before a jury of the damned, bested "the King of Lawyers," the Devil.[6]

[6] Stephen Vincent Benét, "The Devil and Daniel Webster," in *Twenty-Five Short Stories by Stephen Vincent Benét* (Garden City, N.Y.: Sun Dial Press, 1943), pp. 163, 172.

Similarly, while most pronouncements made by courts of what the law means are hardly memorable as literary art, they need to be at least clear and convincing if they are to be understood and enforced. This is especially critical in the decisions handed down in difficult and significant cases, in which a judge tries to summon all his powers of literary and legal persuasion. Supreme Court Justice Benjamin Cardozo made this point in his noted essay on "Law and Literature," in which he dismissed the notion that "a judicial opinion has no business to be literature." What was true for literature generally was especially true for legal writing: form and meaning were intricately related. "The strength that is born of form and the feebleness that is born of the lack of form," Cardozo maintained, "are in truth qualities of the substance. They are tokens of the thing's identity. They make it what it is."

Cardozo stressed above all the importance of persuasive authorial force in any opinion (he could also have been talking about the pleas and briefs of lawyers). His standards were very high, as he called for a form that embodied "sincerity and fire, or the mnemonic power of alliteration and antithesis, or the terseness and tang of the proverb and the maxim." No poet, novelist, or essayist could demand more. After outlining varieties of effective and ineffective judicial styles, Cardozo claimed that attention to literary form was what made certain decisions legal landmarks, as much or more than the solidity of the legal reasoning behind the decision. "It is a false and cramping notion that cases are made great solely or chiefly by reason of something intrinsic in themselves," he contended. "They are great by what we make of them." Citing Chief Justice John Marshall's decision in the famous case of *McCulloch v. Maryland* (1819), in which the Court upheld the charter of the second Bank of the United States and broadly interpreted Congress's powers under the Constitution, Cardozo wondered if the opinion would have been long forgotten and perhaps even overruled "if Marshall had not put upon it the imprint of his genius."[7] G. Edward White comments on this point: "It was Marshall's supreme mastery of the existing rhetorical techniques of his time that gave his admittedly partisan results their unassailable quality."[8]

---

[7] Benjamin N. Cardozo, "Law and Literature," in *Law and Literature and Other Essays and Addresses* (New York: Harcourt, Brace & Company, 1931), pp. 3, 6, 9, 39.
[8] G. Edward White, *The American Judicial Tradition: Profiles of Leading American Judges* (New York: Oxford University Press, 1976), p. 33.

Cardozo's observations are somewhat troubling, however, since they do imply that there is a danger that language and rhetoric, rather than the inherent merits of a legal argument, will become a controlling factor in the effectiveness of a decision or a brief. Literary power in law as well as in literature can be abused, but in law this abuse is potentially more damaging since the power of the state stands behind statutes, legal agreements, and court decisions. The legal profession has been criticized for using its special expertise with words to manage matters to suit itself. Those sensitive to the uses and misuses of words and to threats to democratic society are suspicious of this kind of literary manipulation. They are fearful that it can be easily turned into a refuge of special privilege or a tool for sharpers who mine the statutes for ways to free clients from just obligations or responsibilties, who get patently guilty malefactors off on obscure rules, who draft instruments that delude the simple democratic man, or who otherwise evade the spirit of the law by hiding behind the letter.

For those who interpret the laws, powerful rhetoric may contribute to the force of a judicial decision, but it does not guarantee that the judgment is morally or even legally sound. Since judges often determine what the law means not only in the situation at hand but in other like cases, the way they choose to speak is very important. "The words which have been found in the past are much spoken of, have acquired a dignity of their own," Edward H. Levi explains, "and to a considerable measure control results."[9] This kind of literary power can be used for ill as well as good. Charles A. Miller speaks to this problem in examining the Supreme Court's handling of race. Miller points out how the Court's choice of words has shaped the way important disputes, such as those over the rights of slaves and their descendants, have been understood. He traces a pattern of evasion

---

[9] Edward H. Levi, *An Introduction to Legal Reasoning* (Chicago: University of Chicago Press, 1948), p. 8. Citing the case of *Berkey v. Third Avenue Railway Company*, Levi continues, "As Judge Cardozo suggested in speaking of metaphors, the word starts out to free thought and ends by enslaving it. The movement of concepts into and out of the law makes the point. If the society has begun to see certain significant similarities or differences, the comparison emerges with a word. When the word is finally accepted, it becomes a legal concept. Its meaning continues to change. But the comparison is not only between the instances which have been included under it and the actual case at hand, but also in terms of hypothetical instances which the word by itself suggests. Thus the connotation of the word for a time has a limiting influence—so much so that the reasoning may even appear to be simply deductive."

in American legal documents and decisions—through language choice—of the social and ideological problems created by slavery. Miller states that the American legal system up to the *Brown v. Board of Education of Topeka* desegregation decision of 1954 dealt with race in language characterized by, among other things, indirection, abstraction, euphemism, overblown rhetoric, and supposedly "neutral" nonracial concepts. This included talking about slavery and segregation not in relation to individual rights and freedoms, but in terms of property and interstate commerce. Up to the *Brown* case, the Supreme Court ignored troubling social realities and avoided a decisive confrontation with slavery and its aftereffects, denying many Americans their legal rights.[10]

The collected body of legal writings, practices, and doctrines has other significant literary characteristics and even resembles certain aesthetic forms. The importance of judicial interpretation brings to mind how much the law is, like literature, a written text whose meaning depends on how it is interpreted. People want the law to provide absolute certainties, but like all literary expression legal writing admits to different readings. Citizens, attorneys, and civil servants all interpret the law, and, although the final definitive say as to what the law means is given to the courts, the decisions of judges become part of the legal text and are themselves subject to interpretation.

To be sure, openness to interpretation and ambiguity are sometimes assets in law as in literature. A work of literary art with several possible meanings may have an extra depth that allows it to speak to a wide audience over a great period of time. The universality and timelessness of Hamlet's words (and his situation) are measures of the greatness of Shakespeare's play, or of any art. Similarly, a certain controlled flexibility in the language of legislation or of a legal decision, explicitly or implicitly allowing for interpretation, is frequently important to the continuity of legal institutions amid social change. The Constitution has helped provide a stable legal and social identity for almost two hundred years partly because it has been possible to reinterpret its basic principles to apply to changing realities. Writing that is full of plausible readings, however, is often

---

[10] Miller also observes, "But the law has its own demands and its own logic that accommodate unwillingly either to extensive linguistic manipulation or to pressure for the incorporation of too much of its principal components, order and justice." See Charles A. Miller, "Constitutional Law and the Rhetoric of Race," pp. 196–198.

undesirable in the world of law, where wills are contested, statutes are enforced, and cases are tried. In any given situation, a judge or jury *must* determine what this law or that document means. As Walter Benn Michaels points out, "Judges cannot decide that contracts are ambiguous in the same way and for the same reasons that literary critics can." He adds, however, "but this is not because legal *language* is less tolerant of ambiguity than poetic language is; it is because the institution of the law is less tolerant of ambiguity than the institution of literary criticism is."[11]

The "text" of the law also approaches literary forms because it has narrative, dramatic, and fictive qualities. Legal writing of all sorts forms a collective narrative, a kind of public diary, of American political, social, economic, and intellectual life. This is true in all societies, but particularly in the United States, where so many cultural issues emerge as legal questions. Justice Oliver Wendell Holmes, himself a master of English prose, described the law as forming what he called "a great anthropological document," which he elsewhere likened to a "magic mirror" wherein "we see reflected, not only our own lives, but the lives of all men that have been!" If anything, the law to Holmes was more interesting than much fine literature, even on "literary" terms, because it was more real and alive. "To the lover of the law," he claimed, "how small a thing seem the novelist's tales of the loves and fates of Daphnis and Chloe! How pale a phantom even the Circe of poetry, transforming mankind with intoxicating dreams of fiery ether, and the foam of summer seas, and glowing greensward, and the white arms of women!" He pointed out that the law enabled those who studied it "to discover what ideals of society have been strong enough to reach that final form of expression, or what have been the changes in dominant ideals from century to century."[12]

As a reflector of human values, the law in Holmes's view was also a form of literary prophecy, expressing how those who created it thought people in their society should and would act. One sees an excellent illustration of Holmes's point in the Constitution, which begins with a preamble that is a statement of national purposes (i.e., the need "to form a more perfect Union, establish Justice, insure

---

[11] Walter Benn Michaels, "Against Formalism: The Autonomous Text in Legal and Literary Interpretation," *Poetics Today* 1–2 (1979):33.
[12] Oliver Wendell Holmes, *Collected Legal Papers,* ed. Harold J. Laski (New York: Harcourt, Brace & Howe, 1920), pp. 212, 26.

domestic Tranquility, provide for the common defence, promote the general Welfare, and secure the Blessings of Liberty") from which proceed the articles that follow. Behind the several efforts in the history of the United States to form at least certain parts of American law into a coherent and consistent code is the attempt to make the law a declaration of principles, a written credo of American society.

For Holmes and for many others the law has fulfilled the literary functions of history, prophecy, and sheer aesthetic delight. It is also true that certain specific legal proceedings resemble the drama in the way that they order experience. All social rituals and some in particular (like religious rites) have a special shape and drama, but in few areas of life is this so obvious and important as in the law. Society wants trials to follow their special structure not only for practical reasons of hearing cases but also because that structure is satisfying in some profound way. This suggests that the standards of legal order and aesthetic order are related, and that the individual's and the community's conception of justice is based not only on principles but also on a sense of what is the most emotionally and intellectually pleasing relation of actions.

While actual trials do not have the clarity or simplified order of those common to books and plays, they usually involve a discernible conflict centering around a disagreement or criminal act. The individuals involved in the resolution of this conflict voluntarily or involuntarily assume "parts," be it as judge, juror, prosecutor, plaintiff, defendant, or witness, and they act within strict rules that define how they are permitted to behave in the "performance" of justice. Speech is divided into testimony, questioning, cross-examination, and formal argument, all of which take place before an audience. How each participant "performs" can be important, for a judgment can depend not only on what is said but also on the way it is expressed. The good lawyer is a skillful director as well as author, carefully rehearsing his or her presentation and witnesses, even deciding what clothing (perhaps *costume* is the better word) they should wear in court to enhance their case.

A trial, especially a criminal prosecution, has other dramatic aspects. Like any theater, it holds out at least the possibility of surprise and suspense—unexpected testimony, the breakdown of a witness, the introduction of new evidence, an unanticipated verdict. It is small wonder that court sessions have consistently been a form of popular entertainment throughout American history, particularly before the spread of urbanization and mass communication. Spectators not personally involved in cases often attend or follow news accounts of trials and legal proceedings that involve individuals or actions of some special notoriety (the Watergate hearings and the Patty Hearst trial come to mind as recent examples), but it is also the dramatic nature of the proceedings that draws them. During his opening argument in the murder case around which James Gould Cozzens's *The Just and the Unjust* revolves, assistant district attorney Abner Coates surveys the many who have crowded into the courtroom and becomes aware that "those who performed public duties before an audience became willingly or unwillingly actors, and what they did, whether they wanted it that way or not, became drama."[13] It is not surprising, as John McWilliams explains in his essay in this volume, that so many writers have been attracted to trials as a part of their novels and plays, for few human experiences provide so clearly defined and as promising a dramatic structure.

The "legal fiction," a heritage of Roman and English law, also reveals fundamental ways in which law and literature are interrelated. When the term fiction is used in literature, it refers to writing that invents its own world of characters, actions, and ideas. Fiction is commonly associated with prose narrative, but drama, poetry, and possibly other forms commonly create fictive worlds and characters. Fiction may closely resemble what is understood to be the actual world, and it almost always comments on the nature of actuality. There is some disagreement about the definition of a legal fiction, but the term usually applies to a conception and handling of a case or other legal situation that view the actual facts in a specially contrived way and that even sometimes invent "facts"or conditions known by all involved not to be true. A court or other legal authority usually employs legal fictions not in the expectation of deceiving anyone, but to help resolve a complicated question and to take certain actions.

One such fiction is the concept of *attractive nuisance*, which is sometimes employed where a minor is injured when curiosity or chance leads him or her to some unguarded "attraction," such as a neighbor's swimming pool or a construction site. For the sake of

---

[13] James Gould Cozzens, *The Just and the Unjust* (New York: Harcourt, Brace & Company, 1942), p. 9. Coates, conscious of his shortcomings as a speaker, fears that "his audience was finding the performance, of which he was a part, a poor show compared to what true drama, the art of the theater or the motion picture, had taught them to expect."

establishing the liability of the neighbor or contractor (and encouraging the erection of fences so that accidents of this nature do not happen), it is sometimes assumed that the child was actively enticed into the area of danger. In the action called *trover*, likewise, an individual reclaims property that may have been taken illegally. He does so not through a criminal prosecution but under the presumption that he "lost" the property and someone else "found" it. In both instances the court thus "writes" its own fictive version of what has happened and decides on that basis.

Many other large and small fictions pervade the legal system. In the law's eyes, an adoptive parent is a child's father or mother so far as legal rights and obligations are concerned. A corporation has been declared to be the legal equivalent of a person in its right to make contracts, hold property, and sue other persons or corporations. These legal fictions are not the same thing as a novel or short story, but they do have the imaginative inventive features implicit in the idea of "attractive nuisance"or "trover." Since they often are, as Lon L. Fuller argues, "a metaphorical way of expressing a truth," Fuller calls legal fictions "an illustration of the all-pervading power of the word."[14] Defenders of legal fictions point to them as practical corrective devices in the otherwise necessarily rigid system of the law and say that they reveal that in practice the law is flexible and just. Through such fictions the law makes sure that, whatever the facts of a case, it protects those who need protection (small children, for example) and thus helps guarantee justice in a larger sense.

But the legal fiction generally and specific legal fictions have been attacked. Some have claimed that they are nothing more than a form of deception involving circular reasoning that starts from the conclusions it wants to reach and alters the truth to fit. Whether or not one agrees with the implications of a legal fiction, it is troubling to accept a practice or judgment whose factual basis seems shaky. Critics assert that it is dangerous to tinker with the actual facts of a case, and that a system that needs these fictions is unsound. Fuller states that the legal fiction "represents the pathology of the law" since it reveals that the system requires certain adjustments to work as it supposedly should. His point is that fictions disclose areas where the law as written is inadequate to deal with the situation at hand. The legal fiction reflects the law's struggle with unforeseen problems and "forces upon

[14] Fuller, *Legal Fictions*, pp. 10–12.

our attention the relation between theory and fact, between concept and reality, and reminds us of the complexity of that relation."[15]

The existence of legal fictions of these and more general kinds shows again how much daily experience and especially the legal world depend on such imaginative, "artistic" devices, which also include the special language and rituals of the law. For two hundred years Americans have accepted the "fiction" that the political order invented in the Constitution establishes justice and achieves all the other social goals the Founding Fathers outlined in the preamble. The statutes of national, state, and local legislative bodies base their authority on the fiction that they are the expression of true popular sovereignty. Cases are tried by certain procedures and rules, and the fiction that most citizens accept is that this procedure guarantees fairness, truth, and order. The supreme fiction behind all these devices is that the legal system as a whole enacts "justice." None of this is to say that the system is necessarily unjust, but that even if it were possible to define simply the United States' or any other society's collective ideal of justice, no legal system devised to make that ideal real would be able to work without fictions.

A legal fiction has a different kind of force behind it from conventional fiction, just as legal interpretation has a different power from literary interpretation. A poem, a short story, or a novel may strike the individual reader as in some way true or real by his judgment. It may inspire a feeling or an idea by which he may live his life, and so *become* real to him. The special quality of the legal fiction is that it *is* real because it is enforced as real, whether or not the persons affected agree with its assumptions and conclusions. The defendant required to pay a large judgment and the condemned prisoner on Death Row need no convincing of this fact. That they are "actors" in the "drama of justice" and that this justice may not be absolute but "fictive" does not dismiss the award or ease the pinch of the hangman's noose. People live by the fictions of courts and legislatures because they must respect the authority of the law (and the power of those who enforce it), if also because they accept the smaller and larger fictions either in principle or as solutions to the problems of a functioning legal order.

Difficulties can arise with legal fictions, as others have noted, not because they have no reality but because they have so much. If

---

[15] Ibid., pp. viii–ix.

the legal order that society devises is to approximate justice, it is crucial that this order be based on widely shared democratic and humane principles, and that society's fictions should be felt as true by those who live by them, so that as citizens they enter fully and willingly into them. When legal fictions express only the will of a narrow few whose interests they serve, at the same time ignoring a broad social consensus, then justice itself is not only fictive but false.

II

The American Writer and the Law

American writers have spoken most eloquently about the law on those occasions when they have believed that the justice offered by the American legal system has indeed become false. Their relationship with the law has often—though certainly not always—been an adversarial one. Many writers who by common judgment have defined the American literary tradition have perceived a conflict between their own sense of law and justice and that which they have seen prevail in their time. They have spoken not as isolated individuals but as defenders of American moral and ethical idealism, which they think has been betrayed by the legal system, and they have presented their own work to balance and counteract the more dangerous "fictions" of the law. Depending on the occasion, they have attacked the legal system in and of itself and as an emblem of larger wrongs in American society that the law reflects.

This radical tradition has not always been the dominant one, however. In the early years of the Republic in the late eighteenth and early nineteenth centuries, a number of America's leading literary figures were lawyers or trained in the law, and their legal and literary interests coincided. This period is particularly important in terms of both law and literature because it witnessed the establishment of an American legal system and the development of a national literature, both self-consciously independent from (if still based on) those of the former mother country, England. Speaking of the quarter century between 1810 and 1835, literary historian William Charvat points out that of forty leading cultural critics and men of letters of the time, "twenty had been trained for the law and eight had been members of Congress or a legislature." Of the ten most important critics and editors, he continues, all but two had legal training.[16] John Trumbull, Joel Barlow, Washington Irving, Hugh Henry Brackenridge, William Cullen Bryant, Henry Wadsworth Longfellow, and Richard Henry Dana, Jr., all were practicing lawyers or had some kind of legal background. A prominent legal figure would likely be an avid student of Pope, Addison, Swift, and Johnson, and might well try his own hand at poetry. Dana authored *Two Years Before the Mast* a year before he published *The Seaman's Friend* (1841), which includes a manual of the law of the sea.

A number of reasons made for this striking coincidence of legal and literary minds. The law (along with the ministry and medicine) was one of the leading professional careers open to the educated gentleman of the late eighteenth and early nineteenth centuries, whose schooling in any case would include a study of the law. Likewise, the educated lawyer was no narrow specialist, but was familiar with history and literature, particularly of the classical period, and the political philosophy of the Enlightenment. A legal education in many senses was a literary one. In addition, the tasks and opportunities of the new and expanding nation attracted many individuals with a talent for letters, and several of the best literary minds were thus drawn into the law. Charvat also observes that in an era that preceded strong copyright laws and an established reading and buying public, individuals without independent means could not easily devote themselves to imaginative writing without the income of a profession like the law.[17] This did not cool their love of literature, however, for their legal careers gave them opportunities to master the skills of literary expression. When they could, they combined legal practice with the active pursuit of purer art forms.

Robert A. Ferguson explains that there was a more complex, if related, cause for the appearance of the notable group of lawyer-

---

[16] William Charvat, *The Origins of American Critical Thought, 1810–1835* (New York: Russell and Russell, 1968), pp. 5–6. For more on the intellectual background of America's leaders in the late eighteenth century, see Bernard Bailyn, *The Ideological Origins of the American Revolution* (Cambridge: Harvard University Press, 1967), esp. pp. 22–54.

[17] Copyright is a legal issue that has naturally concerned writers, even if it has not directly affected the quality of their work. Throughout the nineteenth century, American (and foreign) authors complained bitterly about the absence of an international copyright agreement that would prevent the "pirating" of texts without payment of royalties. This problem was not corrected until 1891. The latest major copyright legislation was drafted by Congress in 1976 and went into effect in 1978.

writers in the federal and early national periods. Members of this group believed that writers could have significant public careers that contributed to the strengthening of the new country. This helps account, Ferguson contends, for the strong classical tradition, stressing civic virtue and republican order, that dominates American literature for the first three decades of the national period, and especially for the varieties of neoclassical epic—such as Joel Barlow's *Columbiad*—which appear in this time. This kind of creative work is an indisputably public form—didactic, inspiring, and patriotic— aimed at inculcating the love of liberty that its author believed was embodied in the nation itself.

Ferguson even asserts that the spirit behind such efforts was based partly on their authors' reading of Blackstone's landmark *Commentaries* on English law (1769) and the influence of this work's insistence "upon the clear and reliable nature of existing institutions and laws as fundamental sources of reason, order, and unity." The generation of lawyer-writers hoped that their literary efforts would help support such institutions by singing their virtues. They perhaps produced no great and timeless work, but they stressed values critical in a time of war, economic instability, and political change. "In such circumstances," Ferguson writes, "a search for order took precedence over creativity or originality." The result was that the law and republican ideology "became the basic tools of a civic literature that sought to create a necessary order and sense of country." Each literary lawyer aimed "to apply both professional and artistic talents to national themes." Ferguson concludes, "The combination made particular sense to generations of writers eager to portray their own federal republic as the source and symbol of a new stage in human history."[18]

But beginning in the decades before the Civil War, the two callings of law and literature diverged because the social, political, economic, educational, and artistic conditions that allied them gradually ceased to exist.[19] Since that period, many leading American

---

[18] Robert A. Ferguson, "The Emulation of Sir William Jones in the Early Republic," *New England Quarterly* 52 (1979):20, 24, 25.

[19] Of course, since the early nineteenth century some accomplished American writers, including poets Edgar Lee Masters and Wallace Stevens in this century, have been lawyers. Masters was even for a few years the law partner of Clarence Darrow in Chicago. Darrow himself wrote fiction (see John McWilliams's essay), while contemporary novelist Louis Auchincloss draws directly on his legal experience in his books. On Auchincloss, see Louis Auchincloss, *A Writer's Capital* (Minneapolis: University of Minnesota Press, 1974); and Patricia Kane, "Lawyers at the Top: The Fiction of Louis Auchincloss," *Critique* 7 (1964–1965):36–45.

writers have seen the law not as the foundation of republican freedom and virtue but as defender of the entrepreneurial spirit and a sometimes unjust society.[20] These writers continued a major tradition of dissent that is rooted in the Puritan rebellion from the Church of England and the Enlightenment defense of the American Revolution, and which was reinforced by the Romantic movement in literature, which elevated the artist to prophet of humanity's highest possibilities. They attacked the basis of the social system as it existed in their effort to restore America to the ideals by which they believed it was originally founded and constituted as an independent nation, speaking for a vision of society that has given this country its energizing sense of a special mission in the world since the *Mayflower* landed.

It is not possible here to trace the attitudes toward the law of a large number of writers, but it is worthwhile to look at the work of some of those who have been most outspoken and influential on the subject. The antagonism between the legal ideals of those who are generally accepted as being the most outstanding literary artists of their time and the legal actions of American government has rarely been better expressed than by the writers of the American Renaissance of the middle third of the nineteenth century, who were troubled by the existing social and political order and by the legal system as a central element in that order. Their comments on the law are especially interesting because they include statements about the proper place of art and the artist in American society as well as in relation to American law.

Ralph Waldo Emerson, the central literary figure of this period, believed that literary artists should serve their nation, but that they

---

[20] Some legal historians agree. Morton Horwitz has noted that in the period between Washington's inauguration as the first president and the outbreak of the Civil War, and as the legal profession joined with commercial interests to forward their common causes, a major transformation took place in American law. "Law, once conceived of as protective, regulative, paternalistic and, above all, a paramount expression of the moral sense of the community," writes Horwitz, "had come to be thought of as facilitative of individual desires and as simply reflective of the existing organization of economic and political power." In short, Horwitz maintains, law reflected the market mentality and was oriented to aid the free enterprise system. Once in command by the 1830s, these same interests sought to prevent further transformations in the law that would threaten their preeminence, at the same time working to make the legal system that favored them seem based in abstract ideas of justice and right, and thus neutral and apolitical. See Morton J. Horwitz, *The Transformation of American Law, 1790–1860* (Cambridge: Harvard University Press, 1977), pp. 253–266.

did so best when they were truest to their own sense of right. When society became an inflexible mass of conventions and unquestioned beliefs, it was to be suspected. Speaking out was especially urgent if the worth of most thoughts and actions was judged, as Emerson feared it was, by such debased values as simple profit and loss. Emerson's criticism was sharpest during his early career in the 1830s and 1840s. Although he was a champion of the great promise of his country, and though he did not take it as given that the moral self was necessarily opposed to society, Emerson argued that American social, political, and cultural life was flawed. He was particularly embittered that the legal powers of the land—i.e., the president, Congress, and many state legislatures—pursued the imperialistic Mexican War and tolerated slavery.

Emerson saw the corruption of law on all levels as a symptom of the illness of American society. In his "Ode" to W. H. Channing, written during the Mexican War in 1846, Emerson phrased the problem of the time in specifically legal terms:

> There are two laws discrete,
> Not reconciled,—
> Law for man, and law for thing;
> The last builds town and fleet,
> But it runs wild,
> And doth the man unking.

He then offered a solution:

> Let man serve law for man;
> Live for friendship, live for love,
> For truth's and harmony's behoof;
> The state may follow how it can,
> As Olympus follows Jove.

Emerson used the word *law* here in both a narrow and a broad sense. The "law for thing" is the established order of the marketplace that accommodates the flow of commerce. It has circumscribed the "law for man," the timeless humanistic sense of justice based on friendship, love, truth, and harmony. Strictly speaking, the Mexican War and the system of slavery were "legal" in that all proper procedures had been followed and the official authorities supported or tolerated them—but this was just the trouble. The result was a travesty of true justice that diminished the spiritual worth of man in America. In Emerson's famous lines, "Things are in the saddle,/And ride mankind." It was the writer's special duty to use his gifts of imagination, perception, and expression to become a leader of the party of conscience and justice and to judge society as few legally empowered judges would. It was his responsibility to attack convention, compromise, and expediency, and to champion a social order ruled by the laws for "man" and not for "thing."

Emerson maintained that most citizens had accepted without thinking some of the weaknesses of the social order as a matter of practical necessity. He had very little patience with such an attitude, asserting that the law and all social action must proceed from a sound sense of right and wrong, not from blind adherence to precedent and consistency. In his essay "The American Scholar," Emerson stated that it was the intellectual's duty to speak out in the face of moral outrage, even (or especially) if that outrage was "legal." He believed that a society that permits such outrage is perhaps not worth saving, and that it is in the defense of a code based in interests other than morality and right and justice that this same society is destroyed in any case. "No law can be sacred to me but that of my nature," Emerson remarked in the essay "Self-Reliance." "Good and bad are but names very readily transferable to that or this; the only right is what is after my constitution, the only wrong what is against it." Obviously, one's own "constitution" and not that of state or country was the highest authority in Emerson's kind of judicial review. When they conflicted, it was clear which was to be followed.

Emerson's radicalism was selective and tempered, especially as he grew older, and he advocated a modification, not a complete reform, of the existing legal order. Few extended Emerson's ideas as fully in their radical directions as did his friend and one-time disciple, Henry David Thoreau. As Emerson demanded in "The American Scholar" and "The Poet," Thoreau used his literary powers to examine his society. In the most famous incident during his stay at Walden Pond in the mid-1840s, he was arrested and spent a night in jail rather than pay a tax to support what he considered a corrupt political order. Speaking of legal conditions in his own state in his essay "Slavery in Massachusetts," he declared, "I have not read far in the statutes of this Commonwealth. It is not profitable reading. They do not always say what is true; and they do not always mean what they say." The state's version of justice was untrue and unjust, based as it was on the sacrifice of principle for the sake of a smoothly functioning government.

Thoreau felt particularly antagonistic to the legal system because he believed that it avoided essential issues of justice and law by reducing significant controversy to the simple question of whether or not a particular law or agreement was transgressed. "I do not believe in lawyers, in that mode of attacking or defending a man," Thoreau explained in his "A Plea for Captain John Brown," in which he defended the radical abolitionist who was hanged for his bloody raid on the federal armory at Harpers Ferry in 1859. In adopting this mode, Thoreau continued, "you descend to meet the judge on his own ground, and, in cases of the highest importance, it is of no consequence whether a man breaks a human law or not." A matter that the courts were competent to handle was not worth discussing: "Let lawyers decide trivial cases. Business men may arrange that among themselves. If they were interpreters of the everlasting laws which rightfully bind man, that would be another thing." Lawyers could not deal with profound matters, Thoreau said elsewhere, because the "lawyer's truth" was not truth at all, "but consistency or a consistent expediency."

There was little doubt, Thoreau felt, that the legal system threatened to reduce those who obeyed it to witting or unwitting co-conspirators against the best interests of humankind. The law had become an instrument of violence against right when it cooperated in waging the Mexican War and allowing slavery to continue to exist. He wrote angrily in his journal in 1842, "In war, in some sense, lies the very genius of law." He continued:

> What is human warfare but just this,—an effort to make the laws of God and nature take sides with one party. Men make an arbitrary code, and, because it is not right, they try to make it prevail by might. The moral law does not want any champion. Its asserters do not go to war. It was never infringed with impunity. It is inconsistent to decry war and maintain law, for if there were no need of war there would be no need of law.

He reiterated these ideas in several other places. In his famous essay, "Resistance to Civil Government" (better known as "Civil Disobedience"), written after his stay in the Concord jail, Thoreau sharply attacked majority rule, which in *Walden* he described as desperate and uncontrolled. In *A Week on the Concord and Merrimack Rivers*, he reminded his readers of the dangers of any "monster institution" such as the law to "the honest and simple commonwealth, . . . for it is not to be forgotten, that while the law holds fast the thief and murderer, it lets itself go loose." He was nowhere more outspoken on this topic than when he defended John Brown's raid. Modern society, Thoreau pointed out, was based in violence, and Brown was fighting back. "We preserve the so-called peace of a community by deeds of petty violence every day," he declared. "Look at the policeman's billy and handcuffs! Look at the jail! Look at the gallows!" Those who enforced or even simply tolerated slavery were in effect more anarchic than Brown since they lacked his just purpose.

The moral individual with literary powers had to follow and speak his or her conscience, Thoreau believed, especially when expediency made the opposite course far the easier. Laws should not be enforced and obeyed simply because the prevailing agents of the will of the majority made them. "Any man knows when he is justified, and all the wits in the world cannot enlighten him on that point," Thoreau explained in his plea for Brown. "The only obligation which I have a right to assume," he said in a famous passage from "Resistance to Civil Government," "is to do at any time what I think right." He attacked the notion that injustice was but a "necessary friction of the machine of government," remarking, "but if it is of such a nature that it requires you to be the agent of injustice to another, then, I say, break the law." The individual was not responsible for the mere successful working of the machinery of government, but for the survival of right.

Where did this right exist? Thoreau found it where Emerson did, in what he perceived as the higher laws that he believed all people of conscience saw at work in the natural universe created by God. Obedience to this higher law of principle might violate the much lesser law passed by morally corrupt legislatures. "High treason, when it is resistance to tyranny here below, has its origin in, and is first committed by the power that makes and forever recreates man," he asserted in justifying Brown. It was this higher law Thoreau was seeking to discover and make known when he withdrew from society to live in the cabin he built by Walden Pond and when he subsequently wrote a book about his search. This law was that of the divinity and unity of the creation that nature revealed and that society had ignored or violated. Submission to this higher law paradoxically set the individual free. Thoreau explained in his journal in 1851:

> He who lives according to the highest law is in one sense lawless. That is an unfortunate discovery, certainly, that of a law which binds us where we did not know we were bound. Live free, child of the mist! He for

whom law is made, who does not obey the law but whom the law obeys, reclines on pillows of down and is wafted at will whither he pleases, for man is superior to all laws, both of heaven and earth, when he takes his liberty.

And, finally, who can reveal these higher laws? Who else but the "Man of Genius," the highest sort of artistic sensibility. This "Man of Genius" "is an originator, an inspired or demonic man, who produces a perfect work in obedience to laws yet unexplored." The artist, whether or not a person of genuine genius, is "he who detects and applies the law from observation of the works of Genius, whether of man or nature." Upon reading the Man of Genius's work the common individual is restored to a true sense of right.

Thoreau seemed to be speaking of literary artists as holy legislators who revealed, even if they did not in fact make (a power reserved to God in nature) the higher laws by which humans must live and that ordinary legislators sometimes betray. In this view, he shows his debt to Romantic thought and recalls in particular the English poet Percy Shelley's noted essay, "A Defence of Poetry," in which Shelley asserted that in a visionary sense, "Poets are the unacknowledged legislators of the world." While society might look to its parliaments and congresses for direction in mundane matters, it was the artist who proclaimed the basic truths of life according to which society should be organized. To Shelley, poets and other artists were nothing less than "the institutors of laws, and the founders of civil society, . . . " The poet was not to surrender leadership in important matters of truth and justice to lesser "reasoners and mechanists" who were the acknowledged legislators of the world. The acknowledged legislators would do best to obey the laws the poets reveal.[21]

Both Emerson and Thoreau thus called for literary artists who

[21] Romantic ideas of art, adapted to American conditions, strongly shaped the thinking of the writers of the American Renaissance and still dominate the most widely accepted definitions of literature and the literary artist. Romanticism's history defies a short summary, but in most Romantic thought the artist is a creative genius who follows his or her own intuitions and insights where they lead, and who is not directly concerned with mundane questions (though he or she may well be interested in the ideal of social justice). Insofar as the Romantic artist fulfills his obligations to society, he does so by expressing his own thoughts as freely as possible, sometimes even offering an alternative vision of a more perfect social order. In championing this vision, he refuses to be governed without question by the existing laws and ideas that limit most other citizens. Romanticism is hardly a monolithic ideology, however, and there have been important Romantic artists who have strongly supported the established order, just as there have been those who have advocated revolution.

perceived what others could not see without their help and expressed what others could not say about the higher law that should govern democratic citizens and their representatives in America. This ideal American artist would naturally celebrate the great qualities of the American nation. The poet, said Emerson with another trenchant turn of phrase, "stands among partial men for the complete man, and apprises us not of his wealth, but of the commonwealth." According to Emerson, the poet "is isolated among his contemporaries, by truth and by his art, but with this consolation in his pursuits, that they will draw all men sooner or later. For all men live by truth, and stand in need of expression."

Speaking here in his essay "The Poet," Emerson implied that the literary artist is not a legislator in the sense of being a member of a deliberative body, but an independent social leader who answers a higher call and whose words are accepted by the people. The poet is "the sovereign" who "does not wait for the hero or the sage, but, as they act and think primarily, so he writes primarily what will and must be spoken. . . . " In his vision of an ideal harmonious society, Emerson did not conceive of this poet-sovereign as a tyrant or rebel leader, but as an especially gifted individual who contributed most to society by revealing the truth that was to be understood as such by others in society—including legislators—when they heard it. In short, the poet was a sovereign who truly served society. And, insofar as the poet was dedicated to the harmonious whole, his or her literary and social power was enhanced. The poet's obligation was to study the "nature of things," for "then he is caught up into the life of the Universe, his speech is thunder, his thought is law. . . . " In his poem "Merlin," in which he spoke of the ideal artist, Emerson proclaimed, "The rhyme of the poet / Modulates the King's affairs. . . . "

Emerson observed with regret in "The Poet," "I look in vain for the poet whom I describe." A decade after he wrote these words, however, he received a copy of a book of poems by an individual who consciously and successfully answered his call. In his preface to the first edition of *Leaves of Grass*, Walt Whitman declared that "The United States themselves are essentially the greatest poem." He, too, saw poets not as simple legislators, but as the spiritual if not political sovereigns, lawgivers, and judges of the nation to which they dedicated themselves and their work, who became most powerful when they gave themselves most completely to their country. Whitman proclaimed in the preface:

Of all nations the United States with veins full of poetical stuff most need poets and will doubtless have the greatest and use them the greatest. Their presidents shall not be their common referee so much as their poets shall. Of all mankind the great poet is the equable man. Not in him but off from him things are grotesque or eccentric or fail of their sanity. Nothing out of its place is good and nothing in its place is bad. He bestows on every object or quality its fit proportions neither more nor less. He is the arbiter of the diverse and he is the key. He is the equalizer of his age and land. . . . He supplies what wants supplying and checks what wants checking.

Of course, when one talks of the poet in such terms as these, one is speaking of no common legal figure. Whitman's poet is "no arguer . . . he is judgment. He judges not as the judge judges but as the sun falling around a helpless thing." In Whitman's Romantic democratic ideology, however, the sun-poet rules by serving humanity, by helping the judge do his judging and the lawyer his pleading in harmony with the higher laws that the poet reveals. The result is that every individual's life and the conditions of society are improved spiritually and intellectually. Emerson called the poet a liberating God, and Whitman concurred, stating that poets "are the voice and exposition of liberty," and adding, "Liberty takes the adherence of heroes wherever men and women exist. . . . but never takes any adherence or welcome from the rest more than from poets."

This outlook of Emerson, Thoreau, and Whitman has persisted in the work of America's major writers, who, whether or not they have appealed so explicitly to a higher law based in God's truth, have criticized the legally constituted order and those who maintain and defend it. They have consistently felt it their duty as artists, as individuals of insight and eloquence, to judge American society by their sense of right, and out of this same sense to offer alternative "laws" to live by when the established conditions of life expressed or embodied in the legal system failed to meet their standards.

Examples of writers speaking out against illegality and injustice are common. William Dean Howells, one of the most famous and certainly the most influential figure in American letters of the late nineteenth century—and in most people's eyes a spokesperson for the established social order—shocked his colleagues and his public when he came to the cause of the men hastily and unjustly arrested, convicted, and executed for their alleged role in the Haymarket bombing in Chicago in 1886. These men were prosecuted not on hard evidence but because of their anarchist sympathies and because several of them were foreign-born. In this time of social unrest, the legal authorities and much of the American public were irrationally fearful of radicals and immigrants, and they demanded that villains be singled out and punished.

Howells jeopardized his career in declaring the innocence of the accused and then in asking for clemency after their trial. He published a letter to the editor in the *New York Tribune* in which he criticized the Supreme Court for ignoring substantive issues of justice when it refused the condemned men's appeal on the technical grounds that all the proper procedures were followed. "That court simply affirmed the legality of the forms under which the Chicago court proceeded," Howells observed, adding, "it did not affirm the propriety of trying for murder men fairly indictable for conspiracy alone; and it by no means approved the principle of punishing them because of their frantic opinions, for a crime which they were not shown to have committed." He tried unsuccessfully to recruit additional support, and he was widely condemned for his views. The whole incident accelerated Howells's increasingly troubled view of the state of American society, and in his later work he examined what he saw as the strain of violence and injustice in the world around him.[22]

American writers rallied around few causes since abolition as fervently as they did to protest the execution in 1927 of Italian immigrants Nicola Sacco and Bartolomeo Vanzetti for the murder of two men during a robbery in South Braintree, Massachusetts, in 1920. Many Americans argued that the two did not commit the crime, or at least that the handling of their case was prejudiced and highly irregular. In some ways Sacco and Vanzetti resembled the Haymarket accused. Their defenders believed that the pair were singled out in the shrill xenophobic aftermath of World War I because they were foreigners with unpopular political views. Several noted au-

[22] See Kenneth S. Lynn, *William Dean Howells: An American Life* (New York: Harcourt Brace Jovanovich, 1970), pp. 288–296.

thors, including Edna St. Vincent Millay, John Dos Passos, and Katherine Anne Porter, were active in the various protests and vigils, and their work is the most vivid legacy of the case. Millay's poem, "Justice Denied in Massachusetts," speaks movingly in graceful figurative language of the blight upon the once-blessed land that has been caused by the great injustice:

> Let us go home, and sit in the sitting-room.
> Not in our day
> Shall the cloud go over and the sun rise as before,
> Beneficent upon us
> Out of the glittering bay,
> And the warm winds be blown inward from the sea
> Moving the blades of corn
> With a peaceful sound,
> Forlorn, forlorn,
> Stands the blue hay-rack by the empty mow.
> And the petals drop to the ground,
> Leaving the tree unfruited.
> The sun that warmed our stooping backs and withered the
>   weed uprooted—
> We shall not feel it again.
> We shall die in darkness, and be buried in the rain.[23]

More recently, a very broad representation of members of the American literary community was prominent in the protests against the participation of the United States in what many believed was an illegal and unjust war in Southeast Asia. Several writers, including Norman Mailer and Robert Lowell, played central roles in one of the major early protests against America's deep involvement in Vietnam, the march on the Pentagon in October 1967. Mailer was arrested, and his account of the march in *The Armies of the Night* won the Pulitzer Prize and the National Book Award.

In this book Mailer argued that only the novelist could explain the meaning of the march. The journalist and the historian, he con-

---

[23] Edna St. Vincent Millay, "Justice Denied in Massachusetts," in *Collected Poems of Edna St. Vincent Millay* (New York: Harper & Brothers, 1939), pp. 230–231. Copyright 1928, 1955 by Edna St. Vincent Millay and Norma Millay Ellis.

tended, could not understand it fully because its significance was symbolic and its real history was "interior," inside the psyches of those involved and beneath the surfaces of events, where only the artist could reach. Mailer argued that "no documents can give sufficient intimation: the novel must replace history at precisely that point where experience is sufficiently emotional, spiritual, psychical, moral, existential, or supernatural to expose the fact that the historian in pursuing the experience would be obliged to quit the clearly demarcated limits of historic inquiry."[24] Mailer did not mention the legal system explicitly here (though he discusses it extensively in the book), but his remarks recall Thoreau's argument in regard to John Brown that the legal mind cannot deal with complex and momentous social issues and that the artist is especially gifted to understand and interpret them.

American writers have repeatedly used their "fictions" to explore the breakdown of principle in American law. They have celebrated those who have tried to restore those values vital to humanity which have been lost in the separation of law from what they believe to be fair and right and just, and their audiences have responded to these heroes. Several of America's most beloved works are those that endorse the actions of the individual of conscience in conflict with the law. It is the "lawless" Natty Bumppo in Cooper's *The Pioneers* who has to lecture Judge Temple on what travesties have been committed in the name of the law. The rule of law, Huck Finn discovers, tells him that he should turn Jim in as a runaway slave, but his intuitive sense of right convinces him that he must break the laws of Missouri, or of anywhere else, when they go against those of loyalty, friendship, freedom, and love.

As Maxwell Bloomfield explains in his essay on "Law and Lawyers in American Popular Culture," suspicion of the law and of legal authority permeates popular American literary forms as well. Questions of law, justice, and right and wrong enter into crime literature such as mysteries and thrillers, and they are at the heart of one of the most American of all literary forms, the western. These works often champion the representative of the law—the cop or

---

[24] Norman Mailer, *The Armies of the Night* (New York: New American Library, 1968), p. 284.

frontier marshal—and those who ally themselves with these representatives—including the private eye and self-appointed guardians of justice from Hopalong Cassidy to Batman. But much popular as well as more sophisticated literature questions whether regular legal authority can provide law and order based on truth and justice. Detectives from Poe's Monsieur Dupin to dime-novel hero Nick Carter to Nero Wolfe and Spiderman succeed in spite of the plodding police, and gunslingers from the Lone Ranger to Shane to Superman are frequently outsiders who have to step in to provide justice where legal authority cannot or will not act effectively.

American literature on all levels, furthermore, is full of outlaws who challenge the established rule of law in several ways. The wrongly-punished figure (such as Hawthorne's Clifford in *The House of the Seven Gables*) and the technically guilty but morally innocent character (e.g., Natty Bumppo and Huck Finn) reveal how the law can be mistaken, misguided, or corrupt. The acknowledged lawbreaker (from Hester Prynne to Jay Gatsby and Bigger Thomas) is sometimes in his or her very outlawhood a victim of "the system," and this kind of character is frequently in some important traits nobler than law-abiding society. This irony extends to heroes of popular literary forms as well. One thinks of the film treatment of Butch Cassidy and the Sundance Kid as free spirits of imagination and sensitivity pursued by the agents of corporate America, or of folksinger Woody Guthrie's paean to the outlaw Pretty Boy Floyd as a modern-day Robin Hood who gave groceries to families on relief and whose "crimes" were nothing compared to those of the bankers and lawyers who robbed the poor legally with a fountain pen instead of a six-gun.

In summary, American writers have not been hesitant to attack their country for the petty and gross violations of the ideals of justice it believes it serves. Recently novelist and essayist Ralph Ellison felt obliged to remind his readers "that it is the writer's function precisely to yell 'fire' in crowded theaters, and we do so, of course, through the form in which we work, and the forms of literature are social forms."[25] Ellison was referring to the famous definition of the limits

---

[25] Ralph W. Ellison, "Perspective of Literature," in *American Law: The Third Century*, ed. Bernard Schwartz (South Hackensack, N.J.: Fred B. Rothman & Company, 1976), p. 398.

of free speech, Holmes's assertion in *Schenck v. United States* (1919) that the First Amendment does not "protect a man in falsely shouting fire in a theatre and causing a panic." Ellison's point is that society is full of injustices, "theatres" that are *really* on fire. The problem is that most individuals do not perceive or acknowledge these injustices, and they either persecute the critic for endangering everyone by shouting a false alarm or, worse, simply ignore him. But the perceptive and responsible writer who knows the real danger must continue to speak out if society is not to go up in smoke. The Thoreaus, the Natty Bumppos, and the Huckleberry Finns do much to preserve the basis of the legality they appear to be criticizing or violating.

It is important to keep in mind the extent to which the American writer's criticism of the law has been motivated by patriotism and love for the ideals on which the country is ostensibly based. When writers from Thoreau to Ellison have attacked the condition of justice in their time, they have justified their arguments through such fondly held national principles as individual freedom and unalienable rights, equality before the law, and the will and welfare of the democratic whole. They have found their subject and audience as advocates of responsible citizenship and as guardians of democracy who speak for the welfare of the people against compromise and special interest. They have distinguished themselves from conventional lawyers, whom they have criticized for reducing conflicts based in principle to legalisms and for serving the wealthy or privileged few rather than society as a whole.

In their most bitter attacks on contemporary society, these writers have reminded their readers of the high principles on which the country was founded, of how far the community has strayed from these principles, and of the need to return to them. "What distinguishes the American writer," Sacvan Bercovitch observes, ". . . is his *refusal* to abandon the national covenant." Bercovitch continues, "His identification with America as it ought to be impels the writer to withdraw from what is in America. When he retreats into his art, however, it is characteristically to create a haven for what Thoreau called, 'the only true America.' In effect, the ideals that prompt his isolation enlist individualism itself, aesthetically, morally, and mythically, into the service of society."[26] It is no surprise, then, that an

---

[26] Sacvan Bercovitch, *The American Jeremiad* (Madison: University of Wisconsin Press, 1978), pp. 181–182.

Emerson or a Whitman spoke about the poet as a lawgiver, a Moses who will lead the people to fulfillment of the highest promise of the idea of America.

It should be pointed out again that far from all American writers have criticized or even discussed the law, or have felt that their calling as literary artists placed them in some fundamental opposition to the legal system. Even the most outspoken critics of the law have been selective in their attacks. Nor have these critics by any means been limited to writers but have always included lawyers and judges who have voiced some of the same arguments and added others based on their special expertise. They, too, have been troubled by the possible and actual conflicts between law and justice, necessity and morality, and by situations in which the rule of law has resorted to force and expediency rather than consent and principle. They have agreed with Justice Holmes when he stated in his dissenting opinion in *Lochner v. New York* (1905) that no statute should "infringe fundamental principles as they have been understood by the traditions of our people and our law."

Yet at the same time that Holmes observed in another context that "the law is the witness and external deposit of our moral life," he argued that law and morality were *not* identical, for the law primarily regulated human behavior and did not necessarily formulate ideals and guarantee justice.[27] Holmes and other legal scholars have hoped that American law would always embody the higher principles of which Emerson and Thoreau spoke, and that an appeal to that higher law could be made through the laws of the United States, but they have pointed out that the laws themselves reflect and do not shape the moral well-being of any society and are as good or bad as their social context.

Those who speak in behalf of the legal system argue further that this system is in great measure a practical response to the reality that society does not function by itself, that disputes arise among citizens, and that some individuals commit acts that most members of society would call unacceptable. If society is to be preserved, rights and obligations must be defined, contracts must be made and enforced, disputes must be settled, and criminals must be punished. For these purposes the institution of law exists. Although the legal system must

---

[27] Oliver Wendell Holmes, *The Mind and Faith of Justice Holmes,* ed. Max Lerner (Boston: Little, Brown, 1943), p. 149; Holmes, *Collected Legal Papers,* p. 170. In *Lochner v. New York,* the majority voted to overturn a New York law limiting the hours of work in bakeries.

be sound in principle as well as in procedure if it is to have the support of most citizens and if democracy is to work, occasional faults do appear and the law must try to correct them if it can.

Defenders of the laws and legal authorities, whether poets or lawyers, will admit that the Thoreaus are occasionally right, but they claim that such purists are impractical since they would upset for the sake of a single cause a complicated social organization that is fundamentally sound and that provides principled justice in almost all cases. Where it fails to do so—as, for example, in dealing with certain race-related questions in American history—the fault lies in the make-up of American society generally and does not originate in the law. Where the law does attempt to be the agent of reform—and again the Civil Rights laws and Supreme Court cases come to mind—it often faces the necessary but almost impossible task of reconciling deep-seated and conflicting customs and beliefs. The alternative to the rule of law as it exists, this same defense of the legal system would respond, is a worse system or, if Thoreau's idea that the individual can choose what laws to obey is extended too far, legal anarchy.

Certainly very few American writers have desired anarchy. The highest ambition of Thoreau and other writers with similar sympathies has been to keep the principles of freedom and truth a central concern of all citizens. As artists, they have been especially sensitive to the ways the law has impinged upon their world and has used rhetoric and "literary" forms to substitute the appearance of principles for the real thing. Angered by the abuses of authority and perhaps even jealous of the power of the law, they have been a compensating voice speaking out in an effort to bring the legal order closer to the ideals that they espouse. They have used the power they have—the power of words—to give their ideas the ring of higher truth, and they have presented themselves as lawgivers and judges of a nobler kind, whose art moves the hearts and minds of their readers, as no law can, to an appreciation of the ideal of justice.

Bibliographical Essay

The fields of literature and law are both so rich and so varied that any brief guide to sources and scholarship can only be a list of suggestions for further readings that will open up other possibilities. The list below generally follows the major topics of the main essay in the order in which they were discussed.

The Language of Law

In recent years legal scholars have taken the lead in discussing—and often criticizing—the nature of the language and the expository style with which they work. In *The Language of the Law* (Boston: Little, Brown, 1963), David Mellinkoff describes the language of the law and chronicles its history and use. Mellinkoff calls the law "a profession of words" and argues, "With communication the object, the principle of simplicity would dictate that the language used by lawyers agree with the common speech, unless there are reasons for a difference." Another major study is Walter Probert, *Law, Language and Communication* (Springfield, Ill.: Charles C Thomas, 1972).

Lawrence M. Friedman offers a defense of legal language in "Law and Its Language," *George Washington Law Review* 33 (1964):563–579; while Robert D. Hughes discusses "plain language" in "Some Plain Talk About Plain Language," *Record of the Association of the Bar of the City of New York* 33 (1978):206–211. One recent plain-language law dictionary is Robert F. Rothenberg, ed., *The Plain-Language Law Dictionary* (Baltimore: Penguin Books, 1981). A standard law dictionary is *Black's Law Dictionary*, 5th ed. (St. Paul: West Publishing Company, 1979). George C. Christie speaks about the importance of vagueness in "Vagueness and Legal Language," *Minnesota Law Review* 48 (1964):885–911, as does Edward H. Levi in *An Introduction to Legal Reasoning* (Chicago: University of Chicago Press, 1948). Levi observes, "In an important sense legal rules are never clear, and, if a rule had to be clear before it could be imposed, society would be impossible."

As the title of his book implies, Professor Levi deals with legal language in relation to the world of legal reasoning. This is true about several other works, including Jerome Frank's *Law and the Modern Mind* (New York: Brentano's, 1930). More recently, Professor James H. White has published a very ambitious text (including readings and study questions) on legal thinking and writing, *The Legal Imagination: Studies in the Nature of Legal Thought and Expression* (Boston: Little, Brown, 1973). This excellent and provocative introduction to the subject considers legal writing in a larger "literary" context.

Legal and Literary Interpretation

The issue of complexity of meaning and interpretation in law and literature is a difficult one, made all the more difficult by the fact that legal and literary interpretation have followed different rules and practices. Contemporary legal scholars and literary critics, however, increasingly have been examining their common concerns as readers of texts. This examination includes such matters of interest to both the critic analyzing a poem and the judge interpreting a law or contract as whether it is possible to determine the intent of the poet, the legislator, or the parties in the contract, and whether that intent or any other circumstances relating to the original composition of a text are relevant to its meaning. This discussion has also raised the question of how much the reader determines the meaning of a text, and of whether language is so open to interpretation that in and of itself it has no absolutely determined meaning.

There is much written in the field of interpretation, but for some useful short discussions of some of the problems involved, from the point of view of the judge and lawyer, see Felix Frankfurter, "The Reading of Statutes," in *Of Law and Men: Papers and Addresses of Felix Frankfurter, 1939–1956*, ed. Philip Elman (New York: Harcourt, Brace & Company, 1956), pp. 44–71; Benjamin N. Cardozo, *Law and Literature and Other Essays and Addresses* (New York: Harcourt, Brace & Company, 1931); Kenneth S. Abraham, "Statutory Interpretation and Literary Theory: Some Common Concerns of an Unlikely Pair," *Rutgers Law Review* 32 (1979):676–694; and E. Allan Farnsworth, "'Meaning' in the Law of Contracts," *Yale Law Journal* 76 (1967):939–965. For some recent observations by literary theorists, see E. D. Hirsch, *Validity in Interpretation* (New Haven: Yale University Press, 1967); Richard Jacobsen, "Law, Ritual, Absence: Towards a

Semiology of Law," *University of Hartford Studies in Literature* 9 (1977): 164–174; Stanley E. Fish, "Normal Circumstances, Literal Language, Direct Speech Acts, the Ordinary, the Everyday, the Obvious, What Goes without Saying, and Other Special Cases," *Critical Inquiry* 4 (1978):625–644; and Walter Benn Michaels, "Against Formalism: The Autonomous Text in Legal and Literary Interpretation," *Poetics Today* 1–2 (1979):23–34.

The Law as Literature

Along with Oliver Wendell Holmes, many legal historians have discussed the law as a continuous narrative text with "literary" qualities. Lawrence M. Friedman concedes that legal records of colonial courts may be dreary, "yet among the reports are flashes of extraordinary vividness and color. These records, like no other, lift the veil that hides the face of daily life." Speaking of the Massachusetts Bay Colony, George L. Haskins states that in its court records "we find reflected most clearly the social organization of the colony, its general purposes and aims, and the pressures for change and adaptation resulting from political and economic needs." James Willard Hurst sees formal legal documents as presenting an organized understanding of life in America "because of what they reflect of law's relation to wants, needs, and currents of action and inaction embodied also in other-than-legal institutions, and because they reflect law as a prime instrument for extracting meaning from what always threatens to be a chaotic experience." See Lawrence M. Friedman, *A History of American Law* (New York: Simon & Schuster, 1973); George L. Haskins, "Law and Colonial Society," in *Essays in the History of Early American Law*, ed. David H. Flaherty (Chapel Hill: University of North Carolina Press, 1969), pp. 41–52; James Willard Hurst, "Legal Elements in United States History," in *Law in American History*, ed. Donald Fleming and Bernard Bailyn, *Perspectives in American History* 5 (1971):3–92; and G. Edward White, "The Appellate Opinion as Historical Source Material," in *Patterns of American Legal Thought* (Indianapolis: Bobbs-Merrill, 1978), pp. 74–95.

Milner S. Ball has explored the theatrical qualities of courts. After pointing out the ways in which a court is like a theater, he argues that this similarity is salutary, "encouraging impartiality," "facilitating the judgment process," "redirecting aggression," "providing an image of a legitimate political community." See "The Play's the Thing: An Unscientific Reflection on Courts Under the Rubric of Theater," *Stanford Law Review* 28 (1975):81–115. Lon L. Fuller's *Legal Fictions* (Stanford, Calif.: Stanford University Press, 1967) is a very good introduction. For a discussion of fictions and the links between figurative language and legal language, see Owen Barfield, "Poetic Diction and Legal Fiction," in *Essays Presented to Charles Williams*, ed. C. S. Lewis (Oxford: Oxford University Press, 1947), pp. 106–127. A very influential work on the importance of fictions of all sorts is H. Vaihinger, *The Philosophy of the "As If": A System of the Theoretical, Practical and Religious Fictions of Mankind*, trans. C. K. Ogden (London: Routledge & Kegan Paul, 1965). Finally, for a brief comparison of the function of law and literature as order-making humanistic institutions, see Archibald MacLeish, "Apologia," *Harvard Law Review* 85 (1972): 1505–1511. MacLeish was trained at Harvard Law School before his long career as a poet.

American Writers and the Law

The best way to understand American writers' concepts of the law is to read their works. There are, however, a number of useful studies of the relationship between the law and literary ideologies in American history. The scholar with probably the best mastery of both literary and legal thought was the late Perry Miller, and Book Two, "The Legal Mentality," of his *The Life of the Mind in America* (New York: Harcourt, Brace & World, 1965), is an outstanding account of legal and intellectual history from the Revolution to the Civil War. Probably the finest study of the American literary Renaissance in relation to democratic ideology is still F. O. Matthiessen, *American Renaissance: Art and Expression in the Age of Emerson and Whitman* (New York: Oxford University Press, 1941). John P. McWilliams's *Political Justice in a Republic: James Fenimore Cooper's America* (Berkeley:University of California Press, 1972) is an excellent examination of one major writer's treatment of the law.

For more on the literary lawyers of the early republic, see the writings of William Charvat and Robert A. Ferguson cited in the main essay, as well as Miller's book. Richard Beale Davis also looks at this group in "The Early American Lawyer and the Profession of Letters," *The Huntington Library Quarterly* 12 (1948–1949), 191–205. Anton-Hermann Chroust studies the rise of the legal profession in *The Rise of the Legal Profession in America* (Norman: University of Oklahoma Press, 1965). Of more specific interest on the evolution of the legal profession are two first-rate books, Morton J. Horwitz's *The Transformation of American Law, 1790–1860* (Cambridge: Harvard University Press, 1977); and Maxwell Bloomfield, *American Lawyers in a Changing Society, 1776–1876* (Cambridge: Harvard University Press, 1976). Bloomfield includes a chapter on "Antilawyer Sentiment in the Early Republic."

The Law in Literature

There have been a number of collections and lists of works of literature that discuss the law, some of which focus on legal writings that have a claim to be fine literature. John Henry Wigmore, the distinguished Dean of the Northwestern University School of Law earlier this century, compiled a list of what he called "legal novels." By Wigmore's definition, a legal novel had at least one of the following features: a description of a trial or other legal proceeding; a portrayal of a lawyer, judge, or some aspect of professional life; a delineation of the methods of law in the prosecution and punishment of crime; or a discussion of some point of law. See "A List of One Hundred Legal Novels," *Illinois Law Review* 17 (1922):26–41. Anthologies of law and literature include Ephraim London, ed., *The World of Law: A Treasury of Great Writings About and in the Law*, 2 vols. (New York: Simon & Schuster, 1960); William H. Davenport, ed., *Voices in Court: A Treasury of the Bench, the Bar, and the Courtroom* (New York: Macmillan, 1958); and Louis Blom-Cooper, ed., *The Language of the Law: An Anthology of Legal Prose* (London: The Bodley Head, 1965).

For literary responses to particular actual legal conflicts, the richest example is the Sacco-Vanzetti case. There are many histories and analyses of their trial and appeal. As recently as 1977, Katherine Anne Porter published *The Never-Ending Wrong* (Boston: Little, Brown), which tells of her involvement in the case, as well as that of other writers and intellectuals. Of special interest to students of law and literature are such works in defense of Sacco and Vanzetti as *The Sacco-Vanzetti Anthology of Verse*, ed. Henry Harrison (New York: Henry Harrison, 1927); a similar anthology of poems titled *America Arraigned!*, ed. Lucia Trent and Ralph Cheyney (New York: Dean and Company, 1928); and John Dos Passos's *Facing the Chair: Story of the Americanization of Two Foreignborn Workmen* (Boston: Sacco-Vanzetti Defense Committee, 1927). In 1948 G. Louis Joughin and Edmund M. Morgan published *The Legacy of Sacco and Vanzetti* (New York: Harcourt, Brace & Company), an examination of the impact of the case on American law, society, and literature. Part III (pp. 373–514) discusses the literary impact, and notes that almost 150 poems, six plays (most notably Maxwell Anderson's *Winterset*), and eight novels (including Upton Sinclair's *Boston* and Dos Passos's *U.S.A.*) were directly or indirectly inspired by the case. See also David Felix, *Protest: Sacco-Vanzetti and the Intellectuals* (Bloomington: Indiana University Press, 1965). There are also many studies of a specific writer's handling of certain aspects of the law in his or her time. See McWilliams on James Fenimore Cooper and L. Lynn Hogue, "The Presentation of Post-Revolutionary Law in Woodcraft: Another Perspective on the 'Truth' of Simms's Fiction," *The Mississippi Quarterly* 31 (1978):201–210.

Freedom of Expression

One issue relating to basic rights and freedoms not dealt with in the main essay but of great interest to writers and to students of law and literature is the matter of freedom of expression as protected by the First Amendment. Much of the discussion of the First Amendment (which guarantees freedom of speech and the press, as well as religion, peaceful assembly, and the right to petition the government for a redress of grievances) has centered on what the individual is allowed to write and publish without fear of prosecution and censorship. A good deal of this discussion has involved the regulation of obscenity and pornography. The Laws and court decisions that have declared that obscenity and pornography are not protected under the First Amendment have been enforced not only against texts that most people—even those who would most strongly champion the rights of such texts to be published and read—would deem offensive and of little merit on any grounds, but even against works that have received critical praise and have come to be considered classics. At various times in this century, charges have been brought against the writings of D. H. Lawrence, Theodore Dreiser, William Faulkner, James Joyce, James T. Farrell, and Henry Miller, not to mention Ovid and Boccaccio. One of several fine works on literary censorship is Charles Rembar's *The End of Obscenity: The Trials of Lady Chatterley, Tropic of Cancer, and Fanny Hill* (New York: Random House, 1968).

As noted earlier, the reader is urged to consult literary works themselves for their sensitivity to legal issues. At the same time, the reader should look at the whole range of legal writings and how they function in society with an eye to the significance of their "literary" nature.

1. At the outset of the essay, law and literature are both described as "cultural institutions." Do you agree? How is literature an institution? Is it an institution in the same way that law is?

2. Look through a law dictionary, such as *Black's Law Dictionary*, and try to get a sense of the language of the law. Isolate some terms that seem to be peculiar to the law and put their meaning in your own words. Then look up words that you know are in common and everyday use and compare the legal definitions with those in a conventional dictionary. What is the nature of the differences, if any? If you can locate a plain-language law dictionary, see what added meaning, if any, it offers.

3. Examine a standard legal form or document. This might include a will, a contract (perhaps a lease), an application, a notice, or a license. Look at the way it uses language. Study its diction, its level of abstraction, its verb tenses, its figurative qualities (e.g., use of symbols, metaphor, alliteration, repetition, euphemism), and its whole appearance. Try to characterize it. How would you distinguish it from a poem or a piece of fiction or an essay? Is it useful to try to understand it in these terms?

4. Examine a judicial decision, perhaps in a noted Supreme Court case. These are available in legal texts and in many American history source books, such as Henry Steele Commager's *Documents of American History*. You might want to focus on a decision by a justice known for his literary skills, such as Holmes or Marshall, as well as one by a less accomplished writer. Again, compare these decisions to a poem or short story, or to an essay like Thoreau's "Slavery in Massachusetts" or Shelley's "A Defence of Poetry." How does it make its argument? What are its rhetorical devices and how do these relate to its legal argument?

5. Examine the law as a statement about the nature of humanity. Look in particular at "the supreme law of the land," the Constitution. How is it an expression of a view about the nature of the individual in society? What is this view and how is it expressed? As in questions 3 and 4, consider the way the law uses language and how this relates to its meaning and effect on the reader.

6. Look at a statute, a legal document, or a court decision, and consider the problems of interpretation it poses. Is its meaning clear? What possible ambiguities do you perceive and how important are these to its meaning and usefulness?

7. Consider the proceedings of the law as drama. Is it a misleading oversimplification to think of a trial as a form of theater? In what way or ways is a trial essentially *un*like a play or a novel? What is the importance of the dramatic qualities of other ceremonies with legal implications, such as a

presidential inauguration, a wedding, an induction into the Armed Forces, an execution? What aspects of the law do popular dramatizations (such as television programs about lawyers or police) focus on? If possible, read an actual trial transcript or, better, attend a trial and consider its aesthetic dimensions. For more suggestions along these lines, see John McWilliams's essay in this volume, "Innocent Criminal or Criminal Innocence: The Trial in American Fiction."

8.   Consider legal fictions in relation to literary fictions. Does the fact that both law and literature use the term *fiction* really confuse the issue? Are legal and literary fictions two very different things?

9.   Do legal fictions and literary fictions in some important way compete with one another, each asking us in its special manner to accept its version of reality? Where do they get whatever authority they have in expecting us to believe in them?

10.   Read Barlow's *Columbiad*, or a significant excerpt. Describe its form, its use of language, its level of abstraction, its discussion of its subject matter. In what way or ways do its form and content speak to the legal order of the new American nation?

11.   Thoreau's "Resistance to Civil Government" is one of the most well-known essays by an American writer. Its notions of civil disobedience have guided political movements both in this country and abroad. Compare it, for example, with Martin Luther King, Jr.'s, "Letter from a Birmingham Jail," in which King writes, "One has not only a legal but a moral responsibility to obey just laws. Conversely, one has a moral responsibility to disobey unjust laws." Examine Thoreau's essay carefully to see what kind of political and legal order he proposes. How does it compare with that proposed by the Constitution, or with the way the legal order as you understand it was in Thoreau's time or is today?

12.   Consider a literary text as an explicit or implicit endorsement or critique of the established legal order. You might consider another of Thoreau's essays (or *Walden*), Whitman's "Democratic Vistas" or "Song of Myself," Cooper's *The Pioneers*, Hawthorne's *The Scarlet Letter* or *The House of the Seven Gables*, Twain's *The Adventures of Huckleberry Finn* or *The Tragedy of Pudd'nhead Wilson*, Howells's *A Hazard of New Fortunes*, Dreiser's *An American Tragedy* (again, see John McWilliams's essay), or Mailer's *The Armies of the Night*. Keep in mind that not all writers have attacked the law, and that many (like Dreiser) who have discussed social injustice have not believed in the existence of the "higher laws" that Thoreau described. You might instead (or also) discuss these and other works as guides to how the individual should behave in relation to legal authority.

Innocent Criminal or Criminal Innocence: The Trial in American Fiction

John P. McWilliams, Jr.

Professor of American Literature
Middlebury College

Innocent: (1) Doing no evil; free from wrong, sin or guilt; pure, unpolluted. (2) Free from specific wrong; that is, has not committed the particular offense charged.

Criminal: (1) Of the nature of a crime; more generally, of the nature of a grave offense; wicked. (2) Relating to crime or its punishment. (3) Guilty of crime or grave offense.

The Oxford English Dictionary

I often doubt whether it would not be a gain if every word of moral significance could be banished from the law altogether, and other words adopted which should convey legal ideas uncolored by anything outside the law.

Oliver Wendell Holmes, Jr.
"The Path of the Law" (1897)

Introduction

If justice might be obtained merely through verbal clarity, Holmes's understandably exasperated desire to strip away the moral inference of legal terms would be both practicable and persuasive.* The moral and legal definitions provided by the *Oxford English Dictionary* are, to be sure, problematic, if not inherently self-contradictory. Is an impure, polluted sinner who has committed no particular charged offense to be considered "innocent"? Is an individual, not of wicked nature, but legally guilty of grave offense, to be considered "criminal"?

It is of little use to assert that we might solve these problems if we could separate the realms of legal decision and moral judgment. Both words convey both meanings simultaneously; we persist in hoping that law can serve justice. As long as the very words *innocent, guilty, criminal, law,* and *justice* are used in daily court procedure, so long must moral and criminal law remain confusingly linked in the minds

---

* I would like to acknowledge my thanks to the following individuals for particular suggestions that have helped me immeasurably in the writing of this essay: Daniel Aaron, Sacvan Bercovitch, Gerald Fetner, Robert Gross, David Littlefield, Stephen Presser, G. Edward White, and Morris Wolff.

not only of witnesses, jurors, and the public but of lawyers and judges. Perhaps we should counter Holmes's reasoning by considering that the very vagueness of these double terms is an inevitable consequence of the law's greatest virtue. If legal procedure ever were to devise a set of terms utterly devoid of moral content, human beings would have made of the law both a monument to the factual and logical capacity of the human mind, and a civilization so emotionally dissatisfying, so objectively impersonal, that no human being could abide it, especially Mr. Holmes.

Novelists, who need not make court decisions but are free to fictionalize them, are likely to treasure the very ambiguity of terminology that must be so maddening to practitioners of the law. When the dying Arthur Dimmesdale exclaims to Hester Prynne that they cannot meet in the afterlife because of "the law we broke," Hawthorne immediately associates that "law," not with the seventh commandment of Jehovah, nor with the Puritan theocracy's civil law against adultery, but with an alegal attitude: "We violated our reverence each for the other's soul."[1] Similarly, when Huckleberry Finn finally decides he prefers to "go to hell" rather than turn Jim in as demanded by fugitive slave laws, Twain encourages his reader to admire Huck for consigning himself to some nonexistent heaven because he has acted upon a higher law of human decency.[2] At climactic moments of both novels, Hawthorne and Twain thus encourage us to consider that the deeper definition of the term *law* may be moral rather than civil. To return to the problem of language, both authors are acutely aware that the word *justice* is used to convey such contrary meanings as (1) "Observance of the Divine Law," (2) "Conformity to truth or fact," and (3) "The administration of the law, or the forms and processes attending it."[3]

My purpose is to study how the law functions as a standard for conduct in the four major American novels that climax in a criminal trial: Fenimore Cooper's *The Pioneers* (1823), Herman Melville's *Billy Budd* (1891, 1924), Theodore Dreiser's *An American Tragedy* (1925), and Richard Wright's *Native Son* (1940). Together with lesser novels, these four works comprise a particular fictional

---

[1] Nathaniel Hawthorne, *The Scarlet Letter*, ed. L. Ziff (Indianapolis and New York: Bobbs-Merrill, 1963), p. 241.
[2] Mark Twain, *Huckleberry Finn*, ed. H. N. Smith (Boston: Houghton Mifflin, 1958), p. 180.
[3] The second, third, and fifth definitions of the word *justice* in the *Oxford English Dictionary*.

tradition. Their protagonists (Leatherstocking, Billy Budd, Clyde Griffiths, Bigger Thomas) are all *naif* males whose initial moral innocence is partly caused by their ignorance of society's economic and legal institutions. Confronting an increasingly settled and rigid society that needs to protect life, liberty, and property by statute, all four of them remain unable to express their feelings about either society or their place in it. Their inability to articulate their emotions results in moments of psychological paralysis that are violently released in acts of assault or manslaughter. The plots of all four novels accordingly culminate in criminal trials in which the reader is led emotionally to sympathize with the accused as a victim, but rationally to assent to society's need for preventative criminal sanction.

In all four novels the judge's insistence that courts reach decisions on the basis of deeds, not motives, contributes to a final verdict of guilty. Consequently, the judges' arguments are accorded respect because they are based on convictions of legal principle. To the extent that villainy enters into this fictive tradition, it is associated with the agent of prosecution, be he a justice of the peace, master at arms, county attorney, or state attorney, whose motives may include greed, sadistic curiosity, political preferment, or malice of such magnitude that it must be termed "natural depravity." Billy Budd, Clyde Griffiths, and Bigger Thomas are found guilty of murder and sentenced to death; the severity of Leatherstocking's sentence hastens his decision to leave civilization for the wilderness. None of the four novels, however, ends with that sense of mitigation, mutual understanding, or restoration that often follows the demise of the protagonist in dramatic tragedy. Instead, the reader must question whether any of the participants in the trial, including the accused, has been changed or enlightened by his experience. It is precisely this doubt, however, which intensifies the reader's sense that only the fictive record provided by the novel has been able to reveal the full complexities, if not the truth, of the issues involved in the trial.

We are dealing here with a legal variant of our novelists' abiding need to recreate, in R. W. B. Lewis's phrase, "the American Adam."[4] Unlike many literary works that free the American Adam from society, these four novels show us a paradise corrupted as the novel opens, and then introduce us to an Adam who does not fall

[4] R. W. B. Lewis, *The American Adam: Innocence, Tradition and Tragedy in the Nineteenth Century* (Chicago: University of Chicago Press, 1965).

through his own free will. My concern, however, will not be with the mythic implications of these texts, but with their pertinence to the tradition of American legal thought. All four novels treat the conundrum of majority versus minority rights in a way that directly juxtaposes the individual's supposed right to freedom or absolute justice against society's need for civil order.

The very recurrence of this pattern raises fundamental questions. Why should the best American novels dealing with civil justice all contain plots which encourage the belief that one unaided individual is the worthy adversary, hence the equal in right, of the political state? Why do all these novels end in verdicts of guilt, which, even if they are defensible by criminal statutes, are promptly questioned by alternative standards of divine law or social circumstance? Clearly, these novels reflect the American writer's tendency—ably discussed in Carl Smith's essay—to express patriotic suspicions of the workings of legal institutions in the name of some higher law. Why, however, should this tendency be so prevalent in American literature? To provide even tentative answers to such questions, we will need to consider matters beyond the texts of the novels: (1) differences between the fictional trial and its historical model, (2) the author's political and social attitudes and, most important, (3) broad historical changes in American attitudes toward man-made law as an agent of justice.

One question may be resolved with some certainty at the outset: Why the continued fascination with the criminal law and, more particularly, with murder? There is, of course, the fascination for the atrocity of the deed itself, the dramatic pacing that a novel can gain through the double climaxes of the act of murder and the trial decision. And yet a good criminal law novel, like a good criminal trial, surely is great theater everywhere. Perhaps Jerome Hall brings us closer to the particular pertinence of criminal law for American audiences when he contends, "Criminal law is people's law in a sense that applies to no other department of law. Indeed, for some persons criminal law is the only familiar law because of almost daily actual and vicarious participation in its process."[5] Hall's idea suggests that the criminal trial may have special resonance to the people of a

---

[5] Jerome Hall, "The Basic Dilemma of Criminal Procedure," in *Crime, Law and Society*, eds. A. S. Goldstein and J. Goldstein (New York: Collier-Macmillan, 1971), p. 236. Originally published as "Objectives of Federal Criminal Procedural Revision," *Yale Law Journal* 51 (1942): 723–734.

democratic republic. Not surprisingly, some of the special historical developments of American criminal procedure are directly reflected in these novels: the expanded role of a popularly elected prosecuting attorney, the expanded role of a defense attorney, and heavy reliance on trial by jury, especially during the nineteenth century.[6] Roscoe Pound, however, suggests reasons even deeper than these. In *Criminal Justice in Cleveland* (1922), Pound argues that in a democracy each citizen will believe he can judge criminal guilt as well as any judge; hence "the individual citizen looks only at single cases, and measures them by his individual sense of right and wrong."[7] This assumption lies behind our constitutional guarantee of a jury trial in capital cases; perhaps it also leads an American reader or writer to approach a criminal law novel with a greater investment of individual spirit. As Pound rather testily observes, Americans have always "put into action a conviction that conformity to the dictates of the individual conscience is a test of the validity of the law."[8]

I

Rights

It would be hard to overestimate the effect that theories of Natural Right have had on American legal and political thought.[9] Everywhere that the Founding Fathers turned for intellectual support, they found statements that led them to believe that there existed, somewhere, a set of timeless universal principles, called Natural Law, which were based on Divine Law, but which should in turn become the basis of civil or man-made law. According to these Laws of Nature, all individuals are entitled to have their Natural Rights protected. These individual rights, sometimes left altogether unspecified, were usually thought to include the Rights to life, liberty, security, and property, although what these Rights prescribed in practice was not easy to

---

[6] See J. W. Hurst, *The Growth of American Law: The Law Makers* (Boston: Little, Brown, 1950), pp. 174–175; Roscoe Pound, *Criminal Justice in America* (New York: Henry Holt, 1930), pp. 65, 140, 183; Raymond Moley, *Our Criminal Courts* (New York: Minton, Balch, 1930), p. 20.

[7] Roscoe Pound, *Criminal Justice In Cleveland* (Cleveland: Cleveland Foundation, 1922), p. 565.

[8] Ibid., p. 567.

[9] See Benjamin Fletcher Wright, Jr., *American Interpretations of Natural Law* (Cambridge: Harvard University Press, 1931).

determine. Because these Rights could never be reliably guaranteed in the State of Nature, it was the primary duty of any civil government to secure the Natural Rights of those individuals who had together contracted to form it. In a tripartite republic, it was the special function of the judiciary to guard against incursions on Natural Right, provided of course that the judiciary could rule that a legislative act might be unconstitutional.

The fundamental law was believed to originate neither in statute law nor the common law of England. It existed in the nature of things. Since 1630, American Puritans had believed that civil law should reflect Divine Law, that men covenanted together to obtain, in Winthrop's phrase, the "Civil Liberty" to submit to just authority.[10] Thomas Hobbes had written that "Heaven and earth shall pass, but not one tittle of the law of nature shall pass, for it is the eternal God."[11] John Locke, in a passage even better known to Americans, had contended, "The Law of Nature stands as an eternal rule to all men, legislators as well as others. The rules that they make must be conformable to the Law of Nature—i.e., to the will of God."[12] Sir William Blackstone, author of the *Commentaries* (1768), the textbook by which generations of Americans would learn law, had insisted in his introduction that the "law of nature, being coeval with mankind, and dictated by God himself, is of course superior to any other."[13] The theory of Natural Rights may have originated in Grotius, but it received its greatest support among English political philosophers whose ideas would be used against England by the colonists.

We scarcely need to be reminded that the justification offered for declaring the independence of the United States of America was that they were entitled to separate, equal station by "the laws of nature

[10] Winthrop's famous distinction between Natural and Civil Liberty may be found in his speech to the General Court at Hingham (1635). Roscoe Pound's chapter, "Puritanism and the Law," established important continuities between Puritan and Revolutionary attitudes toward the law (see Roscoe Pound, *The Spirit of the Common Law* [Francestown, N.H.: Marshall Jones & Co., 1921], pp. 32–59). Many of Perry Miller's findings about Puritan notions of covenant and contract may also be found in Pound's essay.

[11] Thomas Hobbes, *The Leviathan* , ed. M. Oakeshott (New York: Collier-Macmillan, 1971), pp. 262–263.

[12] John Locke, *Second Treatise on Civil Government, in Locke on Politics, Religion and Education*, ed. Maurice Cranston (New York: Collier-Macmillan, 1965), p. 65.

[13] William Blackstone, "The Nature of Laws in General," introduction to *Commentaries on the Laws of England, Ehrlich's Blackstone* (San Carlos, Calif.: Nourse Publishing Co., 1959), p. 40.

and of nature's God." Nor need we belabor Jefferson's insistence that only through independence could the colonies guarantee the self-evident truth that "all men . . . are endowed by their Creator with certain inalienable rights."[14] But we should recognize how long and fervently this fundamental rationale for political and legal action would be maintained. Important prerevolutionary pamphlets repeatedly cited the laws of nature as the ultimate source of the colonists' political rights, whether those rights were inherited from the common law or passed by colonial statute.[15] The constitutions of most of the original states echoed the language of the preamble of the Declaration directly. The first ten amendments to the federal Constitution were an attempt to codify individual rights.

Familiarity with the bitter quarrels of 1800 is likely to lead us to assume that the following passage must have been written by a doctrinaire Republican:

> The sacred rights of mankind are not to be rummaged for among old parchments or musty records. They are written, as with a sun beam, in the whole volume of human nature, by the hand of divinity itself; and can never be erased or obscured by mortal power.[16]

The writer, however, was that supposed closet monarchist, Alexander Hamilton. During the next generation, when James Kent, Joseph Story, and Benjamin Wharton compiled their legal texts intended to adapt the common law to America, all three followed generations of precedent in insisting upon "natural, inherent and inalienable" rights as the very basis of law.[17] A goodly number of Chief Justice John Marshall's opinions were cast in terms of "Natural

---

[14] Thomas Jefferson, "The Declaration of Independence," in *The Life and Selected Writings of Thomas Jefferson*, eds. Adrienne Koch and William Peden (New York: Random House, 1944), p. 22. The twenty-five lawyers who signed the Declaration thus testified to their belief in Natural Rights theory.

[15] The most important examples are: James Otis, "The Rights of the British Colonies Asserted and Proved" (1764); John Adams, "A Dissertation of the Canon and Feudal Law" (1765); Benjamin Franklin, "Rules By Which A Great Empire May Be Reduced To A Small One" (1773); Thomas Jefferson, "A Summary View of the Rights of British North America" (1774); James Wilson, "Considerations on the Nature and Extent of Legislative Authority of the British Parliament" (1774).

[16] Alexander Hamilton, "The Farmer Refuted" (1775) in *The Papers of Alexander Hamilton*, ed. Harold C. Syrett et al., (New York: Columbia University Press, 1961), I, 127.

[17] James Kent, *Commentaries on American Law*, ed. O. W. Holmes, Jr. (Boston: Little Brown, 1873), 1:4.

Rights" theory.[18] Perhaps the best measure of the prevalence of the Republic's commitment to a government of Natural and Divine Law is to name a few of the important single cause groups which, during the antebellum period, cited the Rights of Nature in their founding constitutions: The American Antislavery Convention (1835), the Liberty Party (1844), the Free Soil Party (1848), the Seneca Falls Women's Convention (1848) and the Republican Party (1854).

The implications of Natural Rights theory proved to be as important as the idea itself. First, belief in an absolute standard of Natural and Divine Law encouraged the assumption that Law existed independently of any mind that perceived it. During the Revolutionary and antebellum periods, legislators, jurists and writers therefore assumed that law was a harmonium of universal principles they could discover, not a mere set of social rules they must make. Rufus Choate, for example, pronounced the law to be "an independent, superior reason, in one sense out of the people, in one sense above them,—out of and above, and independent of, and collateral to, the people of any given day."[19] Second, Natural Rights theory made the individual the *raison d'être* of the state, yet simultaneously ascribed to individual reason a justification for rebelling against the state. Jefferson, Paine, and Adams were ironically concurring with Blackstone when they argued that individuals have a right not to obey man-made statutes that contradict Natural or Divine Law. (Blackstone had written "no human law is of any validity, if contrary to this [law of nature]").[20] If the state exists for the sake of the individual, the plight of one individual can readily seem a value equal to the whole. In Roscoe Pound's formulation,

> the political and legal theory of the last two centuries makes each citizen the ultimate judge of whether his natural rights are infringed. If, as he sees it, they have been, then he is justified in refusing to obey the precept which goes beyond the permissable limits of lawmaking. . . . The citizen is invited to judge for himself at the crisis of action whether and how far to enforce the law as it stands in the books.[21]

---

[18] See G. Edward White, *The American Judicial Tradition* (New York: Oxford University Press, 1976), pp. 14–15.

[19] Rufus Choate, "The Position and Functions of the American Bar" (1845), in Perry Miller, *The Legal Mind in America* (Ithaca, N.Y.: Cornell University Press, 1962), p. 270.

[20] Blackstone, "The Nature of Laws," p. 40.

[21] Roscoe Pound, *Criminal Justice in America* (New York: Henry Holt, 1930), p. 130. These lectures were delivered in 1923.

John Locke's quasi-biblical pronouncement, "In the beginning, all the world was America,"[22] thus demonstrates why the theory of Natural Rights, despite its British proponents, found its most congenial soil here. To be sure, the ideal of Natural Rights provided revolutionaries with justification for violent acts of civil disobedience. But, by positing an absolute law applicable to each natural man, Natural Rights theorists encouraged the assumption that a nation could indeed be natural. It actually seemed possible that an ideal civil state could be realized within that State of Nature that the sheer expanse of America, above all known places on the globe, promised forever to embody.

There were, however, formidable theoretical as well as practical difficulties in realizing a legal system based on Natural Rights. No one knew, and few even attempted to define, precisely what *Natural Law* or *Divine Law* specifically demanded toward the protection of life, liberty, or property. As Jefferson admitted, "Those who write treatises of natural law, can only declare what their own moral sense and reason dictate in the several cases they state."[23] The expectation that all reasonable men would eventually discover the same fundamental Divine Laws in Nature, an assumption common to Jefferson and Emerson, as well as to such fictional characters as Cooper's Leatherstocking and Melville's Ishmael, would remain a hope neither provable nor disprovable.

An even more vexing problem was to define the justifiable—or socially acceptable—limits of behavior for any individual who claimed to perceive the natural or divine law. American literature as well as American law has been bedeviled by such questions. What law can adequately refute the squatter who claims that God gave the earth in common for a settler's use (Cooper's *The Deerslayer*)? If a humble beehive shows that Nature rewards the industry of republican farmers, can the lawyers and plantation aristocrats of Charleston truly belong to America (Crèvecoeur's *Letters From An American Farmer*)? If the higher law demands that citizens should never, for one moment, resign their consciences to a legislator, must we practice passive resistance in every instance of legal injustice (Thoreau's "On the Duty of Civil Disobedience")? If God speaks through the feelings

---

[22] Locke, *Second Treatise on Civil Government*, p. 37.
[23] Jefferson, "Opinion on the Question Whether the United States Have a Right to Renounce Their Treaties with France" (1793), in *The Life and Selected Writings of Thomas Jefferson*, p. 317.

of the female heart, should a senator follow his wife's advice to defy the fugitive slave law (Stowe's *Uncle Tom's Cabin*)?

Even before the war for independence was concluded, there arose an even more fundamental and pressing problem. The logic of Natural Rights theory demanded that the new Republic create its own body of statute laws, which would correspond to Natural and Divine Law. Although the colonies had governed themselves largely by the English common law and had claimed the common law as their heritage of rights (including the right to resist), the English common law was, after 1775, popularly considered to be a vestige of the old order, deeply compromised by feudal privilege. And yet, even though the Republic was to be a government of laws and not of men, the Republic needed first of all to survive. To survive meant to govern, to govern now, and to govern by some code of laws. The vacuum was to be filled in many ways: partly by state and community statute law, partly by *ad hoc* decrees of ill-trained frontier judges, and partly, we may be sure, by the law of nature. The ultimately dominant solution, however, was to import the English common law and to adapt it, where necessary, to American conditions. Such was the conscious aim and great achievement of James Kent, Joseph Story, and the long tradition of Federalist and Whig judiciary of the early nineteenth century.[24] The importance of this solution for us, however, is to perceive how closely this legal compromise finds its counterpart in American literature. Shortly after hostilities began, there arose a demand for an indigenous, independent literature, new in form to suit new republican values. Although the new forms were not promptly forthcoming, the need for some kind of American literature continued unabated. The consequence was that the Republic's next generation of writers compromised the demand for novelty by adapting British literary forms to American subjects and to American values. There is good reason why Americans never quite knew whether they were proud or ashamed to call Cooper "The American Scott," Bryant "The American Wordsworth," and Irving "The American Goldsmith."

THE PIONEERS

When Roscoe Pound sought evidence to confirm his belief that theories of individual rights had prevailed, perhaps excessively, in

---

[24] See Perry Miller's "The Legal Mentality," Book 2 of *The Life of the Mind in America* (New York: Harcourt, Brace & World, 1965), pp. 99–265.

nineteenth-century American criminal courts, he cited evidence both from court records (the refusal of courts to convict for murder when "honor" was at stake) and from literature. In two of his books, Pound cites Cooper's *The Pioneers* as an accurate rendering of the procedures of criminal law on the early nineteenth-century frontier.[25] To Pound, Cooper's ready sympathy for Leatherstocking's appeals to divine law, Cooper's faith in mild laws, and Cooper's relishing of the crudities of Judge Temple's court all provided fit evidence for Pound's own contentions about judicial individualism.[26] Samuel Walker's recent description of frontier criminal courts emphasizes other practices confirmed in Cooper's novel: the improvised informality of trial procedure, the ease of escaping from jail, the tendency for court day to become a seasonal social event, the respect accorded a judge, and the ludicrous attempt of rural pettifoggers to hide their legal incompetence behind bustle and show.[27]

Almost against Cooper's will, the novel outgrew its modest claim to be "A Descriptive Tale" and confronted a great contemporary issue. Given the national commitment both to Natural Rights and to the March of Civilization, who was the true hero? The gentlemen who relied upon property contracts, man-made law, and votes to build a good society at demonstrable expense to natural liberty? Or the individualist who, relying upon himself and the wilderness around him, pursued without qualification the laws of Nature's God? Cooper's novel personifies these conflicting models of heroism, shows us that they must be mutually exclusive, yet refuses explicitly to sanction one at the other's expense.

Although Leatherstocking exemplifies the just man in a Lockean State of Nature, Judge Temple must bring institutional justice to the State of Civilization. Once Templeton's permanence is assured, Leatherstocking's values become, not less true, but less pertinent. As the life of the hunter yields to the life of the farmer, so must natural justice yield to civil justice. Heroic though the codes of Leather-

---

[25] Pound, *The Spirit of the Common Law*, p. 123; Pound, *Criminal Justice in America*, p. 122. Cooper's novel, published in 1823, actually describes events supposedly transpiring in 1793.

[26] More evidence of the same sort may be found in Joseph Baldwin's *The Flush Times of Alabama and Mississippi* (New York: Appleton & Co., 1853). Observing criminal courts on the southwestern frontier led Baldwin to conclude that "the iron rules of British law were too tyrannical for free Americans. . . . They were unsuited to the genius of American institutions and the American character" (p. 59).

[27] Samuel Walker, *Popular Justice: A History of American Criminal Justice* (New York: Oxford University Press, 1980), pp. 17–27, 108–123.

stocking and Indian John may have been in the forest, they are, at best, magnificent anachronisms within a settled society.

The book opens with a glimpse of Templeton in 1823 in order to emphasize that, long after Leatherstocking's departure, the community has continued to illustrate civilized progress. Templeton now lies, Cooper writes, in a land of "beautiful and thriving villages," "neat and comfortable farms," replete with rich valleys and running streams. Cooper insists upon tracing Templeton's blessings back to political rather than natural merits:

> In short, the whole district is hourly exhibiting how much can be done, in even a rugged country, and with a severe climate, under the dominion of mild laws, and where every man feels a direct interest in the prosperity of a commonwealth, of which he knows himself to form a part.[28]

To Cooper, flourishing frontier communities like Templeton were proof of the validity of a republican polity, because they were founded on the assumption that needy settlers, working industriously and with minimal legal restraint, would create pastoral prosperity. Cooper knew, however, that his assumption was questionable. With what ease necessity can serve as an excuse for selfishness, emulation shade into envy, and hustling descend into prying!

The difficulties begin with the vexing problem of land ownership. The owner of the land may have the right to institute civil laws based on the moral law, but who rightly owns the land? Cooper has created five characters all of whom advance a plausible claim to "own" the land on Judge Temple's patent. Each of these claimants— Indian, dispossessed Tory, present holder of the deed, squatter, manipulating pettifogger—appeals either to natural, moral, or civil law as justification for land ownership and the rights it entails.

The conservation laws that cause the conflict between Leatherstocking and the judge arise from the settlers' inability to adjust their civilization to its environs. Although Leatherstocking and Judge Temple both maintain that the bounties of nature may be consumed only according to a person's need, plundering settlers like Billy Kirby good-naturedly axe the trees, massacre the pigeons, and drag nets for bass, primarily for the senseless pleasure of slaughter.

---

[28] James Fenimore Cooper, *The Pioneers* (New York: New American Library, 1964), pp. 13–14.

The disgust that both the judge and Leatherstocking feel at this outrage on natural law expresses itself in exactly opposite ways. Leatherstocking dramatizes the moral law of nature. Marching up to the scene of a pigeon massacre, he shoots one pigeon and stalks defiantly away from the town sheriff and the justice of the peace, who are busily engaged in killing thousands. Whereas Leatherstocking refuses to force the moral law upon another, Judge Temple, being a magistrate, must develop civil laws to enforce the moral law in which they both believe. The crucial irony of the particular situation, however, is that Leatherstocking falls afoul of Temple's civil law; the depredators whom the law should be restraining not only go untouched but lead Leatherstocking's prosecution. The judge's law against the seasonal netting of the bass is apparently not yet in force; the law against the seasonal killing of deer catches only Leatherstocking. Although Leatherstocking's alegal and individual response dissuades no one, the judge's legalistic, communal response is sadly misused.

Conservation has made the deer law necessary, but neither Leatherstocking nor the judge is primarily concerned about the particular deer or even the particular statute. The deer law is at issue because it has aroused a deeper question: Are there limits to the authority that a just and necessary civil law should have over the individual who has prior natural rights? Conversely, if one's natural rights are disregarded, is violent civil disobedience justified?

Leatherstocking's shooting of the deer and defiance of Templeton's magistrates appeal to Cooper's faith in individuality and freedom. Even at the end of his life, Cooper was to argue for the social benefit of permitting unrestricted personal liberty in the early stages of settlement:

We certainly think that even the looseness of law, legislation, and justice, that is so widely spreading itself over the land, is not exactly unsuited to sustain the rapid settlement of a country. No doubt men accomplish more in the earlier stages of society when perfectly unfettered, than when brought under the control of those principles and regulations which alone can render society permanently secure or happy.[29]

---

[29] James Fenimore Cooper, *New York* (New York: William Farquhar Payson, 1930), p. 48.

No one connected to a community could be more self-reliant than Leatherstocking, who clearly personifies the benefits of his "perfectly unfettered" liberty. Judge Temple openly admits that Leatherstocking is the exceptional frontiersman who has little need of laws designed for a Billy Kirby. Believing in the need to remain unrestrained by statutes, Leatherstocking nonetheless agrees with Locke's Law of Nature, which demands "that being all equal and independent, no one ought to harm another in his life, health, liberty or possessions."[30] Consequently, Leatherstocking insists upon exact adherence to Locke's ideas about the proper use of resources in the State of Nature. Believing that God gave all the world in common, Leatherstocking will appropriate to himself only so much of natural bounty as he can personally use. Once appropriated, however, the natural object, whether it be a deerskin or a hut, becomes personal property.

Whenever Cooper views the judge through Leatherstocking's eyes, he recognizes that statute law impinges upon the rights of natural man. The law now considers Leatherstocking an illegal squatter, yet he was the first white settler of the land. When Judge Temple first descended Mount Vision, years before the era of settlement, he encountered Leatherstocking and was offered the hospitality of his hut. Judge Temple's first glimpse of Leatherstocking thus establishes a crucial property right: "while I was lingering around the spot, Natty made his appearance, staggering under the carcass of a buck that he had slain."[31]

In fact, therefore, natural justice confirms Leatherstocking's claim that "There's them living who say, that Nathaniel Bumppo's right to shoot deer on these hills is of older date than Marmaduke Temple's right to forbid him." Judge Temple publicly admits that Leatherstocking "has a kind of natural right to gain a livelihood in these mountains." Nor is Cooper entirely opposed to the right of the squatter to his kill. He leads the reader to sympathize with Leatherstocking's formulation of natural law: "Game is game, and he who finds may kill; that has been the law in these mountains for forty years, to my sartain knowledge; and I think one old law is worth two new ones."[32]

Leatherstocking violates the deer law, not because he wishes to defy a particular statute, but because he does not recognize the

[30] Locke, *Second Treatise on Civil Government,* p. 20.
[31] Cooper, *The Pioneers,* p. 225.
[32] Ibid., pp. 23, 107, 153.

validity of man-made law at all. In Lockean terms, Leatherstocking has made no voluntary compact with Templeton's citizenry. To him, the criminal law of Templeton is only another encroachment of an evil civilization; its magistrates are meddling snoops. Leatherstocking evidently believes that no criminal law could effectively restrain an individual who wishes to break the moral law. When Oliver Edwards and the judge excitedly participate in the killing of the pigeons and the bass, his fears seem amply justified.

The offense for which Leatherstocking is found guilty, stocked, and imprisoned is not the killing of a deer, but resistance of arrest and assault of an officer of the law. Because Leatherstocking recognizes no distinction between a man and a man with a badge, he defies the law with violence rather than legally punishing its abuses. Confronted with a warrant to search his hut, Leatherstocking openly defies the justice of the peace, strikes him, then threatens deputy Kirby with a rifle when Kirby attempts to serve due process. In court, however, Leatherstocking pleads not guilty to these very charges, acknowledging at the same time that he performed the actions which led to the charges.

If one accepts Leatherstocking's premise, his pleas of not guilty are unchallengeable. Nowhere in the novel does Cooper state that a man-made criminal statute has jurisdiction over so admirable a figure as Leatherstocking, who has prior rights, belongs to an earlier stage of history, and is governed by a superior moral law. In denying Doolittle and Kirby entrance into his hut, Leatherstocking was upholding the Lockean law of natural justice by defending both his liberty and his possessions: "And that all men may be restrained from invading the other's rights, . . . the execution of the law of Nature is in that state put into every man's hands."[33]

Leatherstocking's contempt for the administration of the law in Templeton is fully justified. The justice of the peace and the town's lawyers have no interest in enforcing the deer laws for social benefit. Doolittle and Lippet simply use the deer law as a ruse for satisfying their curiosity about Leatherstocking's hut, discovering the location of his mine, and seizing its nonexistent silver for themselves. In practice, the law is condemning minor infringements but ignoring major ones; moreover, it is used by its devious if absurd representatives for their own selfish, illegal ends.

All of the arguments based upon natural justice, prior right, individuality, and legal misadministration argue eloquently on

---

[33] Locke, *Second Treatise on Civil Government*, pp. 20–21.

Leatherstocking's behalf and are not to be denied. Nonetheless, by the conclusion of the novel, Leatherstocking's opposition to man-made law seems both inappropriate and simplistic. Judge Temple, who first appears to be a hunter with a hasty trigger, finally emerges as a civic leader of unquestionable integrity and strength. Cooper explicitly commends Temple's "native clearness of mind," adding that the judge "not only decided right, but was generally able to give a very good reason for it." [34]

The only means by which Judge Temple can maintain order and restraint, in an undefined and expanding society containing wasters and cheats, is by laws that are strictly enforced and commonly respected. After Temple sentences Leatherstocking, he justifies his decision to his daughter by an appeal to circumstantial fact:

> Society cannot exist without wholesome restraints. Those restraints cannot be inflicted, without security and respect to the persons who administer them. . . . Try to remember, Elizabeth, that the laws alone remove us from the condition of the savages; that he [Leatherstocking] has been criminal, and that his judge was thy father.[35]

Locke had offered three reasons why natural justice cannot prevail in the State of Nature: the lack of established law, the lack of a single judge to decide the law, and the lack of magistracy to execute the law.[36] Judge Temple's words to his daughter remind us that he has managed to provide all three for a settlement newly removed from wilderness.

The judge's legalistic attitudes are ultimately confirmed by the facts of social circumstance; his new community must have the strict discipline of criminal statutes. Temple concludes his charge to Leatherstocking's jury by saying, "Living as we do, gentlemen, . . . on the skirts of society, it becomes doubly necessary to protect the ministers of the law." Such a charge is neither impartial nor based upon precedent, yet it is true. To the man who has purchased legal title to the land, established a prosperous community, and become its judge, Leatherstocking must seem a lawless squatter, an old friend allowed unusual liberties only so long as he remains harmless. When Leatherstocking defies a criminal statute, however, Temple rightly asks Oliver Edwards, "Would any society be tolerable, young man,

[34] Cooper, *The Pioneers*, p. 34.
[35] Ibid., pp. 364–365.
[36] Locke, *Second Treatise on Civil Government*, p. 61.

where the ministers of justice are to be opposed by men armed with rifles? Is it for this that I have tamed the wilderness?"[37]

Leatherstocking's harangues against law and civilization have great impact because they are written in an earthy dialect that contrasts favorably to the formal abstractions of Judge Temple. Leatherstocking's heart, however, is not to be confused with Cooper's reason. Leatherstocking is never willing to consider whether law is necessary in a societal context. Whenever he criticizes man-made law, he refuses to distinguish between a just law badly administered, such as Temple's conservation law, and a statute that is intrinsically unjust. This distinction is crucial. Leatherstocking wrongly assumes that, because magistrate Doolittle is violating his natural right to privacy, man-made law must be inherently evil.

Leatherstocking's trial unexpectedly vindicates the judge's argument for criminal statutes even though both lawyers are comically incompetent. Neither the defense attorney, Lawyer Lippet, nor the prosecuting attorney, Dirck Van Der School, mentions any of the compelling arguments Cooper has carefully constructed. After Judge Temple's rather pointed charge, however, the jury returns surprisingly apt and sophisticated judgments. Leatherstocking is found not guilty of striking and assaulting Hiram Doolittle but guilty of resisting the execution of a search warrant by force of arms.

The two charges arise from the same set of acts but have been rightly separated in law. Although Leatherstocking physically struck Hiram Doolittle, testimony revealed that Leatherstocking had not committed assault, both because Hiram had provoked him and because Hiram had already transferred his power to serve the search warrant to Billy Kirby. But when Kirby became empowered to serve the search warrant, Leatherstocking had confronted him with a rifle. Although Leatherstocking pleads not guilty to both charges, his second plea is legally indefensible. Unable to distinguish the man from his civic office, Leatherstocking can see no wrong in denying entry either to Doolittle or to Kirby. To judge and jury, however, Kirby's belligerence as an individual cannot invalidate Kirby's duty as an officer of the law. The jury decides that proper legal procedure must be upheld, even if it is motivated by questionable purposes. Cooper very evidently sanctions the court's decision. When Elizabeth Temple, acting on the promptings of her heart, tells her father that "in appreciating the offence of poor Natty, I cannot separate the

---

[37] Cooper, *The Pioneers*, pp. 352, 328.

minister from the man," and that "it is immaterial whether it be one or the other," Cooper quietly remarks that his heroine has spoken "with a logic that contained more feeling than reason."[38]

Using the only language he knows, Leatherstocking argues eloquently against his severe sentence by returning to the origin of the conflict:

> Hear me, Marmaduke Temple . . . and hear reason. I've travelled these mountains when you was no judge, but an infant in your mother's arms; and I feel as if I had a right and a privilege to travel them ag'in afore I die. Have you forgot the time that you came on to the lakeshore, when there wasn't even a jail to lodge in; and didn't I give you my own bear-skin to sleep on, and the fat of a noble buck to satisfy the cravings of your hunger? Yes, yes—you thought it no sin then to kill a deer![39]

Appealing though the speech is, Leatherstocking can defend himself only by referring to justice as it had existed in the state of nature. His attempt to justify his present slaying of a deer on grounds that he had once slain deer for Temple's benefit simply cannot stand the test of reason. Throughout the trial, Leatherstocking remains comically unable to understand anything of legal procedure; he even refers to a breach of law as a "sin."

Leatherstocking's conflict with the criminal law of Templeton has made the valley that was once "a second paradise" seem no longer endurable. By burning his hut, Leatherstocking reasserts his right to privacy, but his act is clearly symbolic of the end of the Lockean state of nature within Templeton. Over the ashes of his hut, Leatherstocking denounces "the troubles and divilties of the law," and "the wicked feet and wasty ways" of Templeton.[40] As he concludes, Leatherstocking describes himself with a simile that, from his viewpoint, is magnificently apt:

> And now, when he has come to see the last brand of his hut, before it is melted into ashes, you follow him up, at midnight, like hungry hounds on the track of a worn-out and dying deer. What more would ye have? For I am here—one too many.[41]

Pursuing Leatherstocking's metaphor, we find that all the connotations of shooting the deer have been reversed. To Templeton and the

---

[38] Ibid., pp. 364–365.
[39] Ibid., p. 354.
[40] Ibid., pp. 279, 340.
[41] Ibid., p. 341.

judge, Leatherstocking is the hunter who has killed the deer and brought the law upon his head. To Leatherstocking, he himself is the deer that is being hunted by the hounds of the law and by a statute that, rightly conceived, seems only to promote injustice.

Unless he were to violate his idea of natural justice, Leatherstocking has no choice but to depart westward in retreat from the sounding axes, armed with an ample supply of gunpowder for the rifle by which he enforces natural law. Before departure, however, he indicates how his recent experience has led to his final renunciation. Leatherstocking, like Cooper, often insists that "the law of God is the only rule of conduct."[42] Measuring the law of God against the law of Templeton, Leatherstocking rightly finds man-made law deficient, but for the wrong reasons. Referring to Mohegan's death, Leatherstocking says "he's to be judged by a righteous Judge, and by no laws that's made to suit times, and new ways."[43] Leatherstocking's justifiable sense of injury has led him to blame the judge rather than Doolittle, to confuse a law with its misadministration.

Neither Leatherstocking's misunderstanding of the law, nor his just resentment of it, ever abate. His last words to Elizabeth are a thinly disguised slight upon the workings of her father's court:

> I pray that the Lord will keep you in mind—the Lord that lives in clearings as well as in the wilderness—and bless you, and all that belong to you, from this time till the great day when the whites shall meet the red-skins in judgment, and justice shall be the law, and not power.[44]

Observing only the workings of the law rather than its intrinsic merit, Leatherstocking concludes that man-made law can never correspond to divine law and leaves civilization to seek the absolute in the forest.

Leatherstocking's departure releases him from any social commitment back into the wilderness, where Cooper will proceed to enlarge him, in later novels, into a mythical representation of the heroic, solitary frontiersman. It is crucial to remember, however, that the origin of Leatherstocking's character lies in his paradoxical stance toward the law. Leatherstocking could become Hawkeye, Pathfinder, and Deerslayer only after he had been conceived as a rebel

---

[42] Cooper, *The American Democrat*, ed. G. Dekker and L. Johnston (Baltimore: Penguin Books, 1969), p. 151.
[43] Cooper, *The Pioneers*, p. 403.
[44] Ibid., p. 435.

who utterly rejects man-made law and the social institutions built upon it. Defining the essence of Leatherstocking's character, Cooper was later to insist "The most striking feature about the Pathfinder's character was his beautiful and unerring sense of justice."[45] If an American hero's sense of justice depends upon utterly rejecting man-made laws for the laws of nature's god, we may wonder whether Templeton has paid too great a price for its civilized stability. Leatherstocking has had to take his great qualities outside of American society in order to maintain them.

And yet the legal attitudes of the novel, like its plot, are finally resolved in the judge's favor. Cooper will not allow his reader to forget the following facts: pioneers are conquering nature; either civil law or anarchy will prevail; conservation laws are necessary; Leatherstocking's acts were clearly criminal by legal definition; his innocence (either ignorance of fact or harmlessness of intent) can be maintained only by adhering to anachronistic values. Moreover, the reader must remember Judge Temple's achievements. After the barest minimum of legal training, he has adapted the "common law"[46] to the present conditions of Templeton. At the same time, he has used his political influence to pass conservation statutes through the New York legislature. By both means, he is building a prosperous, decent civilization. Without citing precedents or miring his court in procedural detail, Temple dispenses a justice whose imperfections are more administrative than substantive. His mind may be more attuned to the laws of nature than the laws of nature's god, but the difference in legal practice is hard to determine.

In terms of legal history, Judge Temple thus embodies a workable compromise between reliance on common law precedent, reliance on popular legislative statute, and sheer common sense. After his experience in the Templeton Court of Common Pleas, Leatherstocking would be likely to agree with absolutist Robert Rantoul that "Older, nobler, clearer and more glorious, then, is Everlasting Justice, than ambiguous, baseborn, purblind, perishable Common Law. . . . Judge-made law is *ex post facto* law and therefore unjust."[47] But Cooper might prefer us to perceive Judge Temple as a

---

[45] Cooper, *The Pathfinder* (New York: W. A. Townsend, 1861), p. 143.
[46] Cooper, *The Pioneers*, p. 356.
[47] Robert Rantoul, "Oration at Scituate" (1836), in Perry Miller, *The Legal Mind in America*, p. 223.

refined example of the sturdy abilities shown by Justice Dudley of the New Hampshire Supreme Court during the 1790s:

> They [the lawyers] talk about law—why, gentlemen, it's not law we want, but justice. They want to govern us by the common law of England; trust me for it, common sense is a much safer guide for us. . . . It's our business to do justice between the parties; not by any quirk o' the law out of Coke or Blackstone—books that I never read and never will—but by common sense and common honesty between man and man.[48]

Judge Temple applies common sense and common honesty to purposes of economic development that Cooper believes to be socially progressive. In doing so, the judge illustrates an essential shift in land law which Morton Horwitz has traced in *The Transformation of American Law: 1780–1860*. Horwitz notes that, in early nineteenth-century cases of land ownership, the principle that the first developer had controlling property rights took precedence over the principle that the first settler had the natural right of personal use. In Horwitz's words "the rule of priority, wearing the mantle of economic development, . . . triumphed over natural use."[49] Leatherstocking's departure from Templeton thus represents more than Cooper's nostalgia for a vanishing mode of heroism; it is a fictional enactment of a contemporary legal process.

COOPER AND THE JURY SYSTEM

The continuing variety of state criminal procedures indicates that the American people have never been able collectively to determine the extent to which judicial decisions should be affected by public opinion or immune to it. To be specific, there is no unanimity of state practice concerning any of four central issues: (1) whether juries should judge law as well as fact, (2) whether judges should be elected or appointed, (3) whether a jury verdict need be unanimous, and (4) whether the judge or the jury should have the power of sentencing.[50]

---

[48] Quoted by Bernard Schwartz in *The Law in America* (New York: McGraw-Hill, 1974), pp. 11–12.
[49] Morton Horwitz, *The Transformation of American Law: 1780–1860* (Cambridge: Harvard University Press, 1977), p. 34.
[50] Samuel W. McCart, *Trial By Jury: A Complete Guide to the Jury System* (Philadelphia: Chilton, 1964), pp. 117, 122, 123, 150.

One's response to any of these problems depends on one's intuitive sense of the capabilities of the bench and the citizenry. Until that wonderful moment when we all collectively agree that the democratic majority unquestionably is a fickle mob or an anchor of reason, debate over these practices is likely to continue.

Fenimore Cooper, who was never one to shirk a controversy, devoted his last novel, *The Ways of the Hour*, to a fictionalized version of the celebrated criminal trial of Mary Bodine.[51] It is utterly characteristic of Cooper's longstanding concern for legal matters that he would attempt to reveal the ways of America through extensive study of one court trial. The impetus for the novel, however—like the impetus for *Home As Found* or *The Redskins*—came from a local legal controversy. The New York Constitution of 1846 contained a provision specifying that all state judges, formerly appointed by the governor, were henceforth to be elected by the people. By heritage, education, and experience, Cooper was inclined to the view that disinterested decisions based upon Reason were not likely to be made by politicians whose eyes were fixed upon the next election. While writing *Notions of the Americans*, Cooper had read Alexander Hamilton's warning: "that inflexible and uniform adherence to the rights of the Constitution, and of individuals, which we perceive to be indispensable to the courts of justice, can certainly not be expected from judges who hold their offices by temporary commission."[52] In writing *The Ways of the Hour*, Cooper's fundamental purpose was to test whether an elective bench could disprove Tocqueville's well-known claims that, in America, the tyranny of the majority was finally checked by the stability of the judiciary, and that trial by jury was therefore only "a harmless public school, ever open, in which every juror learns his rights.[53]

---

[51] Like Mary Monson, Mary Bodine was a separated but married woman accused of two murders, theft, and arson. Her lawyers claimed her innocent because, during the night of the crime, she was visiting an abortionist. Three changes of venue had to be granted before a supposedly impartial jury could be found. James Grossman offers interesting speculations about the changes Cooper made in the historical trial (James Grossman, *James Fenimore Cooper* [Stanford, Calif.: Stanford University Press, 1967], pp. 240–241).

[52] Alexander Hamilton, John Jay, and James Madison, *The Federalist Papers* (Garden City, N.Y.: Doubleday, 1966), p. 232.

[53] Alexis de Tocqueville, *Democracy In America* ed. Phillips Bradley (New York: Random House, 1945), 1:294. Convinced of the jury's genuinely educational function, Tocqueville concluded "the institution of the jury raises the people itself, or at least a class of citizens, to the bench of judges" (1:293).

Trial by jury is the focus of such passionate attack throughout the novel that one suspects Cooper of an underlying commitment to it. In an aristocracy such as England, Cooper contends, popular juries have served as a bulwark against the abuses of special privilege. A democratic polity, however, demands a different assessment: To delegate the administration of criminal justice to the people is to give judicial powers to the very forces that a republican judiciary had been created to restrain.[54] When the 1846 New York Constitution created an elective judiciary in the state, Cooper foresaw a form of judicial usurpation in which jurors would begin to make law while elective judges would become too timid to insist on legal precedents. Rotation of office was coming to the bench, with the result that "the whole machinery of justice is left very much at the mercy of an outside public opinion." Although an elected judge must retain the approval of the people who comprise the juries, republican jurors habitually believe the public opinion of a fact rather than the fact itself. The result, Cooper felt, was an ominous reversal of roles: "What I most complain of is the fact that the jurors are fast becoming judges."[55]

Cooper uses the narrative of the criminal case to demonstrate the jury's abilities to make law and to distort justice simultaneously. Mary Monson, a rich gentlewoman who has dwelt as a refined outsider in a provincial town, is falsely accused of murder, robbery, and arson. In the absence of all but scant circumstantial evidence, popular prejudice against the wealthy and the cultivated is the lever by which the jurors can be moved.

Neither jurors nor audience are bothered by demagoguery because they are incapable of recognizing it. The problem of responding to judicial injustice falls upon the lawyers who, as often in Cooper's novels, are divisible into two recurrent types. Thomas Dunscomb is an aging, wealthy Christian gentleman, trained in common law, and quite fond of abrasive opinions. Timms, a Yankee sharpster using the law for self-advancement, has risen professionally above his class origins but resents the gentry he tries to emulate. Dunscomb believes that the practice of common law could discover timeless judicial principles, if only democracy would leave the judiciary alone. Timms knows that potentially profitable law is

---

[54] James Fenimore Cooper, *The Ways of the Hour* (New York: W. A. Townsend, 1862), p. 290.
[55] Ibid., pp. 287, 18.

being made every day by popular juries whose opinions he must sway. Dunscomb and Timms closely resemble the two antebellum images of the lawyer—trained neoclassic gentleman versus frontier pettifogger—which Maxwell Bloomfield so ably discusses in the following essay. Cooper's rendering of the status of the two types, however, reveals his awareness of the great social and legal change that has taken place by mid-century. Unkempt, rude, and rural though Timms is, Timms represents the future (he is on his way to the State Senate), because he knows popular prejudice and because he is undeterred by scruples of legal principle. Dunscomb, embodiment of the old guard, is dangerously out of touch with contemporary practice.

The legal chicanery surrounding the trial of Mary Monson vindicates Dunscomb's gravest fears about the mindlessness of popular juries. All the instances of jury tampering never induce the reader to conclude, however, that Mary will not receive justice. The district attorney, after making a canting speech about Mary's aristocratic ways, delivers a surprisingly restrained and impartial summation to the jury. The judge's charge correctly specifies that the circumstantial evidence against her is flimsy and debatable. Believing that Mary should and will be acquitted, the reader is then stunned by the jury's verdict of guilty; the judge has no recourse but to sentence Mary to hanging.

The cause for the jury's disregard for facts and reason emerges only on reflection. Searching to explain the jury's contempt for the judge's opinion, we recall that Mary's judge has been elected under the new constitution, and must therefore curry popular favor rather than lead opinion. We recall Timms's contemptuous observation: "You will remember that our judge is not only a bran-new one, but he drew the two years' term into the bargain. No, I think it will be wisest to let the law, and old principles, and the right, and *true* liberty, quite alone; and to bow the knee to things as they are."[56]

Mary Monson's trial ends in her acquittal, not because the ways of American justice establish her innocence, but because the man she has been convicted of murdering appears in the courtroom. Because all of Dunscomb's fears about a failing judicial system seem confirmed, he concludes that America cannot be saved unless repressive measures are adopted. Dunscomb asserts that the masses should be

[56] Ibid., p. 228.

given "all power that they can intelligently and usefully use; but not to the extent of permitting them to make the laws, to execute the laws, to interpret the laws." And he is prepared to contend that true liberty demands severe curtailment of liberty of the press: "As respects proceedings in the courts, there never will be any true liberty in the country, until the newspapers are bound hand and foot."[57]

To what extent is the reader asked to share Dunscomb's reactionary opinions? Cooper clearly dissociates himself from Dunscomb's vehement attacks on recent divorce laws, women's property statutes, and the codification of the common law by David Dudley Field. The reader remains unsure whether Cooper's approval of Dunscomb's opinions of American facts extends to Cooper's approval of Dunscomb's reactionary solutions. Dunscomb himself clearly desires a return to an appointive judiciary and an end to trial by jury. Cooper's preface, however, acknowledges that, despite the many injustices of jury trials, "the difficulty is to find a substitute."[58]

Sprawling and tedious though *The Ways of the Hour* unquestionably is, the novel stands, like many of Cooper's other novels, at the beginning of a long tradition in American letters. Melville, Twain, Dreiser, Darrow, and Cozzens were all to construct novels around a murder trial in which a jury would pronounce a morally innocent person guilty, not because of legal reason but because of legal unreason and some quirk of popular prejudice. But the persistent attack on jury trial by American novelists has, in none of these instances, been accompanied by the offering of any better procedure for determining criminal guilt. In fact, Cozzens and Auchincloss have expressed disquieting fears that the decreasing use of jury trials in criminal cases (due to the waiver privilege) may be leading to greater criminal injustice. The writing of fiction may set one apart from, and sometimes above, the people, but trial by jury is a right that even the sourest American seems unwilling utterly to relinquish. Despite all its faults, as Cooper knew, "the difficulty is to find a substitute."

PRACTICALITY, OR THE LAST ASSIZES

Even though Billy Budd is hung on a British ship by a British court according to British martial law, Melville explores the law's

---

[57] Ibid., pp. 86, 140.
[58] Ibid., p. vii.

relation to justice through terms particularly pertinent to the American tradition of legal thought. Addressing the drumhead court he has rather secretively convened, Captain Vere challenges his officers to determine the standard by which Billy is to be judged:

> In natural justice is nothing but the prisoner's overt act to be considered? How can we adjudge to summary and shameful death a fellow creature innocent before God, and whom we feel to be so?—Does that state it aright? You sign sad assent. Well, I too feel the full force of that. It is Nature. But do these buttons that we wear attest that our allegiance is to Nature? No, to the king. Though the ocean, which is inviolate Nature primeval, though this be the element where we move and have our being as sailors, yet as the king's officers lies our duty in a sphere correspondingly natural? So little is this true, that in receiving our commissions we in the most important regards ceased to be natural free agents.[59]

Before one concludes that Edward Vere's reasonings are merely those of an office holder whose "settled convictions" have hardened into expediency, it is crucial to recognize the universal principles that Vere not only concedes but insists upon. He compels his court to recognize that natural justice and natural right exist. He insists that, according to natural justice, divine justice and "the private conscience," Billy Budd is "innocent" of murder because Billy bore "no malice" against John Claggart.[60] (Sir Edward Coke's phrase "with malice aforethought" had remained the legal definition of first-degree murder in civil criminal courts.)[61] Only Vere's personal testimony enables the court to recognize that Billy struck Claggart because Billy's anger at Claggart's malice had no other outlet. Vere even tells his court "Before a court less arbitrary and more merciful than a martial one, that plea [of innocent intent] would largely extenuate. At the Last Assizes, it shall acquit."[62] Like Leatherstocking, Captain Vere cites natural and divine law as a way of criticizing human law. One of *Billy Budd*'s great ironies is that Vere's honesty in admitting counterargument has provided his critics the words with which to condemn him.

---

[59] Herman Melville, *Billy Budd, Sailor (An Inside Narrative)*, ed. H. Hayford and M. Sealts (Chicago: University of Chicago Press, 1962), p. 110.
[60] Ibid., pp. 62, 111, 106.
[61] M. Cherif Bassiouni, *Substantive Criminal Law* (Springfield, Ill.: Charles C Thomas, 1978), pp. 232–235.
[62] Melville, *Billy Budd*, p. 111.

Vere rests his argument for hanging a morally innocent man on grounds of both practical benefit and legal precedent. He is, of course, absolutely correct to insist that the king's officers take an oath to obey the king's laws, and that the Articles of War prescribe death for striking a superior officer "under any pretence whatsoever." Nor does Vere take refuge behind duty or his inability to change the law. He argues that, in his particular situation, he must act neither as casuist, moralist nor "psychologic theologian." The threat that the rebellious outbreaks at Spithead and the Nore might spread mutiny to the *Bellipotent* leads him genuinely to believe that the well-being of the ship excuses the moral (not legal) injustice done to Billy. Whether Vere exaggerates the threat of rebellion or not, his essential response to the decision is that of a pragmatist: "It is a case practical," he says, "and under martial law practically to be dealt with."[63]

Vere's commitments to natural law and divine justice extend only so far as natural law coincides with the Benthamite standard of the greatest good of the greatest number. Vere accedes to arguments of natural right and innocence of intent only until he perceives that the good of the ship might be threatened by them. His preferences clearly emerge in his reversal of the Enlightenment's association of human faculties with political values. Whereas Jefferson and Madison had associated Natural Rights with human Reason, and privilege with passion for the past, Captain Vere associates the argument from Natural Law with the feelings ("warm hearts") and entrenched statutes with right reason ("cool heads").[64]

The words of Starry Vere's speech reflect the tension between the legal assumptions of French Revolutionaries and English counter-revolutionaries. Because Billy is impressed from *The Rights of Man* to a ship named the *Bellipotent*, whose captain is an historically minded traditionalist of passionate intelligence, it has long been evident that the issues of Billy's trial subsume fundamental disagreements between the thought of Edmund Burke and Thomas Paine. Melville's historical fictions, however, had never been antiquarian entertainments written about a separable past; they had recast contemporary issues in historical terms. Although Vere's concepts of natural and human justice may derive from Burke, they bear startling similarity to contentious arguments about the criminal law recently

---

[63] Ibid., pp. 180, 108, 110.
[64] Ibid., p. 111.

advanced by America's most prominent legal thinker. Holmes's *The Common Law*, published in 1882, four years before Melville began writing *Billy Budd*, directly attacks the assumption that the law exists primarily to safeguard individual rights.

Like Captain Vere, Holmes is prepared to argue that "Public policy sacrifices the individual to the general good. . . . Justice to the individual is rightly outweighed by the larger interests on the other side of the scales."[65] Just as Vere argues that divine justice must be violated so that social order be preserved, so Holmes insists, "Theory and fact agree in frequently punishing those who have been guilty of no moral wrong." Holmes clearly believes that the defensible reason for punishment of criminals is not justice to a sinner, but society's need to protect itself. With evident delight, Holmes forces readers to consider that, in daily fact, "the law does undoubtedly treat the individual as a means to an end, and uses him as a tool to increase the general welfare at his own expense." Holmes and Vere agree that "Prevention would . . . seem to be the chief and only universal system of punishment." All readers of *Billy Budd* recall Starry Vere's disturbingly cogent argument that, if he as captain is to pass judgments in accord with divine law, all impressed sailors aboard the *Bellipotent* should be immediately freed. When Holmes wishes to prove that society's survival must and will take precedence over "the dogma of equality," he cites the same example: "No society has ever admitted that it could not sacrifice individual welfare to its own existence. If conscripts are necessary for its army, it seizes them, and marches them, with bayonets in their rear, to death."[66]

Starry Vere is enforcing a code of martial law, but his argument to the court proceeds, not by contrasting martial law to criminal law, but by contrasting Divine Law with man-made statutes. Our judgment of the procedures Vere uses in conducting the trial thus affects our judgment not merely of martial law but of the consequences for any legal system once the individual's rights are conceived to be secondary to society's self-protection. Before convening the drumhead court, Vere calls Billy "fated boy," then says of Claggart "struck dead by an angel of God! Yet the angel must hang." Because Vere's regard for his ship has clearly led him to prejudge Billy's trial, his

---

[65] Oliver Wendell Holmes, Jr., *The Common Law*, ed. Mark DeWolfe Howe (Cambridge: Harvard University Press, 1963), p. 41. Oliver Wendell Holmes, Sr., had been Melville's physician during the 1850s.
[66] Ibid., pp. 38, 40, 40, 112, 37.

procedures are means to a foregone conclusion. The ship's surgeon, "a self-poised character . . . of grave sense and experience," is convinced that proper and politic legal procedure would have been to confine Billy until an admiralty trial could be held on shore.[67] Vere himself elects the officers who will serve as the jury. Vere is the sole witness, assumes the roles of both prosecution and defense attorney, charges the jury to find Billy guilty, and then forces the decision. Although the officers who make up the jury ask occasional questions, Captain Vere personally sets procedures and directs the flow of argument.

Vere's honesty leads him to disclose the true facts, but there is no procedural separation of judicial functions by which Vere's interpretation of those facts could be effectively challenged. Melville never considers whether Vere tries Billy according to the stipulated procedures of martial law. Instead, Melville condemns Vere's procedures by comparing them to the most un-American of civil criminal systems: "The maintenance of secrecy in the matter, the confining all knowledge of it for a time to the place where the homicide occurred, the quarterdeck cabin; in these particulars lurked some resemblance to the policy adopted in those tragedies of the palace which have occurred more than once in the capital founded by Peter the Barbarian."[68]

Melville was well aware that tyrannical procedures can result in a just decision. Whether Melville asks us to condone or condemn the court's decision to hang Billy Budd has been a subject of debate for fifty years. Not until the genesis of the manuscript was carefully studied did readers become aware of a third possibility—that *Billy Budd* might be a work of calculated ambiguity in which Melville sought to confront the reader with an insoluble question.[69] The similarities between the ideas of Vere and Holmes suggest, however, that Melville's insoluble irony is not simply that divine justice cannot be embodied in human statutes. Instead, Melville may be asking us to recognize that any truly just decision would have solved the impossible task of simultaneously protecting the natural rights of the individual and the needs of social order.

The similarity of Vere's and Holmes's arguments also suggests that Melville's perception of the problem of criminal justice has diverged

---

[67] Melville, *Billy Budd*, pp. 99, 101, 100.
[68] Ibid., p. 103.
[69] See Hayford's and Sealt's "Editors' Introduction" to *Billy Budd*, pp. 1–12.

from the ideas of his eminent father-in-law, Chief Justice Lemuel Shaw of the Massachusetts Supreme Court. Although Shaw, like Vere, warned against "the encroachment of a wild and licentious democracy," worried about "the irregular action of the mere popular will," and supported the authority of informed judges over presumably irrational juries, Shaw was also a constant and vigorous defender of due process rights for the accused—as Vere clearly is not.[70] Lemuel Shaw's most famous criminal conviction involved the citing of a doctrine of "implied malice" by which the burden of disproving "malice aforethought" would be shifted to the defendant.[71] Vere clearly absolves Billy of any malicious intent but hangs Billy on the Holmesian grounds that both societal expediency and written statute demand it.

Although interpretations of the judicial issue in *Billy Budd* may, like Ahab's doubloon, tell us more of the interpreter than of the novella, every reader is nonetheless impelled by the nature of the plot to reach his own decision. Toward that decision, three or four new considerations may here be added. First, a comparison of the novella's trial to its historical prototype suggests that Melville has lent Captain Vere's decision considered intellectual dignity. In 1842 Captain Alexander Slidell Mackenzie of the U.S. Navy brig *Somers* summarily hung three members of his crew for mutiny without any formal trial before a military court. In his own defense, Mackenzie could thus offer no appeal to statute, but simply stated, "Their lives were justly forfeited to the country, and the honor and security of its flag, required that the sacrifices, however painful, should be made. In the necessities of my position I found my law, and in them also I must trust to find my justification."[72] The contrast between Mackenzie's pathetic but dangerous plea for necessity and Vere's reasoned speech leads us to consider seriously whether, as Vere's name and nickname suggest, Melville's captain may indeed speak the truth of the stars.

Second, we need to restore a balance to our assumptions about Melville's attitudes toward law. Critics of *Billy Budd* rightly point out that Chapters 70 through 72 of *White-Jacket* comprise a direct, impassioned attack on the Articles of War. During his thirties,

---

[70] Leonard W. Levy, *The Law of the Commonwealth and Chief Justice Shaw* (New York: Harper & Row, 1967), pp. 315, 282–289.
[71] Ibid., p. 321.
[72] Harrison Hayford, *The Somers Mutiny Affair* (Englewood Cliffs, N.J.: Prentice-Hall, 1959), p. 42.

Melville had clearly believed the Articles of War to be a barbarous, inquisitorial code, dating from the tyrannical Stuarts, and wholly inimical to "the indigenous growth of those political institutions, which are based upon that arch democrat Thomas Jefferson's Declaration of Independence."[73] Between 1849 and 1886, however, Melville's attitudes toward law and revolution had become increasingly less dependent on a standard of individual natural rights. His volume of poems on the Civil War is filled with welcoming references to the eventual "victory of LAW." When troops put down the New York draft riots of 1863, Melville conceded that such repression was a "grimy slur on the Republic's faith," yet accepted the sad necessity that wise, Draconian troops must come "in code corroborating Calvin's creed."[74] We should therefore not be surprised to discover that the narrator of *Billy Budd* refers, quite unironically, to the "irrational combustion" and the "red meteor of unbridled and unfounded revolt" ignited by the French Revolution. In similar fashion, Melville denounces Napoleon as "this French portentous upstart from the revolutionary chaos."[75] Those who would find in Melville a constant adherence to political beliefs based on the Rights of Man should pause to consider that Melville's view of the effect of the French Revolution is quite indistinguishable from Captain Vere's.

In face of these facts, however, we need to consider the one paragraph in which Melville seems to offer his personal assessment of Vere's decision. Unfortunately, this paragraph is the most awkwardly written passage in the entire novella:

In the jugglery of circumstances preceding and attending the event on board the *Bellipotent*, and in the light of that martial code whereby it was formally to be judged, innocence and guilt personified in Claggart and Budd in effect changed places. In a legal view the apparent victim of the tragedy was he [Claggart] who had sought to victimize a man blameless; and the indisputable deed of the latter [Billy], navally regarded, constituted the most heinous of military crimes. Yet more. The essential right

---

[73] Herman Melville, *White-Jacket or the World in a Man-of-War*, ed. Hennig Cohen (New York: Holt, Rinehart & Winston, 1967), p. 296.
[74] From "Dupont's Round Fight" and "The House-Top" in *The Battle-Pieces of Herman Melville*, ed. Hennig Cohen (New York: T. Yoseloff, 1963), pp. 49, 90.
[75] Melville, *Billy Budd*, pp. 54, 66.

and wrong involved in the matter, the clearer that might be, so much the worse for the responsibility of a loyal sea commander, inasmuch as he was not authorized to determine the matter on that primitive basis.[76]

The first two sentences of the passage force us to recognize the familiar disparity between legal and moral definitions of innocence and guilt. But the last two sentences are truly crucial, for they insist that considerations of moral justice form "the essential right and wrong," which amounts to "more" than the "legal view." Thus Melville's final assertion that moral standards are a "primitive basis" for judgment can only be intentionally ironic. Nonetheless, much still depends on the tone of the entire last sentence. If read ironically, the sentence forces us to conclude that Vere has used a cloak of responsibility and practicality to avoid having to face moral right. If read without irony, the sentence forces the sad recognition that, in our flawed world of war, loyalty and responsibility often leave an honorable commander no satisfactory choice.

Reasons for the insolubility of issues of justice extend beyond Melville's rendering of the trial. To treat *Billy Budd* as if its subject is the trial and death of a particular man in a particular historical setting is to limit severely the reach of Melville's narrative. Throughout the tale, Melville's imagery suggests that Billy Budd represents prelapsarian Adam, Claggart represents Satan, and Captain Starry Vere represents God. The narrative thus transpires on two levels simultaneously: the trial of William Budd, foretopman, and a modern reenactment of the Fall of Man.

If the implications of the allegorical level are pursued to their logical end, we recognize how thoroughly dissillusioned Melville's religious views have become. No longer permitted to live on *The Rights of Man,* Billy is impressed into the depressingly hierarchical but contemporary world of the *Bellipotent.* Precisely because Billy has not yet "been proffered the questionable apple of knowledge," he proves unable to understand the sheer malignancy of Claggart, whom Melville calls "the scorpion for whom the Creater alone is responsible." The modern Adam's innocence, however, emerges as moral virtue in action. Billy's ignorance renders him verbally defenseless, and his verbal defenselessness leads him to kill John Claggart. In Melville's reenactment of *Genesis,* the very innocence of

[76] Ibid., p. 103.

Adam thus enables him to rid the world of Satan; Billy's blow causes Claggart's body to resemble a "dead snake."[77] As recompense for ridding the *Bellipotent* of the agent of evil, however, God then sentences Adam to death, enabling Billy's allegorical referent to shift from Adam to Christ. We are left to infer that the modern Adam does not fall because of his own free will (Billy's stutter was his birthright), and that God punishes those who rid the world of evil.

The killing of Claggart thus assumes two contradictory meanings. Legally, it is a killing of one's superior officer, but spiritually it is a purification of "natural depravity."[78] Billy's innocence only compounds the interpretative dilemma. Billy may be innocent of any intent to kill Claggart, but he is equally innocent of any noble purpose of combatting evil. We can conclude only that Melville has transposed a biblical myth depending on free will into a modern context where criminal acts are caused by compulsive psychological drives. Claggart cannot annul the elemental evil in him; Billy cannot avoid striking Claggart; Vere could never have decided to free Billy. All play psychologically predetermined roles in a decision whose consequences are persistently linked to tragedy. Wherever justice may reside in such a world is left almost altogether to the reader's devising

The two levels of interpretation do not fit well together, either in logic or consistency of tone. Those passages that direct us toward allegorical meanings are evidently of special significance to the author, yet the reader experiences them as intrusions upon a narrative. At no point does Melville attempt to resolve conflicting inferences of meaning between the two levels. We are never led to consider, for example, how Billy could simultaneously be the Handsome Sailor, Adam, Baby Budd, Christ, and a foretopman guilty of homicide. Such difficulties are not simply those of an aging author who, in an unfinished text, was superimposing one meaning upon another. *Billy Budd* was written at a time when basic assumptions about jurisprudence in America were undergoing an immense change. Like men who came of age in the 1840s, Melville inherited his culture's belief in a timeless set of universal principles that, deriving from God, demanded that natural rights be specified in civil law. Like many thoughtful men of the 1870s and 1880s, however, he was beginning to suspect that natural rights, if they existed at all,

[77] Ibid., pp. 52, 78, 99.
[78] Ibid., p. 75.

must give way to the general welfare. Maturing at the height of the era of Kent and Story, Melville wrote *Billy Budd* when the legal realists were gathering momentum. Is it any wonder, then, that *Billy Budd* can, almost simultaneously, remind us both of Holmes's *The Common Law* (1882) and Milton's *Paradise Lost* (1660)?

====================   **II**   ====================

Realities

The helpless longing that the poor outsider of Dreiser's era often felt for the glamour and power of wealth had a legal as well as an economic cause. During the late nineteenth century, the clout of industrial capital was being strengthened by two parallel movements in American legal thought. The Fourteenth Amendment of 1868, conceived as a protection of Negro civil rights, was broadly interpreted to mean that the persons of a corporation could not be "deprived of life, liberty or property without due process of law."[79] In 1868 the influential constitutional jurist T. M. Cooley argued that any legislative transfer of private property would be unconstitutional: "The bill of rights in American constitutions forbids that parties shall be deprived of property except by law of the land; but if the prohibition had been omitted, a legislative enactment to pass one man's property over to another would nevertheless be void."[80]

Although protection of private property may have become, as James Willard Hurst has argued,[81] a policy for releasing economic growth rather than protecting inherited wealth, it was nonetheless true that the prime rights that government was supposed to protect had regressed from life, liberty, and the pursuit of happiness (Jefferson) to life, liberty, and property (Locke). Even in the early nineteenth century, "the increased instrumentalism of American law," to use Horwitz's phrase, had repeatedly led judges to conceive of the law as a means of promoting economic growth.[82] Such growth, however, had often been defended as a benefit for the common

---

"The United States Constitution, Amendment XIV," in Edward S. Corwin, *The Constitution And What It Means Today* (New York: Atheneum, 1965), p. 304.
[80] T. M. Cooley, *A Treatise on The Constitutional Limitations* (Boston: Little, Brown, 1927), p. 356.
[81] James Willard Hurst, *Law and the Conditions of Freedom in the Nineteenth-Century United States* (Madison: University of Wisconsin Press, 1964), pp. 6–19.
[82] Horwitz, *Transformation of American Law*, p. 28.

weal and supported by the argument from moral law. As industrialization accelerated in the 1870s and 1880s, freedom for economic growth was perceived as the individual's right to pursue his own economic choices with whatever capital he possessed.

Paramount attention was given to devising statutes that would guard absolute freedom of economic contract against governmental intrusion. At the 1900 meeting of the American Bar Association, American law was declared to have been nearly perfected because "There is . . . complete freedom of contract; competition is now universal, and as merciless as nature and natural selection."[83] Progress was thought to be inevitable as long as an open field existed in which only the fittest would survive. To determine who would be fittest, each individual, whether factory worker, immigrant, or industrialist, must have the right to choose to make a contract, and then abide by it. The application of such axioms led quite logically to the beliefs that strikes and unions should remain illegal, that laissez faire was natural law, and that poverty impeded no one's freedom of choice. Even though labor unrest, urban slums, Jim Crow laws, and vast extremes of wealth and beggary were the visible consequences of these beliefs, progress presumably decreed that individuals were being rewarded by their merits. Equality of right demanded no concern for inequality of condition because Darwinian selection had replaced universal reason as the law of nature.

During the heyday of these ideas there arose, almost simultaneously, the two movements known to scholars of both literary and legal history as *Realism*. The many fundamental similarities between the chief literary realists (Howells, Twain, James, and their "naturalist" successors, Crane, Norris, Dreiser) and the chief legal realists (Holmes, Pound, Darrow, Hand, Cardozo, Frank) are as revealing as they are unrecognized. Both groups of realists drew from the heritage of Social Darwinism, yet simultaneously attacked it. Realists opposed the very notion of universality, denied the existence of *a priori* ideas, and insisted that law, like evolution, was an ongoing process. The world did not exist for the development of the autonomous individual. The individual, who had largely been formed by external forces, should be regarded merely as one thread in the societal carpet. When considering the implications of these assumptions for the governing of society, however, the realists

---

[83] Bernard Schwartz, *The Law In America* (New York: McGraw-Hill, 1974), p. 115.

diverged from the heritage of Social Darwinism. Whereas the strict Social Darwinist insisted that society will progress only if the individual is left free to fail, the realists concluded that the paramount social interest demanded legal protection against the social injustices being wrought by natural laws of economic selection.

The crucial tenet of both literary and legal realism is that ideas no longer have any existence outside of the mind which perceives them. Howells's *Criticism and Fiction* (1892) attacks the falsity of all literature that seeks to promote universal ideas, to declare absolute truths, or to sermonize about morality.[84] Particular people are to be described as they exist in a social context; they are not to be judged by any preexisting system of values. Similarly, Holmes insists that "the first requirement of a sound body of law is, that it should correspond with the actual feelings and demands of the community whether right or wrong."[85] A law, then, does not correspond to any external principle. Holmes's famous dictum, "The life of the law has not been logic; it has been experience,"[86] at once denies that law has metaphysical origins and simultaneously forces us to conceive of law as a product of social conditions. Its purport is very like the equally famous dictum of Henry James: "There is . . . no more nutritive or suggestive truth . . . than that of the perfect dependence of the 'moral' sense of a work of art on the amount of felt life concerned in producing it."[87]

The chief casualties of the realist movements were the traditions of literary romance and legal theories of natural rights. James's dislike of Hawthorne's allegory and Twain's scorn for Cooper's inaccurate abstractions are both based on the premise that the otherworldly settings and moral absolutism of romance have no place in a relativistic, perhaps Godless world. The same premise underlies Clarence Darrow's impatience with the false reasoning supporting the Single Tax movement: "I grew weary of Henry George's everlasting talk of 'natural rights,'" Darrow acknowledged. "If

---

[84] William Dean Howells, *Criticism and Fiction* (1891) (Cambridge, Mass.: Walker-de-Berry, 1962), pp. 10–11, 73, 95–99.
[85] Holmes, *The Common Law*, p. 36.
[86] Ibid., p. 5.
[87] Henry James, "Preface," *The Portrait of a Lady*, ed. Leon Edel (Boston: Houghton Mifflin, 1963), p. 6. Compare Richard Wright's phrasing in *Native Son:* "The degree of morality in my writing depended upon the degree of felt life and truth I could put down upon the printed page" (Richard Wright, "How Bigger Was Born," in *Native Son* [New York: Harper & Row, 1966], p. xxxi).

'natural rights' means anything, it means that individual rights are to be determined by the conduct of Nature. But Nature knows nothing about rights in the sense of human conception. Nothing is so cruel, so wanton, so unfeeling as Nature."[88]

If Nature seemed to cede no Rights to Man, then the very basis for founding law upon protection of the individual became vulnerable to attack. The opening of Roscoe Pound's *Criminal Justice in America* (1923) summarizes the consequences of this change succinctly:

> Today jurists approach the law from psychology rather than metaphysics. They think of the scope and subject matter of law from the standpoint of the concrete desires and claims of concrete men in civilized society, not from the standpoint of the abstract qualities of the abstract individual, nor from the standpoint of the logical implications of the abstract individual free will.[89]

All assumptions of "self-evident truths," "individual rights" and "divine law" thus seemed untenable simultaneously. Holmes's adage "no concrete proposition is self-evident" should be read as an attack upon the preamble to the Declaration of Independence, as well as an explicit comment on Herbert Spencer.[90] The Bill of Rights was to be defended, not because it declared Man's self-evident Natural Rights, but because it was a socially beneficial part of the federal Constitution. We may presume that Melville was fully aware of the contemporary relevance of Billy Budd's impulsive exclamation, "And good-bye to you too, old *Rights-of-Man*."[91]

To the Realist, law and literature were tools to be made, not truths to be discovered. The Transcendentalists had been confident that a word was ultimately a sign of a spiritual fact. The literary Realists, many of whom had been journalists, saw the word as an often inaccurate, man-made way of describing objects and their relations. Benjamin Cardozo's redefinition of the meaning of "natural law" for

---

[88] Clarence Darrow, *The Story of My Life* (New York: Scribner's, 1932), p. 53.
[89] Pound, *Criminal Justice in America*, p. 4.
[90] Oliver Wendell Holmes, Jr., "The Path of the Law" (1897) in *American Social Thought*, ed. Ray Ginger (New York: Hill and Wang, 1961), p. 65.
[91] Melville, *Billy Budd*, p. 49. Compare Billy's farewell to Learned Hand's insistence that "The Bill of Rights . . . are the altogether human expression of the will of the state conventions that ratified them" (Hand, *The Bill of Rights* [Cambridge: Harvard University Press, 1958], p. 3).

his generation subsumes the same change: "That expression then meant that nature had imprinted in us, as one of the very elements of reason, certain principles of which all the articles of the code were only the application. The same expression ought to mean today that the law springs from the relations of fact which exist between things."[92] Only if the palpable world were to be perceived as a process of ever-changing fact could laws or words continue to be valued for their "natural" qualities.

Both Howells and James had asserted that the literary realist should allow his characters to work out their own destiny in their own particular situations; he should not add judgmental reflections on the way his characters have performed in predetermined plots.[93] When Roscoe Pound formulated the way in which the spirit of the common law could best function in the twentieth century, his approach was equally empirical:

> The judge makes the actual law by a process of trying the principles and rules and standards in concrete cases, observing their practical operation and gradually discovering by experience of many causes how to apply them so as to administer justice by means of them.[94]

Pound here celebrates the judicial method that individuals as different as Jefferson, Rantoul, Leatherstocking, and perhaps even Melville had greatly feared—the making of merely human law to fit present, shifting conditions.

To the realists, law should become an everchanging process, not a fixed body of ideas or statutes. At the very least, intelligent man-made law could maintain social order by fitting human practices to human needs. As Cardozo put it, "Statutes are designed to meet the fugitive exigencies of the hour."[95] More commonly, however, the legal realists looked to law as a means toward future prediction, rather than toward expediency or timeless revelation. Holmes

---

[92] Benjamin Cardozo, *The Nature of the Judicial Process* (New Haven: Yale University Press, 1921), p. 102. Excerpts from Benjamin Cardozo, *The Nature of the Judicial Process* are reprinted with the permission of Yale University Press.
[93] Howells, *Criticism and Fiction*, pp. 104, 119–120. James, "The Art of Fiction" (1884) in *The Future of the Novel*, ed. Leon Edel (New York: Vintage Books, 1956), pp. 10–19, 26.
[94] Roscoe Pound, *The Spirit of the Common Law* (Francestown, N.H.: Marshall Jones & Co., 1921), p. 176.
[95] Cardozo, *The Nature of the Judicial Process*, p. 83.

insisted "the prophecies of what the courts will do in fact, and nothing more pretentious, are what I mean by the law."[96] Somewhat later, Cardozo refined Holmes's idea in an attempt to establish a consensus: "We shall unite in viewing the law as that body of principle and dogma which with a reasonable measure of probability may be predicted as the basis for judgment in pending or in future controversies."[97]

Despite the disclaimers of modesty, the import of these statements is finally both pretentious and progressive. Cardozo, Pound, Brandeis, and even Holmes all looked to the law as a positive force in constructing a better-ordered, more livable society. To this end, however, they expected lawyers and judges to bring to their decisions knowledge beyond Blackstone and the casebooks. All four men demanded that the ideas of philosophical pragmatism and the findings of the new social sciences (sociology, psychology, economics) should be considered in the forming of a judicial decision. Similar demands were made of the literary Realist and Naturalist. Frank Norris and Sinclair Lewis consciously set out to do quasi-sociological research before writing *The Octopus* and *Babbitt.* Theodore Dreiser not only modeled *An American Tragedy* rather closely on the Gillette murder trial; he read deeply in Jacques Loeb's *The Mechanistic Conception of Life* as a way of understanding the mind of Chester Gillette.[98]

Legal realists, literary realists and literary naturalists all recognized that concern for the autonomous individual must henceforth be balanced, if not outweighed, by the needs of society at large. Roscoe Pound repeatedly attacked what he called "the simplistic starting point of the criminal law of the last century . . . the belief that a criminal was a person possessed of free will who, having before him a choice between right and wrong, had freely and deliberately chosen to go wrong."[99] Pound's purpose in attacking the assumption of criminal free will was not to arouse sympathy for supposedly helpless victims, but to force the reader to recognize that changeable social forces caused criminal conduct. America's transformation from a decentralized rural economy to an urban industrial economy clearly demanded, Pound believed, that the individual must now become subordinate:

[96] Holmes, "The Path of the Law," p. 59.
[97] Benjamin Cardozo, *The Growth of the Law* (New Haven: Yale University Press, 1924), p. 44.
[98] Ellen Moers, *The Two Dreisers* (New York: Viking, 1969), pp. 240–260.
[99] Pound, *Criminal Justice In America*, p. 122.

When houses are scarce and landlords are grasping, Blackstone's proposition that the public good is in nothing more essentially interested than in the protection of every individual's private rights is not the popular view. A crowded, urban, industrial community looks to society for protection against predatory individuals, natural or artificial, and resents doctrines that protect these individuals against society for fear society will oppress them.[100]

Pound's purpose in citing *The Pioneers* was to show that the rural conditions for which Templeton's "mild laws" were suited are no longer present in modern America.[101]

Throughout the late nineteenth century, the position of the individual in the legal system was full of anomalies. The Bill of Rights was a part of the federal Constitution, but the Supreme Court was not enforcing the Bill of Rights on the states. Liberty of contract and protection of property were regarded as primary individual rights, but they were used to keep poorer citizens in positions where economic freedom of choice was impossible to obtain. The response of the legal realists was itself somewhat confusing. As Pound's previous statement suggests, they proposed to subordinate certain individual rights (liberty of contract) in order to enable the legal system to better support the economic needs of all individuals. Two tendencies were nonetheless emerging from these changes. The first was the increasingly widespread assumption that individuals are not autonomous, do not possess free will, and are therefore not solely responsible for their acts. The second was a shrinking of the justification for civil disobedience. If divine law does not exist, and natural law is red in tooth and claw, what "higher law" could be cited to sanction the moral virtue of legally criminal individualists? Roscoe Pound's opinion was unequivocal: "Assertions of a super-legal right of private judgment, such as were made habitually by statesmen, publicists, and lawyers of the nineteenth century, are anachronisms."[102]

The attitudes of legal realism clearly surface in Mark Twain's *The Tragedy of Pudd'nhead Wilson*. Like *The Ways of the Hour*, Twain's

[100] Pound, *The Spirit of the Common Law*, pp. 102–103.
[101] *The Pioneers*, Pound says, shows us how "our common law polity presupposes an American farming community of the first half of the nineteenth century; a situation as far apart as the poles from what our legal system has had to meet in the endeavor to administer justice to great urban communities at the end of the nineteenth and in the twentieth century" (*The Spirit of the Common Law*, p. 124).
[102] Pound, *Criminal Justice In America*, p. 131.

novel culminates in a small-town murder trial in which a morally and legally innocent outsider is assumed by the townspeople to be guilty, partly because of circumstantial evidence, and partly because of prejudice against foreigners. Despite his scorn for Cooper, Twain's own attitudes toward trial by jury, the tyranny of public opinion, and the mean-minded follies of small-town prejudice are essentially Cooper's attitudes expressed in the darkest shades of humor. Twain has none of Cooper's lingering faith in the restraining power of judicial character. Judge York Leicester Driscoll may be, like Judge Temple or Thomas Dunscomb, a highly respected Christian gentleman, but Judge Driscoll's naive faith in the "laws" of the honor code of the First Families of Virginia (FFV) utterly blinds him to Tom Driscoll's worthlessness. The law of honor even leads Judge Driscoll to urge Tom to fight duels rather than "crawl to a court of law."[103] The FFV honor code, because it condones aristocracy, duelling and slavery under the guise of Christian gentility, becomes a substitute "law" that not only induces Roxy to exchange her black baby for the Judge's adopted white baby, but creates an atmosphere in which Tom will murder Judge Driscoll to retain his genteel position, knowing that all townspeople will suspect a foreigner, and not Tom, of the deed.[104] The townspeople's desire to hang Italian immigrants for the murder of Judge Driscoll, thereby enabling the real murderer to retain his false status as a white gentleman, is apt confirmation of Roscoe Pound's withering comments upon the "higher law" supported by nineteenth-century southern courts.[105]

Ironically, however, the xenophobia that seems sure to prevail at the trial is disarmed by proof of Tom Driscoll's guilt. And yet, the vindication of the court's decision does not exonerate the court system. Truth and reason can enter Dawson's Landing's courtroom only from outside it, when David ("Pudd'nhead") Wilson, an ostracized village atheist who has never established a law practice because he graduated from an Eastern law school, agrees to become the Italians' defense attorney. Because of his clear-sighted cynicism, Pudd'nhead enables justice to prevail in court, not by citing Natural Rights, case precedents, or the logic of circumstances, but by the discovery of undeniable tangible fact. Pudd'nhead's use of finger-

---

[103] Mark Twain, *The Tragedy of Pudd'nhead Wilson* (New York: Harper & Row, 1964), pp. 93, 96.
[104] Ibid., p. 93.
[105] Pound, *Criminal Justice In America*, pp. 128–129.

prints to reveal both the murderer and the exchange of babies is a twentieth-century technique that derives from the empirical assumptions of legal realism.[106] The literary effect of Puddn'head's anachronistic use of fingerprints in the 1850s, however, is ultimately disillusioning. The stupidity of the gaping courtroom audience suggests that justice prevails in criminal law only when legal judgments are based on clear physical evidence introduced in opposition both to public opinion and accepted courtroom practice.

DREISER AND DARROW

After *An American Tragedy* had gained Dreiser controversial popularity, he succinctly expressed his novel's purpose in a letter:

> I had long brooded upon the story, for it seemed to me not only to include every phase of our national life—politics, society, religion, business, sex—but it was a story so common to every boy reared in the smaller towns of America. It seemed so truly a story of what life does to the individual—and how impotent the individual is against such forces. My purpose was not to moralize—God forbid—but to give, if possible, a background and a psychology of reality which would somehow explain, if not condone, how such murders happen—and they have happened with surprising frequency in America as long as I can remember. [107]

The historical source for Clyde Griffith's "story," Chester Gillette's murder of a factory worker whom he had made pregnant, was clearly meant to serve as the seed for an all-inclusive study of a representative national tragedy. Dreiser's statement also suggests a revealing similarity between the novel's purposes and the tenets of legal and fictional realism. Dreiser assumes, as did Social Darwinists, that the individual is controlled by external forces. To moralize about one's subject, whether by presuming the existence of universal laws or pontificating about ethical imperatives, is an unforgivable falsification. Instead, one is to use the insights of psychology to provide an explanation for societal patterns. Fiction must adhere as closely as

---

[106] Walker, *Popular Justice*, p. 187. Walker reveals that "the fingerprint method of identification had arrived in the United States in 1904." Twain had undoubtedly learned of fingerprint detection in Europe; *Pudd'nhead Wilson* (1892) was published before fingerprinting was known in America.

[107] Letter to Jack Wilgus, April 20, 1927, in *Letters of Theodore Dreiser*, ed. Robert Elias (Philadelphia: University of Pennsylvania Press, 1959), 2:458.

possible to fact; to recast an historical trial helps to justify the ambition inherent in the novel's title.

Dreiser's controlling purpose—to provide a "background and psychology of reality" for a murder trial—thus demands a technique quite different from the novels of Cooper, Melville, or Twain. Like Wright's *Native Son, An American Tragedy* does not arrive at the fictive account of a historical trial until part three of a lengthy novel. Both Wright and Dreiser insist on detailed rendering of the long foreground of the accused's life, in order to provide the "psychology of reality" necessary for a twentieth-century understanding of life. Although Twain, Melville, and Cooper had also reserved trial scenes for narrative climax, the opening sections of their novels had not been concerned with a presumably objective account of the criminal's developing psyche, but with diverse matters of religious, economic, or amatory interest.

The form of the criminal trial novel has been fundamentally altered to accord with the changing conception of criminality. Assuming that a criminal act is the outcome of social and psychic conditioning, Dreiser and Wright seek to disclose causative conditions that a court trial per se cannot accurately or fully reveal. Dreiser was well aware of his premise that only fiction could reveal the sources of historical crime:

> In my examination of such data as I could find in 1924 relating to the Chester Gillette–Billy Brown case, I became convinced that there was an entire misunderstanding, or perhaps I had better say non comprehension, of the conditions or circumstances surrounding the victims of that murder *before* the murder was committed.[108]

Two years earlier, Roscoe Pound had publicly lectured on the same failing of the criminal justice system: "The lawyer's interest is in the machinery of prosecution and conviction and the machinery of mitigation. With what goes on before the commission of an offence, with the conditions which generate offenders and ensure a steady grist to the mill of criminal justice, the lawyer is not concerned."[109] To Pound, the circumstances that cause crime must be revealed so that a judge can rightly exercise discretion in sentencing. To Dreiser, those

[108] Theodore Dreiser, "I Find the Real American Tragedy," *Mystery Magazine*, 11 (1935): 88.
[109] Pound, *Criminal Justice in America*, p. 34.

circumstances must be recreated because they are the forces of life itself; without an understanding of them, no judgment oñ realities can be made.

From the "tall walls" of Kansas City to the corridors of the Green-Davidson Hotel, to the shrinking room of the Griffiths' collar factory, to the narrow rowboat, and finally to Clyde's prison cell, *An American Tragedy* is filled with images of the enclosing and confining of the self.[110] In all three of the novel's settings, we observe how social and economic forces create, in passive individuals, intense longings for wealth, sex, and power—longings that those same social forces then frustrate. Clyde's yearnings for the inner rooms of the Green-Davidson, for Hortense Briggs, for a house on Wykeagy Avenue, and for Sondra Finchley, depend on the degree to which they are on display as socially forbidden fruits. The class structure of American society is tragically unchangeable because the moneyed, the beautiful, and the powerful are able to arouse and frustrate desires without suggesting any alternative system of value. Dreiser once said that Chester Gillette "was really doing the kind of thing which Americans should and would have said was the wise and moral thing to do had he not committed murder."[111] If the novel may be said to contain villainy, it resides in a system of social values that creates longings, frustrates those longings, but then condemns the few people who are driven to illegal but feasible means of reaching them.

The very first sentence in which Clyde Griffiths is described provides the key to his character: "The boy moved restlessly from one foot to the other, keeping his eyes down, and for the most part only half singing."[112] Enticed by worldly symbols he has been taught to disapprove, Clyde is forever paralyzed with indecision, yet unable to analyze why. In a crucial summary passage, Dreiser says of him:

> To say the truth, Clyde had a soul that was not destined to grow up. He lacked decidedly that mental clarity and inner directing application that in so many permits them to sort out from the facts and avenues of life the particular thing or things that make for their direct advancement.[113]

[110] Theodore Dreiser, *An American Tragedy* (New York: New American Library, 1964), p. 7.
[111] Dreiser, "I Find the Real American Tragedy," p. 88.
[112] Dreiser, *An American Tragedy*, p. 9.
[113] Ibid., p. 169.

Like Billy Budd and Bigger Thomas, Clyde is a passive responder, resorting to childish expressions because he is unable to articulate the sources of his contradictory longings and fears. Unlike Billy and Bigger, however, Clyde was meant to respond in patterns characteristic of American youth. Dreiser once noted with evident pleasure, "I have had many letters from people who wrote 'Clyde Griffiths might have been me.'"[114]

The death of Roberta Alden is not rendered as an act around which to debate issues of natural or divine law, but as an inevitable outgrowth of environmentally determined character in a particular situation.[115] As soon as Clyde grows old enough to feel the "chemisms" of sexual attraction, he struggles with contradictory responses toward women: desire to possess their beauty and money, disapproval of his own sexuality, responsibility toward a woman one has "corrupted," fear of the danger and shame of public exposure. When Clyde, longing for Sondra Finchley, learns of Roberta's pregnancy, the collision of all four feelings renders him wholly unable to reach any reasoned decision. During the crucial moment before Roberta's death, Clyde is paralyzed by the same confusions. Silently drifting in a rowboat over dark waters, Clyde fantasizes Roberta's death as a desired atrocity completed without agency. When Roberta rises to dispel his visible inner torment, Clyde flings out hatefully and fearfully at her with his camera, not intending murder but compulsively desiring to "free himself of her . . . presence forever."[116] After Roberta recoils from the blow, Clyde rises to right the boat and to apologize. Although the capsizing of the boat is therefore unintended, Clyde's subsequent refusal to help the drowning Roberta is clearly a conscious decision resulting in her death.

Dreiser's careful reconstruction of Clyde's life up through this scene shows how utterly inappropriate the legal conception of murder is to judge Clyde's actions. During a postpublication interview, Dreiser acknowledged that Clyde's trial was intended to show how "the snap judgments of juries are inadequate in those knife-edge cases . . . where there is a subtler distinction to be made than the one

---

[114] F. O. Matthiessen, *Theodore Dreiser* (New York: William Sloane Associates, 1951), p. 191.
[115] In a letter of 1931, Dreiser referred to Roberta's drowning as "the planned culmination of a series of inescapable circumstances" (Elias, *Letters of Theodore Dreiser*, 2:511).
[116] Dreiser, *An American Tragedy*, p. 492.

between black and white."[117] First-degree murder, for which Clyde is tried and convicted, assumes both malice aforethought and deliberate intent. Clyde had wished Roberta obliterated but had not been able to bring himself to deliberate commission of the act. The crucial issue at stake here is the very premise of nineteenth-century American criminal justice—the belief in the freedom of the will. The deterministic way in which Clyde's entire life has been recreated convinces us that such concepts as "will," "intent," "malice," and "aforethought," are too crude to be applied to twentieth-century conditioning of human life.

The one crucial factual change Dreiser made in the Chester Gillette case was to alter the assault weapon from a tennis racquet to a camera, thereby obscuring even further the question of Clyde's intent.[118] Dreiser's remarkable success in recreating a homicide for which the very terms of law seem no longer adequate was acknowledged by Clarence Darrow, who told Dreiser that "on the basis of the novel, it would be impossible to determine Clyde's guilt."[119]

Even though all the facts are known to the reader, the sheer complexity of the evidence and the false categories of criminal law render any truly just decision impossible. The men who fill official roles in the court trial scarcely even attempt to discover the truth. Although prosecuting attorney Mason begins his opening statement by charging that Clyde "plotted for weeks the plan and commission of it [Roberta's 'drowning'], and then, with malice aforethought and in cold blood, executed it,"[120] Mason never reconsiders the applicability of these terms to Clyde's acts. He simply assumes that, because Clyde is bearded, employed, and of age, Clyde must be responsible for whatever consequences occurred while he was rowing.

Extraneous arguments become the very substance of Clyde's trial. The prosecution attempts to gain sympathy by casting Clyde as a sophisticated city seducer who corrupted the heart of a pure country maiden. Belknap, chief counsel for the defense, argues that Clyde is innocent of murder because he is a "mental and moral coward" afflicted with fear. Jephson, the assistant counsel for the defense, later tries to prove that Clyde had a noble and merciful "change of heart" toward Roberta.[121] Neither the legal officials nor the accused is

[117] Robert Elias, *Theodore Dreiser: Apostle of Nature* (Ithaca: N.Y.: Cornell University Press, 1969), pp. 222–223.
[118] See Moers, *Two Dreisers*, pp. 199–200.
[119] Elias, *Dreiser: Apostle of Nature*, p. 222.
[120] Dreiser, *American Tragedy*, p. 640.
[121] Ibid., p. 669, 695.

troubled by the many lies which all knowingly devise and promulgate. Unlike Cooper and Twain, Dreiser implies that the adversary system must obscure truth because its participants are motivated by gaining victory rather than revealing fact or deciding justice.

Clyde's trial illustrates faults of criminal procedure that Roscoe Pound was then denouncing. Pound's presumption that jurors are usually prejudiced and incompetent to judge either law or facts is reflected in Clyde's jury, all but one of whom are religious, married rubes "convinced of Clyde's guilt before he ever sat down."[122] District Attorney Mason, who seeks to be elected judge, arranges a special session for Clyde's trial and loses no opportunity either of gaining publicity for the case or of appealing to the prejudices of the jury and the courtroom. Observing that "where judges are chosen by direct primary followed by popular election, the need of keeping in the public eye in order to ensure reelection has made the judicial Barnum a characteristic feature of the American Bench," Pound therefore concludes that ambitious public prosecutors pose the greatest danger of all: "Undoubtedly the bane of prosecution in the United States of today is the intimate connection of the prosecutor's office with politics."[123]

To Pound and to Dreiser, the tendency to make a criminal trial into a local theatrical is directly dependent on reporters who try cases in public print, thereby assuring that the open courtroom will be filled with bias. During Clyde's trial, the rowboat is brought in for absurd demonstrations, and one irate woodsman in the audience cries out "Why don't they kill the God-damned bastard and be done with him."[124] Monetary motives dominate from the trial's beginning, when Clyde's uncle purchases less than the fullest efforts of defense lawyers, to its finish, when the one wavering juror is pressured into voting guilty lest his druggist business suffer.

In keeping with the tenets of legal and literary Realism, none of the participants in Clyde's trial argues from premises of Natural Rights or Divine Law. Facts stand for nothing beyond themselves; behavior is explained, not by moral laws, but by psychological needs and communal beliefs. The most telling aspect of this shift is that Theodore Dreiser condones it as well as accedes to it. Only two characters ever judge Clyde by standards of divine law. Clyde's fundamentalist mother affirms her son's innocence of intent by telling

[122] Ibid., p. 639.
[123] Pound, *Criminal Justice In America*, pp. 191, 183.
[124] Dreiser, *An American Tragedy*, p. 721.

reporters "whether or not the jury has found him guilty or innocent is neither here nor there in the eyes of Him who holds the stars in the hollow of His hand." Reverend MacMillan, himself unsure whether Clyde is morally guilty of murder, tells the governor that he knows of no legal reason why Clyde should be pardoned: "As his spiritual advisor, I have entered only upon the spiritual, not the legal aspect of his life."[125] Both Duncan MacMillan and Clyde's mother are associated with a profession and a way of thinking that are powerless, passé, and discredited. More important, both characters assume that legal and moral judgments are in fact quite separate kinds of decisions. Religious though they are, their expectations of criminal law are utterly distinct from those of the American Puritans, who conceived of a statute as a punishment for sin. Divine and man-made law have become wholly severed.

The participants in the trial are equally unable, however, to accept the premise of psychological and social causation that Dreiser has so painstakingly demonstrated in the unfolding of Clyde's life. When Clyde had contemplated drowning Roberta, he had never been able to concede that it was he, Clyde Griffiths, who was planning murder. Instead, he had attempted to project his dark desires unto some "Devil's whisper," "genie," "black rebus," or "Giant Efrit that had previously materialized in the silent halls of his brain."[126] At no time during his imprisonment does Clyde consider possible social or psychological causes for his feelings. Trapped within accepted modes of thought, he torments himself with the insoluble questions of whether he is morally or legally guilty. Neither Mason nor Belknap nor Jephson wishes to unravel the skein of determinism that has brought Clyde to his present straits. To do so would not be in the prosecution's interest and would not be an effective argument for the defense to use on the jury or the audience.

An unexpected irony of the trial's outcome is that the jury's decision is not even made in accord with the inappropriately simplistic canon of first-degree murder. Judge Oberwaltzer correctly charges the jury that Clyde's intent to murder, but not his motive, is legally pertinent to the decision. Oberwaltzer rightly insists that Clyde's failure to rescue Roberta once she was in the water does not constitute first-degree murder. Dreiser's recounting of testimony has revealed, however, that the audience and jury, rightly impressed by

[125] Ibid., pp. 743, 803.
[126] Ibid., pp. 440, 464, 467, 471.

Clyde's weak negligence, have turned Belknap's defense plea against him and are wrongly convicting Clyde for being a "mental and moral coward."

Clyde's trial thus shows us Dreiser's recognition that his own assumptions about criminality and civil justice are well in advance of the popular attitudes of the 1920s. *An American Tragedy* affirms the new assumptions both of the legal realists and of the most notorious criminal defense lawyer in American history. The forces driving Clyde toward manslaughter nicely illustrate Clarence Darrow's startling speech to prisoners in the Cook County Jail in 1902:

> I really do not in the least believe in crime. There is no such thing as a crime as the word is generally understood. I do not believe there is any sort of distinction between the real moral conditions of the people in and out of jail. One is just as good as the other. The people here can no more help being here than the people outside can avoid being outside. I do not believe that people are in jail because they deserve to be. They are in jail simply because they cannot avoid it on account of circumstances which are entirely beyond their control and for which they are in no way responsible.[127]

Dreiser provides a similar explanation for the presence of the twenty men who wait beside Clyde on Death Row. None of the twenty had deliberately chosen to commit a criminal act: "each one . . . had responded to some heat or lust or misery of his nature or his circumstances."[128]

Passages from Darrow's speeches summarize the reasons why Clyde's life had ended in jail and death: "Nine tenths of you are in jail because you did not have a good lawyer, and, of course, you did not have a good lawyer because you did not have enough money to pay a good lawyer." "A child is born with no ideas of right or wrong, just with plastic brain, ready for such impressions as come to him, ready to be developed." "If there is such a thing as justice, it could only be administered by one who knew the inmost thoughts of the man to whom he was meting it out."[129] Darrow spoke the last two of these quotations during his celebrated defense of Leopold and Loeb, delivered while Dreiser was writing *An American Tragedy*.

[127] Clarence Darrow, "Address to the Prisoners in the Cook County Jail," in Arthur Weinberg, *Attorney for the Damned* (New York: Simon & Schuster, 1957), pp. 3–4.
[128] Dreiser, *An American Tragedy*, p. 767.
[129] Weinberg, *Attorney for the Damned*, "Address to the Prisoners of the Cook County Jail," p. 7; "Defense of Leopold and Loeb," pp. 54, 43.

If criminality is conditioned behavior and free will is a mirage, the entire system of criminal law can readily seem an anachronistic outrage. A chapter of Darrow's autobiography that summarizes his lifetime of experience in criminal courts is tellingly titled "The Blind Leading the Blind." If we make needed allowance for Darrow's professional habit of cynical overstatement, his findings apply perfectly to the experience of Clyde Griffiths. The causes of criminal acts, Darrow concludes, are buried in the obscurity of the womb or of one's youth. Circumstances and accidents bring forth latent psychological impulses driving individuals to commit acts legally defined as criminal. Our confusion of moral guilt and legal guilt turns the courtroom into a theater where "there is always the same morbid audience absorbing the details." Through playing on such morbidity, "the prosecutor hopes and expects to be judge."[130] Juries habitually assume guilt; the accused seeks mercy and not justice; only the judge ever desires a decision according to law. Because criminal statutes do not recognize that cause and effect, rather than free will, determines human actions, our criminal procedure has become an "archaic, costly and pernicious system"[131] that is not adapting to a rapidly changing world. Recognizing that Dreiser's novel had reaffirmed his own convictions about the judicial system, Darrow promptly praised the book's "fanatical devotion to truth," told Dreiser "of course my philosophy is practically the same as yours," and later undertook to defend *An American Tragedy* against a charge of obscenity.[132]

Clarence Darrow's novel, *An Eye For An Eye* (1905), attacks both the *lex talionis* and the American system of criminal justice unsparingly. Committed to realistic fiction since writing "Realism Versus Idealism in Literature and Art" (1899), Darrow recreates an autobiographical monologue of a condemned murderer in order to

[130] Clarence Darrow, *The Story of My Life* (New York: Scribner's, 1932), p. 352.
[131] Ibid., p. 356.
[132] Matthiessen, *Theodore Dreiser*, p. 208; Kevin Tierney, *Darrow: A Biography* (New York: Crowell, 1979), pp. 386–388. Helen Dreiser recalled a chance meeting between Dreiser and Darrow in 1927: "As [Dreiser] was walking through the train, he was surprised to meet Clarence Darrow. 'Well,' said Dreiser, 'where are you going?' 'Why, I'm going to the trial of your book in Boston,' Darrow replied. 'As you know, I think you have written a great novel and I want to do anything I can to defend it.' Dreiser was delighted. On the way up they had much to talk about, for Darrow and Dreiser had a parallel philosophy, in that they agreed that no one was really guilty if his conditioning environment was understood. Darrow told Dreiser that after reading *An American Tragedy* it would be impossible to determine Clyde's guilt on the basis of the book" (Helen Dreiser, *My Life With Dreiser* [Cleveland: World Publishing Co., 1951], pp. 162–163).

demonstrate the law's indifference to the facts of urban poverty. Jim Jackson, a parentless Chicago slum child, leaves school at twelve, works in the stockyards and trainyards, participates in the Pullman strike, and then marries a stolid waitress by whom he has a child, only to sink ever deeper into patterns of peddling, poverty, and debt. Driven to violence by his environs, Joe eventually kills his embittered wife with a poker, hides her body in a gravel pit, and flees to Georgia, where he is captured, brought back to Chicago, tried for first-degree murder, and sentenced to execution.

Unlike Dreiser, Darrow grants that his drearily ordinary protagonist has committed first-degree murder by legal definition. By allowing Jim to describe the circumstances that drove him to commit murder, Darrow clearly intends to attack both capital punishment and the very idea that retribution is the defensible purpose for criminal deterrence. Because Jim tells his story after his legal innocence is lost, his simple vernacular voice proves an effective means for Darrow to reveal the press's lust for punishment, the jury's mean-minded sadism, the political ambitions of prosecutors, and the madness of hanging men of confused mind. Jim shows us how the legal system has almost succeeded in persuading criminals not to regard the societal causes of their deeds:

> I haven't time to tell you all about my peddlin'; anyhow, it ain't got much to do with the case, not much more'n any of the rest. My lawyer always said any time I told him anything "well, what's that got to do with your killin' her," and the judge said about the same thing whenever we asked any questions. He couldn't see that anything I had ever done had anything to do with it except the bad things.[133]

Unfortunately, Darrow's confining of the narrative to Jim Jackson's point of view also diminishes his novel's achievement. By not allowing consideration for social as well as individual needs, Jim's narrative becomes merely a vehicle for Darrow's legal criticisms. A worse offense is that Darrow's determination to allow Jim to exonerate himself leads to frequent lapses in fictional credibility. Jim tells us of his great love for pets and children and dwells on his selfless generosity in giving half a peck of potatoes to a starving woman.

---

[133] Clarence Darrow, *An Eye For An Eye*, ed. R. B. Shuman (Durham, N.C.: Moore Publishing Co., 1969), p. 46.

Darrow's choice of a fictional point of view thus suggests how readily a realist who confuses fictional truth with angry propaganda could be inadvertently led into sentimentality.

CREATIVE CRIME

When *Native Son* was published in 1940, many reviewers sensed the close affinity between Wright's novel and *An American Tragedy*. Clifton Fadiman wrote in *The New Yorker*:

> *Native Son* does for the Negro what Theodore Dreiser in *An American Tragedy* did a decade and a half ago for the bewildered, inarticulate white. The two books are similar in theme, in technique, in their almost paralyzing effect on the reader, and in the large brooding humanity, quite remote from special pleading, which informs them both.[134]

Such a sense of general likeness stems from the many similarities of detail through which Richard Wright seems consciously to place his book within a Dreiserian tradition. Bigger and Clyde are both inchoate adolescents trapped in poor families dominated by religious mothers. While Bigger and his friends watch the double feature of *Trader Horn* and *The Gay Woman*, they are unknowingly being conditioned in the same allure of unobtainable power and unobtainable rich women that had so entranced Clyde Griffiths. Bigger's smothering of Mary Dalton, like Clyde's "flinging out" at Roberta, is motivated by an uncontrollable need to obliterate a woman whose presence has aroused fear and guilt over his violation of American sexual taboos. During both trials, popular rage against the wrong done to a presumably pure woman is fomented by the prosecution until a rational decision becomes an impossibility. Extorted confessions, tyranny of the press, politically motivated prosecutors and theatrical restagings of crime are common to both trials. State Attorney Buckley is almost indistinguishable in character from District Attorney Mason; Reverend Hammond's religious appeals to Bigger seem as outmoded as those of Reverend MacMillan; both Clyde and Bigger go to their deaths fearful, alone, and unsure of their guilt.

Wright's acknowledgement of the impact of Dreiser's fiction ("I

---

[134] Clifton Fadiman, review of *Native Son*, *The New Yorker*, March 2, 1940, p. 52.

was overwhelmed")[135] should not lead us to assume any discipleship, nor should the many similarities between *Native Son* and Dreiser's masterpiece lead to the facile, still repeated conclusion that *Native Son* is "the Negro *American Tragedy*."[136] Wright has adopted the naturalistic techniques and plot situation of *An American Tragedy*, not merely to apply Dreiser's vision to the black race, but to lead the reader toward altered psychological and legal understanding through a new rendering of Dreiser's material.

One could certainly find in *Native Son* a wealth of evidence to prove that Bigger Thomas is, like Clyde Griffiths, the creation of societal forces and therefore innocent of criminal intent, however guilty he may be of criminal motive. In "How Bigger Was Born," Wright insisted that Bigger was the "product of a dislocated society . . . a dispossessed and disinherited man . . . resentful toward whites, sullen, angry, ignorant, emotionally unstable, depressed and unaccountably elated at times, and unable even, because of his own lack of inner organization which American oppression has fostered in him, to unite with members of his own race."[137] Like Clyde, Bigger is paralyzed by the conflicts between his desire to possess society's symbols of worth, his wordless feeling that society bars him from attaining them, and a shame of self caused by shame of low status. The "murders" for which both young men are convicted are uncontrollable, violent expressions of their need to free themselves from guilt by obliterating the symbol of their guilt. Accepting all the values by which American society defines upward mobility, Bigger and Clyde cannot articulate the reasons for their recourse to violence. Bigger can no more think "I hate myself because society believes I am a nigger" than Clyde can say "I dislike myself because society, while condemning unwed mothers, bars my marriage to a rich man's daughter." Perhaps the clearest expression of the extent to which Bigger Thomas is a product of his society's values is his unchanging response to Bessie Mears. Whereas Bigger neither consummated his desire to rape Mary nor killed her intentionally, he bullied Bessie into an abandoned house, forced himself upon her sexually, and then, with malice aforethought, bludgeoned her to death with a brick. And yet, neither the prosecuting attorney nor the defense attorney nor the judge nor the people nor even

[135] Richard Wright, *Black Boy* (New York: Harper & Row, 1966), p. 274.
[136] Review of *Native Son*, *New York Times Book Review*, March 3, 1940, p. 2.
[137] Richard Wright, *Native Son* (New York: Harper & Row, 1966), pp. xx–xxi.

Bigger himself is ever much concerned with the charges concerning Bessie. The stereotype of "the nigger" is all important to Bigger's trial, but a Negro's person simply does not count, in trial or in life.

Although Wright reconfirms Dreiser's thoroughly deterministic explanation of criminal behavior, he differs sharply with Dreiser's portrayal of its psychological effect. From the outset, Bigger Thomas exemplifies the failing Robert Penn Warren perceived in Clyde: "the most important thing shrouded from his sight is his own identity."[138] And yet, the act of killing affects Bigger's sense of identity in a way Dreiser could not imagine. Roberta's death had redoubled Clyde's self-doubt, forcing him deeper into a spiritual paralysis caused by the conflict between moral guilt and cowardice, between shame and desire. The act of killing Mary Dalton, however, frees Bigger Thomas by giving him an identity. Without a trace of moral disapproval, Wright concludes of Bigger: "He had murdered and had created a new life for himself. It was something all his own, and it was the first time in his life he had had anything that others could not take from him."[139] By asserting mastery over a white person who made him feel guilt and shame, Bigger separates himself from the world of victimized blacks and master whites. In his new isolation there is not only an emerging sense of self, but an ability to see the impoverished conditions of the Black Belt in accurate comparative terms.

Wright enables his reader to understand why Bigger, unknowingly denying the most basic Christian axiom about criminal behavior, could truly feel that "his crime seemed natural."[140] Knowing only the amoral responses of an urban slum Bigger can associate the word *natural* only with the word *inevitable*. Unlike Clyde Griffiths, who was half convinced by the spiritual rigor of Reverend MacMillan, Bigger scorns and defies Reverend Hammond. Even after Bigger has been recaptured, he clings to his feeling that his self has been formed by murder:

> I don't know. Maybe this sounds crazy. Maybe they going to burn me in the electric chair for feeling this way. But I ain't worried none about them women I killed. For a little while I was free. I was doing something. It was wrong, but I was feeling all right.[141]

---

[138] Robert Penn Warren, *Homage to Theodore Dreiser* (New York: Random House, 1971), pp. 124–125.
[139] Wright, *Native Son*, p. 101.
[140] Ibid., p. 101.
[141] Ibid., p. 328.

This contrast between the two young men is sustained to the end. Clyde Griffiths sinks limply into the "terrible chair, his eyes fixed nervously and, as he thought, appealingly and dazedly on him and the groups surrounding him."[142] As Boris Max leaves Bigger for the last time, Bigger manages a "faint, wry, bitter smile" because he believes that, in some indefinite sense, "what I killed for must've been good! . . . It must have been good. When a man kills, it's for something. . . . I didn't know I was really alive in this world until I felt things hard enough to kill for 'em."[143]

Whereas the guilty doubt of Clyde Griffiths reflects his lingering commitment to Protestant moral values, Bigger Thomas's tentative grasp on an identity recalls Dostoevsky's Raskolnikov and anticipates Camus's Meursault. Through the act of murder, all three men experience new psychic power more intensely than old moral guilt. Because Wright believes that murder can be an act of self-creation, he must continually redefine traditional moral and legal terms in a new psychological context. A plausible legal defense against the charge of murder might have been that Mary Dalton's death was an unpremeditated accident. Wright grants this traditional defense ("though he had killed by accident. . . ") but almost immediately shifts the meaning of the term: "And in a certain sense, he knew that the girl's death had not been accidental. He had killed many times before, only on those other times there had been no handy victim or circumstance to make visible or dramatic his wish to kill."[144]

By legal definition, Bigger Thomas did not rape Mary Dalton, even though he is condemned in court for having done so. Wright, however, asks his reader to believe that Bigger was a rapist in spirit:

> Had he raped her? Yes, he had raped her. Every time he felt as he had felt that night, he raped. But rape was not what one did to a woman. Rape was what one felt when one's back was against a wall and one had to strike out, whether one wanted to or not, to keep the pack from killing one.[145]

Bigger's smothering of Mary starts a chain of events that drive Bigger from a legal state of freedom to a legal state of imprisonment. According to traditional Christian thought, such a violation of God's law should show how Bigger's spirit is bound to forces of evil. Wright,

---

[142] Dreiser, *An American Tragedy*, p. 881.
[143] Wright, *Native Son*, p. 392.
[144] Ibid., p. 101.
[145] Ibid., pp. 213–214.

however, declares, "Never had his [Bigger's] will been so free as in this night and day of fear and murder and flight."[146]

All three examples illustrate one pattern. Wright selects a term associated with a legal condition, then redefines the term as a mental attitude that is a response to social conditioning, not individual will. This continuing process of redefinition serves to subordinate legal deed to psychological health as the valid standard of judgment. At certain moments, Wright is even led to the verge of condoning crime, as well as explaining it, on grounds of its psychological benefit. Dreiser and Darrow, not to mention Holmes, would surely have been appalled at the extent to which psychological and sociological thinking could subvert all sense of traditional ethics.

It is within this perspective of a reworking of fictional conventions that we can best understand the most debated aspect of Wright's novel—Defense Attorney Boris Max's seventeen-page speech on behalf of Bigger Thomas. We must consider, first of all, that Max's speech is different in kind from both its historical and fictional models. Eighteen-year-old Robert Nixon, a Negro handyman who killed Mrs. Florence Johnson with a brick while robbing her apartment, had been convicted of murder by a jury trial in 1938.[147] Like Dreiser's decision to change Gillette's murder weapon, Wright's decision to change the victim of the bludgeoning from Mary Dalton to Bessie Mears greatly lessens the degree of willful intent attributable to the specific trial charge.

Unlike the pleas in all the novels previously discussed, Wright arranges for Boris Max to have Bigger plead guilty to the charge of murder. Boris Max's long speech thus becomes, not a defense of Bigger's legal innocence, but a plea to the judge to mitigate Bigger's sentence from execution to life imprisonment. Critics who, following James Baldwin, criticize Max's speech as "one of the most desperate performances in American literature"[148] should remember that Max's long uninterrupted plea follows a legal practice. More important, the change in the kind of defense speech alters the content of the speech itself. Wright does not wish Boris Max to interest us, as Dreiser had, in the applicability of legal definitions of first- or second-degree

[146] Ibid., p. 225.
[147] See Michel Fabre, *The Unfinished Quest of Richard Wright* (New York: William Morrow, 1973), p. 102; and Kenneth Kinnamon "*Native Son*: The Personal, Social and Political Background," *Phylon*, Spring 1969, pp. 68–71.
[148] James Baldwin, *Notes of a Native Son* (New York: Bantam Books, 1955), p. 32.

murder to the factual circumstances of a homicide. Instead, Wright frees Boris Max to direct the trial toward disclosure of the psychological and economic forces that cause thousands of Bigger Thomases to commit crime. In effect, Boris Max ceases speaking as a defense lawyer and addresses the court as a criminologist whose assumptions about causation are fundamentally Marxist.

Much of Max's speech affirms in abstract terms the crucial experiential truths that Bigger could never articulate. Behind the sadism and racial prejudice vented on Bigger by white Chicago lie "fear and hate and guilt," but most especially "the long trailing black sense of guilt stemming from that wrong [slavery]." Bigger Thomas regrettably had no soul because he was "like a weed growing from under a stone, . . . springing from a soil plowed and sown by all our hands." Precisely because society denied him an identity, the act of murder became "the first full act of his life; it made him free, gave him the possibility of force, of action, the opportunity to act and to feel that his actions carried weight." Mary Dalton may be dead, but "the truth is, this boy did *not* kill" because he had "no motive as you and I understand motives." Bigger's homicide was "as instinctive and inevitable as breathing or blinking one's eyes. It was an act of *creation!*"[149]

Boris Max's plea thus redefines the meaning of the terms *innocent criminal* and *criminal innocence* as they have applied to Leatherstocking, Billy Budd, and Clyde Griffiths. Bigger committed rape and murder; in attitude, he committed them countless times. And yet, because he had to create himself through these acts, and not through words, he remained fundamentally innocent in motive. This notion of innocence, however, involved Wright in one fundamental contradiction. He could plausibly contend that crime was not a deed: "This Negro boy's entire attitude toward life is a *crime*. . . . His very existence is a crime against the state." He could also, equally plausibly, have Boris Max say to Mr. Dalton "you rent houses to Negroes in the Black Belt and you refuse to rent to them elsewhere. You kept Bigger Thomas in that forest! You kept the man who murdered your daughter a stranger to her and you kept your daughter a stranger to him."[150] In order to retain for Bigger a higher innocence, however, Wright has been led to ascribe free will and

---

[149] Wright, *Native Son*, pp. 357, 358, 364, 366, 366.
[150] Ibid., pp. 366–367; 150.

social responsibility to whites who control the Black Belt but to deny free will and social responsibility to blacks who are victimized by it.

Boris Max announces to the judge "I do *not* claim that this boy is a victim of injustice, nor do I ask that this court be sympathetic with him.". A few sentences later, he repeats his point even more insistently: "Let us banish from our minds the thought that this is an unfortunate victim of injustice. Max's purpose in offering so startling a contention is to force the court to recognize that *injustice* can exist only when the legal system allows for equality. When social conditions wholly preclude equality, there can be no justice even if legal procedures are equitable. Hence Max insists "What is happening here today is not injustice but oppression, an attempt to throttle or stamp out a new form of life." "The very concept of justice rests upon a promise of equal claims," Max says, "and this boy here today makes no claim upon you."[151] Such reasoning, however valid it may be, can have no pertinence toward the decision of the court. Boris Max is attempting to use one representative case to indict an entire society, yet he asks a judge within that society's criminal system to mitigate punishment to an individual, not because of any legal injustice, but because of the nature of the social order. He would redress wrongs done to a legal criminal by exposing an oppressive social order of which the court is an extension. In legal and psychological strategy, Max's plea is bound to fail.

The futility of Max's plea should lead us to qualify the common assumption that he readily supports revolutionary Communist ideas. It is true that Max applies arguments of economic class to the Black Belt, and equally true that he warns of "another civil war" in which the rage of the oppressed will topple skyscrapers. Boris Max, however, clearly fears revolutionary violence and refrains from ever stating that the 12 million Negroes who constitute a "separate nation" should ever fight for independence. Instead, he explicitly argues that Americans' "inalienable rights, among which are life, liberty and the pursuit of happiness" entitle them to be "caught up, absorbed in a meaningful task or duty to be done, a task or duty which in turn sheds justification and sanction back down upon their humble labors."[152] Because such language better fits an advocate for the New Deal than for the John Reed Society, we may wonder whether Richard Wright's commitment to Jeffersonian notions of

---

[151] Ibid., pp. 358, 358, 361, 358.
[152] Ibid., pp. 369, 364, 365, 365.

inalienable rights may be stronger than even he realized. In "How Bigger Was Born," Wright was to contend that Bigger Thomas, however inarticulate,was filled with repressed rage precisely because he had in him a "dammed up, buried and implied" desire to seek out his own fate, a desire based on the cultural assumption that "The Bill of Rights is a good legal and humane principle to safeguard our civil liberties."[153]

No matter how Wright's readers respond to Max's words, their substance is clearly wasted upon the court. Bigger himself "had not understood the speech." In summation, Prosecuting Attorney Buckley twice reminds the court that "the law is holy," then displays how holiness is practiced by referring to Bigger as a "black lizard" who needs to be killed "to keep from scuttling on his belly farther over the earth and spitting forth his venom of death!" The impartial decision that Boris Max had hoped the jury might deliver proves to be just as illusory as the impartiality of a jury. Bigger's judge sentences him to death with but one sentence of explanation: "In view of the unprecedented disturbance of the public mind, the duty of this Court is clear."[154]

Such judicial pandering to popular racial prejudice reflects historical practice. Samuel Walker notes that, after the passage of the Fourteenth Amendment, "the criminal justice system was one of the major instruments of white supremacy."[155] It was widely presumed that the stability of the court system could continue only as long as courts periodically acted out the retributive desires of the people. Holmes was inclined toward this view, and Roscoe Pound shows us how long it lingered:

> Moralists and sociologists no longer regard revenge or satisfaction of a desire for vengeance as a legitimate end of penal treatment. But jurists are not agreed. Many insist upon the retributive theory in one form or another, and Anglo-American lawyers commonly regard satisfaction of public desire for vengeance as both a legitimate and a practically necessary end.[156]

The circumstances of the decisions in the cases of Clyde Griffiths and Bigger Thomas suggest that the retributive theory, much to both

---

[153] Ibid., pp. xxiv–xxv.
[154] Ibid., pp. 370, 373, 373, 380–381.
[155] Walker, *Popular Justice*, p. 119.
[156] Pound, *Criminal Justice In Cleveland*, p. 113.

authors' distaste, is very much an unspoken component in judicial decisions. Dreiser's interest in legal reasoning and legal procedure had impelled him toward a traditional concern with law as an institutional system. In a world where murder becomes creative and lawyers refer to the accused as a subhuman ape, the legal system must seem something more than an institution. Richard Wright would surely have agreed with Morris Raphael Cohen who, in the same year that *Native Son* was published, declared that "the criminal law represents the pathology of civilization."[157]

III

Uncertainties

The novels we have discussed demonstrate the continuing grasp that individualism has held on the American mind. However much Dreiser and Wright may insist that any individual is a mere pawn amid social forces, the very structure of their novels illustrates that Clyde Griffiths and Bigger Thomas, pathetically ordinary and confused though they be, nonetheless matter a very great deal. When American authors successfully imagine a resonant legal controversy they repeatedly pit a helpless outsider against the forces of the community, and then induce the reader to believe that the single individual's interest should be accorded at least equal consideration.

Melville, Twain, Darrow, Dreiser, and Wright all explicitly designate that their works are to be experienced as tragedies. These are not tragedies, however, to which we may apply such older definitions as a noble individual's inner flaw, the fall of a man of high estate, or cleansing through pity and fear. Nor could all these works (save Darrow's) seem tragic if they merely aroused sympathy for a little person victimized by social injustice. The tragic consequences of these guilty verdicts do not fall on the community or the individual but on the community through what has happened to a representative individual. Is this not a particularly communal and egalitarian conception of what legal tragedy is?

The individuals who are accused of murder are almost always tried for the right deed but by the wrong standard. Recall the

---

[157] Morris Raphael Cohen, "Moral Aspects of the Criminal Law," *Yale Law Journal* 49 (1940):1024.

similarly compulsive way in which Billy Budd kills Claggart, Jim Jackson kills his wife, Clyde Griffiths kills Roberta, and Bigger Thomas kills Mary Dalton. Do not all of these killings fit, almost exactly, the legal definition of involuntary manslaughter?

> Involuntary manslaughter is an unintentional homicide where the death of the victim is not intended nor contemplated, but the act causing death is done in such a manner that it is neither innocent nor accidental homicide.[158]

Billy, Jackson, Clyde, and Bigger physically strike out because of their uncontrollable need to obliterate rather than from a deliberate wish to kill.

Why then, we should ask, have not the authors chosen to try the accused by the appropriate charge? To answer that Melville, Dreiser, and Wright were all faithfully following the trials of their historical models may be generally true, but it begs the question of the authors' intent in their initial choices. Evidently, American writers have selected historical trials in which, because neither charge nor punishment quite fits the crime, we can readily see the inability of society either to devise a just criminal code (Melville), or its inability, because of oppressive social forces, to apply it rationally (Dreiser and Wright). Even though appeals to notions of divine or natural right may make late nineteenth- as well as twentieth-century writers uncomfortable, they have nonetheless chosen to recreate historical trials in which an individual's merits or needs or even "rights" are somehow denied.

The persistence and strength of this viewpoint are measured by the slighting of its opposite. When James Gould Cozzens's *The Just and the Unjust* was published in 1942, the *Harvard Law Review* judged Cozzens's work to be "one of the best legal novels the reviewer has ever read," "the best account I know of the daily life of ordinary lawyers," a book that "every law student ought to read." "It is extraordinary," the reviewer concluded, "that an author who is not a lawyer could have written this book."[159] Sixteen years later, *Time Magazine* flatly declared "*The Just and the Unjust* is the best American novel ever fashioned about the law."[160] Even if we discount

[158] Bassiouni, *Substantive Criminal Law*, p. 269.
[159] Zachariah Chafee, Jr., review of *The Just and the Unjust, Harvard Law Review* 56 (1943):833–836.
[160] *Time Magazine*, September 2, 1957, p. 76.

the last statement as exaggeration, we are faced with an anomaly. A fine novel, dealing accurately with legal institutions, has virtually dropped from sight, while the tradition of Cooper, Melville, Twain, Dreiser, and Wright continues to fill paperback shelves and college courses.

Part of the cause may be inferred from the praise of another reviewer, who sneered at the popularity of Arthur Train's Ephraim Tutt on the one hand, and of westerns that romanticize vigilantism on the other:

> Imagine a murder trial with no noble prosecutor, no rugged defender, no victimized defendants, no purple moments. That's what Cozzens gives us in this book, and that, by the way, is what most murder trials are.[161]

Upon opening *The Just and the Unjust*, we note immediately how far outside the traditions of American legal fiction Cozzens's novel lies. The book begins with a long list of the court's docket entries, taken almost verbatim from an historical trial of 1935. The narrative begins at the beginning of the trial and ends at trial's end. It includes sections of little-revised trial transcripts together with descriptions of the participant's extralegal activities during the trial days.[162]

The change in fictional form both reflects and creates great changes in legal attitude. The controlling point of view belongs neither to the accused nor the defense lawyer nor the judge but to that chief villain of tradition, the prosecuting attorney. Unlike each of the novels discussed, *The Just and the Unjust* never provides us the author's presumably objective account of the crime. Instead, the reader is placed in the same position as a juror; he must sift through chaotic testimony in order to try to determine whether the accused's deeds suit the definitions of murder according the Pennsylvania statutes. In American trial novels from Cooper through Wright, the omniscient point of view had encouraged the reader to believe that one can accurately know the facts of a case, even though there may be no just way of deciding the case in a human court. Cozzens's novel

---

[161] Arthur Garfield Hays, "Yankees in the Courtroom," *The New Republic*, August 1942, p. 205.
[162] For information about the historical trial that Cozzens studied (*Commonwealth v. Wiley and Farrell*) and its relation to *The Just and the Unjust*, I am indebted to Morris H. Wolff's "The Legal Background of Cozzens' *The Just and the Unjust*," *Journal of Modern Literature* 7 (September 1979):505–518.

challenges this entire tradition by immersing us directly and wholly within trial proceedings, thereby showing that there can be no omniscient view by which the truth, if there is any, could be determined. We encounter the case only after it has entered the judicial system; the long foreground provided by Dreiser and Wright is thereby made to seem quite irrecoverable.

Confused by conflicting testimony from little-known individuals, Cozzens's reader cannot finally determine the exact chronology of the events leading to the homicide. Four habitual criminals named Bailey, Howell, Basso, and Leming kidnapped another criminal, William Zollicoffer, drove him to a bungalow outside Childerstown, Pennsylvania (Doylestown in actuality), kept him imprisoned for a few days, drove him to a local bridge, shot him, and then, weighting the body, pushed it into a river. At the time the trial opens, Bailey is dead, Leming's trial has been severed from the trial of the other three defendants, and Basso has decided to stand mute. There is no way of determining who was the killer, who were the accessories, the degree of intent, or the controlling motive. Because the trial is made to bear no grand national issues, the unfolding of testimony often seems deliberately tedious.

Puzzling through the questions and responses, Cozzens's reader is forced to recognize truths that Jerome Frank was soon to describe in *Courts On Trial* (1950). The presumption of rules of evidence, Frank wrote, could be expressed by the equation $R \times F = D$—a legal Rule applied to a given set of Facts results in a correct Decision. Actually, however, witnesses observe the past inaccurately, or remember the past inaccurately, or do not know pertinent facts, or express accurate memories inaccurately, or deliberately lie. A truer apothegm, Frank concluded, would acknowledge that "Facts are Guesses," that Rules are interpreted differently, and that the rectitude of any Decision depends on both variables, among others.[163]

Cozzens's title allows the reader to assume that the just can be separated from the unjust. When the title phrase is actually used, however, we learn that a judicial decision is a "solemn mystery in which, all jumbled together, the just entered into judgment with the unjust."[164] Near the end of the novel,

[163] Jerome Frank, *Courts on Trial* (Princeton: Princeton University Press, 1950), pp. 14–36.
[164] James Gould Cozzens, *The Just and the Unjust* (New York: Harcourt, Brace and Co., 1959), pp. 12–18.

Cozzens's sensible protagonist, Assistant District Attorney Abner Coates, wearily remarks:

> Getting to the bottom of things like that was impossible. You just had to take the practical view that a man always lied on his own behalf, and paid his lawyer, who was an expert, a professional liar, to show him new and better ways of lying.[165]

Using different sorts of terms, Frank and Cozzens are both contending, not that truth may not exist, but that no courtroom procedures could ever disclose it. Whether an adversary system is adopted or not, every decision must be rendered according to the courtroom presentation of presumed facts, rather than the historical facts themselves. Any trial is therefore self-reflexive; judgment is passed on history only as it is reenacted through legal procedure.

Cozzens's novel inverts many of the conventions of American legal ficton. A criminal trial may be drama but, like Abner Coates' opening statement, most of it is "a poor show compared to what true drama, the art of the theater or the motion picture, had taught them to expect."[166] Lawyers, Abner notes, love to waste time complaining about how lawyers waste time. The defendants in Cozzens's novel are neither heroic loners nor innocent naifs. They are unsavory, small-town thugs with drearily long criminal records. While the Howell-Basso trial drags on, we watch Abner Coates prosecuting other cases, postponing still others, attending town socials, and proposing a workable marriage. We overhear offhand bathroom and barroom conversations by which lawyers make deals affecting court decisions. Abner Coates disposes of Darrow's theory that criminality depends on economic servitude by first admitting inequality of condition, but then insisting on selfishness of motive: "Criminals might be victims of circumstance in the sense that few of them had a fair chance; but it was a mistake to forget that the only 'fair chance' they ever wanted was a chance for easy money."

Cozzens recasts the longstanding attack on trial by jury in a particularly effective manner. According to legal statute, Howell and Basso clearly should be judged guilty of first-degree murder, no matter who pulled the trigger. No one disputes that Zollicoffer was

---

[165] Ibid., p. 330. Quotations from *The Just and the Unjust* by James Gould Cozzens are reprinted by permission of Harcourt Brace Jovanovich, Inc.
[166] Ibid., pp. 9, 323, 38.

first kidnapped (a felony) and then shot with the collusion of all four men. According to Pennsylvania law, any murder committed in the perpetration of a felony "should be deemed murder in the first degree." Although Judge Vredenburg charges the jury carefully, the jurors wholly ignore the law and convict Howell and Basso only of second-degree murder, because they have been swayed by the clever, diversionary arguments of the cynical defense attorney, Harry Wurtz. In fact the decision proves the jury to be very much as Abner Coates had described: "The truth was, it would never cross your mind to ask the opinion of any one of them on a matter of importance."[167]

Because of the jury's illegal leniency, Howell and Basso receive twenty-year sentences, whereas Leming, who had turned state's evidence, and who surely had not pulled the trigger, receives life imprisonment. Both the prosecuting attorneys and the two judges are outraged, while Harry Wurtz is delighted to admit that the jury has overruled the law. However, when Abner Coates expresses his anger to his father, Judge Philander Coates, the old judge suddenly inverts the traditional, expected attack on the ineptitude of juries:

> The ancient conflict between liberty and authority. The jury protects the Court. It's a question how long any system of courts could last in a free country if judges found the verdicts. It doesn't matter how wise and experienced the judges may be. Resentment would build up every time the findings didn't go with current notions or prejudices. Pretty soon half the community would want to lynch the judge. There's no focal point with a jury; the jury is the public itself. That's why a jury can say when a judge couldn't, 'I don't care what the law is, that isn't right and I won't do it.' It's the greatest prerogative of free men. They have to have a way of saying that and making it stand. They may be wrong, they may refuse to do the things they ought to do; but freedom just to be wise and good isn't any freedom. We pay a price for lay participation in the law; but it's a necessary expense.[168]

The judge's words are a magnificent rebuttal, one that earns the reluctant consent of both Abner Coates and the reader. Unlike previous American novelists, Cozzens is prepared to argue that individual injustices caused by the people must be permitted in order

[167] Ibid., pp. 369, 375.
[168] Ibid., pp. 427–428.

to ensure that the larger judicial structure of legal freedom be preserved. Cozzens's argument depends on subordinating individual interests to the good of the whole in a manner that neither Dreiser nor Wright, despite all their determinism, would ever have countenanced.

The protagonists of *The Just and the Unjust* are all officials who serve the court system: Judge Irwin, Judge Vredenburg, District Attorney Martin Bunting, Assistant District Attorney Abner Coates, and his father Judge Philander Coates. All are cut from the same cloth—cautious, honest, responsible to the law and to society, and inclined toward commonsensical cynicism about human nature. Cozzens's admiring characterization of these honest, small-city practitioners suggests how deeply he shared in the longstanding American distrust of the slick Wall Street corporate lawyer—a distrust that Maxwell Bloomfield's essay will explore in detail.

Convinced of the overall decency of American community life, Cozzens's lawyers have learned the necessity of making moral compromises for the sake of greater good. The compromises that Cozzens condones are precisely those that Dreiser and Wright had most scorned. Morally revolted by extorted confessions, Martin Bunting nonetheless accepts them because extortion cannot be proven, and because many criminals who would otherwise be freed are thereby convicted. Cozzens's novel reevaluates the supposedly corrupting connection between state prosecutors and democratic politics. Like Mason and Buckley, Abner Coates needs to gain a conviction in a notorious local trial in order to be elected to higher office. He also needs the help of the local Republican county boss, a rather sleazy and frankly manipulative pol named Jesse Gearhardt. After rejecting Jesse's help because it involves favoritism and probable future trade-offs, Abner is chided by Martin Bunting for his ethical innocence:

> Nobody's making you be district attorney. If you run, it must be because you want to. If you went into the primaries and tried to get the nomination on your own, do you know what you'd get? About twenty write-ins. If you ran as an independent, do you know what you'd get? You'd get the pants licked off you. Now, why don't you act your age? This isn't the college debating society election where you vote for the other fellow to show how modest you are. You may be the best man for the job, and I think you are; but nobody's going to bring it to you on a platter.[169]

---

[169] Ibid., p. 365.

Because Abner clearly is the best person for the job, Cozzens has maneuvered his reader into preferring pragmatic moral compromise to wasted moral absolutism. From the inside perspective of the lawyer and the politician, the distant criticisms of an elective prosecutor made by Cooper, Dreiser, and Wright smack of self-indulgent moralism.

Cozzens considered himself no less a realist than Dreiser or Wright. In 1934 he stated "I simply put down, when I write, what the things I have seen and known look like to me."[170] By 1958 his creed had changed hardly at all: "I have no thesis except that people get a very raw deal from life. To me, life is what life is."[171] And yet, realism had led Cozzens to write a novel that controverted nearly every legal conviction that Dreiser or Wright had advanced. The fundamental difference between Cozzens and his predecessors is, ironically, that he has even less faith in the human race than they. Whereas Wright holds forth latent hopes for a better economic and social order, Cozzens's view is that societies of ceaseless human folly can only be held together by the received wisdom that is the law. Judge Coates tells his son that the law is "the stronghold of what reason men ever get around to using."[172] Nine years later, Cozzens would declare his high regard for law even less equivocally: "If the law has a single fault or flaw, I lay that to the unfortunate intrusion of the human element—a fallibility and unreasonableness of mankind that enters to disturb the law's own august order of right and reason."[173]

So reverential a phrase as "august order of right and reason" should not lead us to conclude that Cozzens has returned to the assumptions of Kent and Story. To Cozzens, the reasonableness of the law is entirely of human origin and has nothing whatever to do with divine law or natural law. Law is, rather, that body of common-sensical wisdom by which a flawed but worthy civilization can be least violently maintained. With so minimal a faith in human capabilities, it is small wonder that Cozzens, perhaps thinking of Wright as well as Steinbeck, once declared "I couldn't read the proletarian crap that came out in the '30s; again you had sentimentalism—the poor oppressed workers."[174] Such statements perhaps suggest why

---

[170] Frederick Bracher, *The Novels of James Gould Cozzens* (New York: Harcourt, Brace and Co., 1959), pp. 12–18.
[171] *Time Magazine*, September 2, 1957, p. 78.
[172] Cozzens, *The Just and the Unjust*, p. 109.
[173] *Bucks County Law Review* 1 (1951):302.
[174] *Time Magazine*, September 2, 1957, p. 76.

Cozzens's belligerent legalistic conservatism continues to be heard, if at all, as an iconoclastic voice from America's waspish, small-town Republican past.

USES OF CONFUSION

Herbert L. Packer's *The Limits of the Criminal Sanction* (1968) establishes a useful distinction between two recurring models for the purpose of criminal justice: the due process model and the crime control model. Under our adversary system, many citizens have believed that the defendants, who are assumed innocent, must have their constitutional rights to due process protected to the fullest. People of this persuasion are also likely to believe that the criminal law exists to reform the criminal as well as to protect society. Many other citizens, however, assume that it is the criminal laws themselves that need protection. They contend that only strict law enforcement and efficient police surveillance will ever enable society to control crime.[175] Although Packer's models conflict with one another, both have their roots in our constitutional system. Any hope for a decent, just society under a democratic policy surely demands a regard for the merits of both. The problem is, in any given situation, to discover that point of compromise at which due process and crime control, the rights of the individual and the needs of society, can most fairly be protected.

If we apply Packer's models to the fiction under consideration, we may crudely surmise that Cooper and Cozzens would have favored the crime control model; that Dreiser, Darrow, and Wright would have favored the due process model; and that Melville and Twain seem genuinely ambivalent. Packer's terms are especially useful, however, as a way of summarizing broad trends in recent judicial thinking. During the 1950s and 1960s, the Warren Court vastly expanded an accused individual's rights to due process by guaranteeing that the accused be informed of his or her legal rights, be provided a lawyer, and not be subjected to unwarranted searches and seizures. It further ruled that an extorted confession is inadmissible evidence. During the 1970s, the temper of the Warren Court

---

[175] Herbert L. Packer, *The Limits of the Criminal Sanction* (Stanford, Calif.: Stanford University Press, 1968), pp. 149–173.

has still been discernible in arguments made in support of the individual's rights to control his or her own body (abortion), to privacy (wiretapping) and to an inhabitable environment (pollution and no-smoking laws).[176] In the 1970s, however, adherents of the crime control model gained increased support, not simply through the law-and-order slogans of politicians, but through the movements to restore capital punishment, to limit plea bargaining, and to reduce judicial discretion by requiring "flat-time sentencing" of criminal court judges.[177]

Unfortunately, the parallels we have traced between the spirit of legal thought and the spirit of legal fiction seem to have broken down recently. Whether the past two decades are too close to discern lasting patterns, or whether the parallels indeed do not exist, one must at least acknowledge that the criminal novels which have gained greatest public attention do not partake of the spirit of either the Warren Court or its aftermath. There is, however, a decided similarity of kind among the novels themselves. Works like Truman Capote's *In Cold Blood* (1965), Vincent Bugliosi and Curt Gentry's *Helter Skelter* (1974) and Norman Mailer's *The Executioners's Song* (1979) all belong to a genre that may be called the naturalistic atrocity saga. Characteristics common to all three include the following: recreating brutal and highly publicized multiple murders, retracing the lives of the criminal(s) to give a psychological explanation for seemingly unmotivated atrocities, exhaustive investigative reporting, and sheer length.[178]

It is a misnomer, of course, to refer to these works as novels. Capote calls *In Cold Blood* a "nonfiction novel";[179] Bugliosi and Gentry quote and footnote thousands of sources about Charles Manson's family; Mailer subtitles *The Executioner's Song* "A True Life Novel." These works blend realistic principles of fictional method, reportorial description, and sociological research into a genre that aims at breaking down the distinction between fiction and history, even as it calls attention to it. Capote, Bugliosi, and Mailer satisfy, to the limit of any reader's capacity, the legal realist's

[176] See Schwartz, *Law in America*, pp. 236–256, and G. E. White, *American Judicial Tradition*, pp. 359–368.

[177] Walker, *Popular Justice*, pp. 243–251.

[178] Capote, p. 384; Bugliosi and Gentry, p. 664;. Mailer, p. 1050.

[179] From George Plimpton's 1966 *New York Times Book Review* interview with Truman Capote, reprinted in *Truman Capote's In Cold Blood: A Critical Handbook* (Belmont, Calif.: Wadsworth, 1968), p. 25.

demand for objective sociological and psychological study of the roots of crime.

The vividness and objectivity of such works have accompanying drawbacks. Investigation has been so thorough that the authors become reluctant to select important details from the whole. The author of a nonfiction novel aims so intently at factual objectivity as to become unwilling to judge characters or to argue a position. The world of the criminal, from early life to crime, from trial to execution, is merely to be rendered whole for the reader to judge. The reader thus experiences a criminal's life as a sequence of happenings that may have a sense of inevitability about them but that are not placed within any larger context. If these three works have any common purpose, it is to show suburban middle-class Americans how closely the criminal world impinges on them, how suddenly and destructively it can explode into their seemingly ordered life. Perhaps this is a worthy purpose, but we should not forget that both the matter and manner of these books have been shrewdly calculated for notoriety and sales.

Nonfiction criminal novels offer no solutions for the improving of criminal procedures because they offer no solutions for the causes of criminality. Richard Hickock, Perry Smith, Charles Manson, and Gary Gilmore are the products of so deprived an upbringing, so rootless an adolescence, that their utter amorality seems unchangeable. Innocence is hardly their undoing. Neither priest nor lawyer nor judge nor parole officer can effectively touch their need to exalt themselves through the power of senseless violence. The nation seems too large, its population too mobile, for crime control to be effective. In the face of such bloodletting, due process guarantees seem only a nicety.

The grim hopelessness that pervades these works little resembles the affirmative spirit of the Warren Court, but it does presage the mood of many who presently administer the criminal justice system. Samuel Walker concludes his history of American criminal justice as follows:

> By the end of the 1970s, many criminal-justice experts felt at an impasse. Never before had public awareness of criminal justice been so high. And never before had the experts themselves understood the actual process of the administration of justice as well. The research revolution of the 1970s had produced an unprecedented outpouring of data on criminal justice. Yet, the experts were not sure what to do with all this knowledge. The

experience of the previous fifteen years had left them deeply chastened. The "wars on crime" promised first by Lyndon Johnson and then by Richard Nixon had both failed to achieve their stated objectives. Moreover, the false promises had generated a potent backlash of disillusionment. The experts were inclined to promise less, and, for the most part, were unwilling to venture firm predictions about the future of criminal justice.[180]

Because, as Henry Adams long ago predicted, human knowledge has accelerated far faster than our ability to control it, neither sociologically minded criminologists nor sociologically minded novelists wish to presume to suggest answers.

If Walker's description of the prevailing mood is accurate, we might surmise that another infusion of the pragmatic spirit of legal realism is sorely needed. Good legal principles, the realists had suggested, were to be made in decision, not discovered through research. However cynical Holmes liked to sound about universals, the last words of "The Path of the Law" remind us that a properly trained lawyer might "catch an echo of the infinite, a glimpse of its unfathomable process, a hint of the universal law."[181] Cardozo reminded his readers that the value of the concept of justice lay precisely in its being, not a discoverable entity, but "an aspiration, a mood of exaltation, a yearning for what is fine or high."[182] Even Roscoe Pound, staunch advocate of crime control though he was, grudgingly admitted, "Jurists of the law-of-nature school were not wholly in error in insisting that appeal to the conscience of the citizen, appeal to his reason, was the foundation of the authority of the legal order, and so of the precepts of a body of laws."[183]

There is nothing new in a mood of baffled uncertainty about law. Those who now believe that "nothing works," that there are no better principles to be wrought,[184] might find a timely expression of their feelings in a passage written by Cardozo in 1921:

I was much troubled in spirit, in my first years upon the bench, to find how trackless was the ocean on which I had embarked. I sought for

---

[180] Walker, *Popular Justice*, p. 252.
[181] Holmes, "Path of the Law," p. 74.
[182] Cardozo, *Growth of the Law*, p. 87.
[183] Roscoe Pound, *The Formative Era of American Law* (Boston: Little, Brown, 1938), p. 28.
[184] Walker, *Popular Justice*, p. 247.

certainty. I was oppressed and disheartened when I found that the quest for it was futile. I was trying to reach land, the solid land of fixed and settled rules, the paradise of a justice that would declare itself by tokens plainer and more commanding than its pale and glimmering reflections in my own vacillating mind and conscience. I found, with the voyagers in Browning's "Paracelsus," that the real haven was always beyond. As the years have gone by, and as I have reflected more and more upon the nature of the judicial process, I have become reconciled to the uncertainty, because I have grown to see it as inevitable. I have grown to see that the process in its highest reaches is not discovery, but creation; and that the doubts and misgivings, the hopes and fears, are part of the travail of mind, the pangs of death and the pangs of birth, in which principles that have served their day expire, and new principles are born.[185]

Whereas contemporaries seem to regard the apparent flux of principles as grounds for hopelessness, Cardozo had learned to value legal uncertainty precisely because it stimulated worthy efforts to resolve it. Many American novelists have shared Cardozo's quest; many have found a similar consolation in its bafflement. But surely anyone concerned with the wonder of language—legal or literary—can appreciate Cardozo's ability to convey "the nature of the judicial process" in appropriate metaphors of paradise, voyaging, pioneering, and rebirth. Perhaps it is well to end with such a passage because, in its words and cadences, legal experience and literary eloquence have become indissolubly one.

[185] Cardozo, *The Nature of the Judicial Process*, pp. 166–167.

Bibliography

The alphabetized bibliography that follows is not meant to provide a comprehensive list of major writings pertaining to American law and literature, although it contains many of them. It is rather a record of those writings that have been essential to the thought of my essay. The bibliographic note is intended both to indicate special debts and to provide suggestions for students beginning the study of law and American literature.

For general histories of the law as an institution, I am indebted to Lawrence Friedman's *A History of American Law* and to Samuel Walker's *Popular Justice: A History of American Criminal Justice*. G. Edward White's *The American Judicial Tradition* provides an invaluable history of the changing legal attitudes held by America's most distinguished judicial figures since the era of John Marshall. In their collection of essays titled *Crime, Law and Society*, Abraham and Joseph Goldstein have gathered major statements about the purposes of criminal law and its relation to the ideal of justice. Morton Horwitz's recent study, *The Transformation of American Law: 1780–1860*, is a stimulating analysis of the ways in which economic realities influenced legal attitudes and practices during the antebellum period.

Although detailed study of the relationship between American literature and American law is yet in its infancy, beginnings have been made, two of which have proven especially helpful to me. Perry Miller's "The Legal Mentality," Book 2 of *The Life of the Mind in America*, suggests ways in which legal attitudes have shaped American political thought and selected political fiction. Patricia Kane's pioneering dissertation "Legal Fictions: The Law in the American Novel" studies the changing characterization of lawyers in the works of major American novelists. There have been recent studies of the way the law, as institution or as concept, has been treated by individual writers; those most helpful for my purposes are listed in the bibliography.

For the interested layman, literature about the law can seem a thicket of incomprehensible, dull casebooks, overspecialized "issue" studies, and lengthy academic histories. Perhaps the best beginnings for anyone interested in the essential spirit of American law are Benjamin Cardozo's *The Nature of the Judicial Process* and Roscoe Pound's *The Spirit of the Common Law.* Designed for both a lay and a professional audience, these two short works are not only of immense historical importance. They are models of informed legal thought and expressive English prose.

Baldwin, Joseph G. *The Flush Times of Alabama and Mississippi: A Series of Sketches.* New York: Appleton & Co., 1853.

Bassiouni, M. Cherif. *Substantive Criminal Law.* Springfield, Ill.: Charles C Thomas, 1978.

Blackstone, William. *Commentaries on the Laws of England. Ehrlich's Blackstone.* San Carlos, Calif.: Nourse Publishing Co., 1959.

Bracher, Frederick. *The Novels of James Gould Cozzens.* New York: Harcourt, Brace & Company, 1959.

Brown, Richard Maxwell. *Strain of Violence: Historical Studies of American Violence and Vigilantism.* New York: Oxford University Press, 1975.

Capote, Truman. *In Cold Blood.* New York: New American Library, 1965.

Cardozo, Benjamin N. *The Growth of the Law.* New Haven: Yale University Press, 1924.

Cardozo, Benjamin N. *Law and Literature And Other Essays And Addresses.* New York: Harcourt, Brace & Company, 1931.

Cardozo, Benjamin N. *The Nature of the Judicial Process.* New Haven: Yale University Press, 1921.

Castle, John F. *The Making of An American Tragedy.* Dissertation, University of Michigan, 1952.

Cohen, Morris Raphael. "Moral Aspects of the Criminal Law." *Yale Law Journal* 49 (1940):987–1026.

Cooley, Thomas M. *A Treatise on the Constitutional Limitations.* Boston: Little, Brown, 1868.

Cooper, James Fenimore. *The American Democrat.* Edited by George Dekker and Larry Johnston. Baltimore: Penguin Books, 1969; originally published 1838.

Cooper, James Fenimore. *The Pioneers.* New York: New American Library, 1964; originally published 1823.

Cooper, James Fenimore. *The Ways of the Hour*. New York: W. A. Townsend, 1862; originally published 1850.

Cozzens, James Gould. *The Just and the Unjust*. New York: Harcourt, Brace & Company, 1942.

Darrow, Clarence S. *An Eye For An Eye*. Durham, North Carolina: Moore Publishing Co., 1969; originally published 1905.

Darrow, Clarence S. *Attorney for the Damned*. Edited by Arthur Weinberg. New York: Simon & Schuster, 1957.

Darrow, Clarence S. *The Story of My Life*. New York: Scribner's, 1932.

Dreiser, Helen. *My Life With Dreiser*. Cleveland: World Publishing Company, 1951.

Dreiser, Theodore. *An American Tragedy*. New York: New American Library, 1964, originally published 1925.

Dreiser, Theodore. "I Find the Real American Tragedy." *Mystery Magazine* 11 (1935):11, 98.

Elias, Robert H. *Letters of Theodore Dreiser*. Philadelphia: University of Pennsylvania Press, 1959.

Elias, Robert H. *Theodore Dreiser: Apostle of Nature*. Ithaca, N.Y.: Cornell University Press, 1970.

Fabre, Michel. *The Unfinished Quest of Richard Wright*. New York: William Morrow, 1973.

Frankel, Marvin. *Criminal Sentences: Law Without Order*. New York: Hill & Wang, 1973

Friedman, Lawrence M., *A History of American Law*. New York: Simon & Schuster, 1973.

Goldstein, A. S., and Goldstein, J., eds. *Crime, Law and Society*. New York: Free Press, 1971.

Grossman, James. *James Fenimore Cooper*. Stanford, Calif.: Stanford University Press, 1967.

Hall, Jerome. "The Basic Dilemma of Criminal Procedure." *Yale Law Journal* 51 (1942):723–34.

Hamilton, Alexander; Jay, John; and Madison, James. *The Federalist Papers*. Garden City, N. Y.: Doubleday, 1966.

Hand, Learned. *The Bill of Rights*. Cambridge: Harvard University Press, 1958.

Hand, Learned. *The Spirit of Liberty: Papers and Addresses of Learned Hand*. New York: Knopf, 1952.

Hayford, Harrison. *The Somers Mutiny Affair*. Englewood Cliffs, N.J.: Prentice-Hall, 1959.

Holmes, Oliver Wendell, Jr. *The Common Law*. Cambridge: Harvard University Press, 1963; originally published 1882.

Holmes, Oliver Wendell, Jr. "The Path of the Law," in *American Social Thought*. Edited by Ray Ginger. New York: Hill & Wang, 1961.

Horwitz, Morton. *The Transformation of American Law 1780-1860*. Cambridge: Harvard University Press, 1977.

Hurst, James Willard. *The Growth of American Law: The Law Makers*. Boston: Little, Brown, 1950.

Hurst, James Willard. *Law and the Conditions of Freedom in the Nineteenth-Century United States*. Madison: University of Wisconsin Press, 1956.

Jefferson, Thomas. *The Life and Selected Writings of Thomas Jefferson*. Edited by Adrienne Koch and William Peden, New York: Random House, 1944.

Kane, Patricia. *Legal Fictions: The Lawyer in the American Novel*. Doctoral Dissertation, University of Minnesota, 1961.

Kent, James. *Commentaries on American Law*. Boston: Little, Brown, 1873; originally published 1826-30.

Levy, Leonard. *The Law of the Commonwealth and Chief Justice Shaw*. New York: Harper & Row, 1967.

Lewis, Anthony. *Gideon's Trumpet*. New York: Vintage Books, 1964.

Locke, John. *Second Treatise on Civil Government, Locke on Politics, Religion and Education*. Edited by Maurice Cranston. New York: Collier-Macmillan, 1965; originally published 1690.

Mailer, Norman. *The Executioner's Song*. Boston: Little, Brown, 1979.

Malin, Irving. *Truman Capote's In Cold Blood*. Belmont, Calif.: Wadsworth, 1968.

Matthiessen, F. W. O. *Theodore Dreiser*. New York: William Sloane Associates, 1951.

McCart, Samuel W. *Trial by Jury*. Philadelphia: Chilton, 1964.

Melville, Herman. *The Battle-Pieces of Herman Melville*. Edited by Hennig Cohen. New York: T. Yoseloff, 1963; originally published 1866.

Melville, Herman. *Billy Budd, Sailor (An Inside Narrative)*. Edited by Harrison Hayford and Merton M. Sealts, Jr. Chicago: University of Chicago Press, 1962; originally published 1924.

Melville, Herman. *White-Jacket or The World in a Man of War*. Edited by Hennig Cohen. New York: Holt, Rinehart & Winston, 1967; originally published 1850.

Miller, Perry. *The Legal Mind in America*. Ithaca, N. Y.: Cornell University Press, 1962.

Miller, Perry. *The Life of the Mind in America*. New York: Harcourt, Brace & World, 1965.

Moley, Raymond. *Our Criminal Courts*. New York: Minton, Balch & Co., 1930.

Moers, Ellen. *Two Dreisers*. New York: Viking, 1969.

Packer, Herbert L. "Two Models of the Criminal Process," in *The Limits of the Criminal Sanction*. Stanford, Calif.: Stanford University Press, 1968.

Pound, Roscoe. *Criminal Justice in America*. New York: Henry Holt & Company, 1930.

Pound, Roscoe, et al. *Criminal Justice in Cleveland*. Cleveland: Cleveland Foundation, 1922.

Pound, Roscoe. *The Formative Era of American Law*. Boston: Little, Brown, 1938.

Pound, Roscoe. *The Spirit of the Common Law*. Francestown, N. H.: Marshall Jones Co., 1921.

Schwartz, Bernard. *The Law in America: A History*. New York: McGraw-Hill, 1974.

Silberman, Charles E. *Criminal Violence, Criminal Justice*. New York: Vintage Books, 1980.

Story, Joseph. *Commentaries on the Constitution of the United States*. Boston: Hilliard, Gray & Co., 1833.

Tierney, Kevin. *Darrow: A Biography*. New York: Thomas Y. Crowell, 1979.

Tocqueville, Alexis de. *Democracy in America*, Edited by Phillips Bradley. New York: Vintage Books, 2 vols., 1945; originally published 1835.

Twain, Mark. *The Tragedy of Pudd'nhead Wilson*. New York: Harper & Row, 1964; originally published 1894.

Walker, Samuel. *Popular Justice: A History of American Criminal Justice*. New York: Oxford University Press, 1980.

Warren, Robert Penn. *Homage to Theodore Dreiser*. New York: Random House, 1971.

White, G. Edward. *The American Judicial Tradition*. New York: Oxford University Press, 1976.

Wright, Benjamin Fletcher. *American Interpretations of Natural Law*. Cambridge: Harvard University Press, 1931.

Wright, Richard. *Black Boy*. New York: Harper & Row, 1966; originally published 1945.

Wright, Richard. *Native Son*. New York: Harper & Row, 1966; originally published 1940.

STUDY QUESTIONS

1. Are there words in addition to *innocent* or *criminal* that have both legal and moral meanings? What is the effect of these double meanings on our perception of the workings of legal institutions?

2. Why have people since the time of the Old Testament insisted on a distinction between man-made law and some "higher law" of divine or natural origin?

3. Why were Americans living between 1770 and 1860 especially concerned that there be a correspondence between man-made law and divine or natural law? How is this concern evident in *The Pioneers* and *Billy Budd*?

4. What differing attitudes have American novelists assumed toward trial by jury? Why was the validity of a jury's decision so acute an issue during the nineteenth century?

5. How did attitudes toward the purpose of the law change during the late nineteenth century? Why did these changes occur?

6. What are the similarities between legal realism and literary realism? To what degree do *An American Tragedy* and *Native Son* partake of the spirit of legal realism?

7. Consider Oliver Wendell Holmes's attitudes toward criminal justice. Are these attitudes reinforced by today's television crime shows?

8. What are the advantages and disadvantages of recreating an historical trial in a novel rather than in a case summary? Reduce *Billy Budd* to a one-page summary and then compare the summary to the novel.

9. Is it logical to assume that, at any given historical period, the spirit of legal thought will be reflected in novels that concern the law? Do you believe that such a correspondence exists today?

10. Why have American novelists lent such weight to individual rights in their rendering of legal issues? In this regard, compare any of the American novels to famous European novels about the law such as Dickens' *Bleak House* or Kafka's *The Trial*.

LAW AND LAWYERS IN
AMERICAN POPULAR CULTURE

Maxwell Bloomfield

Professor of History
Catholic University of America

To understand any society, anthropologists tell us, one must look beyond formal institutions to customary practices and pervasive cultural values. That cautionary advice seems especially applicable to an inquiry into the relationship between American law and an evolving social order. In common-law countries, such as the United States, a wide gulf often separates the black-letter law of statutes and court decisions from the "living law" that people acknowledge and act on in their daily lives. Legal rules that contradict cherished popular attitudes are likely to pose serious enforcement problems for democratic governments, which rely on public opinion to sustain their actions. Those who help to shape public opinion thus play a necessary and important mediating role between the dispensers and the recipients of legal rules and regulations. Ordinary citizens derive their impressions of the legal system largely from the newspapers and magazines they read, the novels they buy, the movies and television programs they watch. Although these sources of information all tend to distort reality, laypeople look to them for guidance in evaluating the social impact of the law and its practitioners.

From the days of the early Republic to the present, creative writers have regularly introduced legal issues and characters into their work. Even the most arcane subjects, such as codification or the reform of common-law pleading, have been fictionalized and presented to the public as entertainment. American audiences, habitually suspicious of those who wield power, have always welcomed simplified expositions of law and politics. The legal-mindedness of the average American impressed scores of foreign visitors in the nineteenth century, including Alexis de Tocqueville, who developed a theory of cultural diffusion to explain the intimate bond between law and the popular imagination:

> Scarcely any political question arises in the United States which is not re-solved, sooner or later, into a judicial question. Hence all parties are obliged to borrow, in their daily controversies, the ideas, and even the language, peculiar to judicial proceedings. As most public men are, or have been, legal practitioners, they introduce the customs and technicalities of their profession into the management of public affairs. The jury extends this habitude to all classes. The language of the law thus becomes, in some measure, a vulgar tongue; the spirit of the law, which is produced in the schools and courts of justice, gradually penetrates beyond

127

their walls into the bosom of society, where it descends to the lowest classes . . . [1]

The continuing popularity of novels and films that deal with criminal justice, minority rights, and professional ethics confirms Tocqueville's analysis. As lawyers achieved unprecedented political power and social acceptance in the decades following the American Revolution, a multitude of writers began to celebrate their achievements and to criticize their failings. Few of these authors are remembered today; they were seldom original thinkers or impressive literary stylists, such as Emerson, Thoreau, and other figures discussed in the preceding essays. Despite their aesthetic deficiencies, however, the minor writers of the last two hundred years have produced a rich and largely unexplored body of legal literature that chronicles every aspect of professional life.

In the pages that follow, I shall rely principally on such neglected source material, with an occasional glance at the works of some major authors. I draw no sharp line between "elite" and "mass" culture, since those categories have little relevance to a discussion of legal issues. Today's comic strips and television programs, like the dime novels and story papers of the nineteenth century, portray lawyers and their work in terms that are indistinguishable from those found in serious fiction and drama. *Popular culture*, as used in this essay, thus encompasses any legally related material designed for a general audience, regardless of its actual distribution or influence. Only by adopting such a broad-gauged perspective can one begin to appreciate the manifold ways in which lawyers have impressed themselves upon the consciousness of other social groups.

Just as the bar has never been a monolithic institution, the "public" has always included diverse constituencies whose interests and attitudes have not been fairly represented through the mass market. Students of popular culture cannot afford to overlook the views of the legal system expressed in children's books, religious tracts, the literature of women and minorities, or utopian and radical fiction. Such specialized works often examine legal themes—from professional recruitment and training to judicial power and institutionalized racism—that are ignored or minimized in more commercially successful publications.

---

[1] Alexis de Tocqueville, *Democracy in America*, ed. Andrew Hacker (New York: Washington Square Press, 1964), p. 106.

This introductory survey will focus on the interplay between law and various forms of popular literature in two historical periods: the antebellum years of the early nineteenth century and the era of Progressive "reform" and modernization at the turn of the twentieth century. Each of these periods witnessed the creation of a distinctive set of cultural values that defined the terms of legal and literary discourse for several generations. In the early nineteenth century, Americans self-consciously constructed an ideology of laissez-faire republicanism that suited the needs of a society of small farmers and tradesmen. By the early twentieth century, an industrial society turned away from its agrarian past and established the intellectual foundations of the welfare state, to which we still—with much grumbling—adhere. The organs of popular culture in each period facilitated the process of value change by encouraging audiences to reflect upon the workings of the legal and political system.

I

Legal Fictions of a Model Republic

Oh! accurst let Him *rave,*
And no Lenity save,
Who dares plant a nettle *on WASHINGTON's grave!*

"The Birth-day of Freedom" (1814)

Early American writers, as Carl Smith has noted in the opening essay, were strong nationalists who celebrated the uniqueness of their country's infant institutions and urged other nations to emulate the American example. For each of them the term *republicanism* provided a common frame of reference. As defined by the revolutionary generation, *republicanism* connoted most obviously a representative form of government, based on popular sovereignty and limited in its powers by a written constitution. But republican ideology encompassed social as well as political values. It called for a society of self-reliant freeholders, who should be encouraged to pursue wealth and status with a minimum of governmental interference. The most important function of law, according to the republican creed, was to facilitate economic growth and social mobility by releasing private entrepreneurial energies. Competition and self-help were to replace the colonial ideals of paternalism and security as the nation moved from a ruler-subject model of social organization to one based on the principle of free exchange between equals.

This libertarian ethic found early fictional expression in a number of plays dealing with the American Revolution. Such dramas as John Daly Burk's *Bunker-Hill; or, The Death of General Warren* (1797) and William Dunlap's *The Glory of Columbia: Her Yeomanry!* (1803) emphasized the limited and legalistic aims of the rebels and praised the sturdy farmer as a model citizen-soldier. "What are your boasted English laws to us, or any laws, which sanctify injustice?" cries General Warren to a British officer on the eve of the Battle of Bunker Hill.[2] The Americans are fighting, he asserts, to defend their lives and property from the lawless power of King and Parliament. Later, in a dying vision, Warren glimpses the democratic future that awaits his countrymen:

> O might I look into the womb of time
> And see my country's future destiny:
> Cou'd I but see her proud democracy,
> Founded on equal laws, and stript entire,
> Of those unnatural titles, and those names
> Of *King,* of *Count,* of *Stadtholder*, and *Duke,*
> Which, *with degrading awe*, possess the world:
> My cheered soul, would gather life anew,
> And parting from my body, as the dove
> Sails from her nest, would singing soar to heaven. . . .
> O God protect this land—I faint—I die.
> Live the Republic. Live; O live, forever.[3]

The play concludes with a solemn tableau, as Warren's body lies in state in the American camp, surrounded by grieving troops whose banners proclaim republican slogans: "THE RIGHTS OF MAN," "LIBERTY AND EQUALITY," "HATRED TO ROYALTY," and "A FEDERAL CONSTITUTION."

Not content with exploiting the native revolutionary tradition, playwrights also ransacked the past for other examples of popular struggles against tyranny. Despite their exotic settings, these historical dramas likewise preached the lessons of nineteenth-century republicanism. A case in point is Robert T. Conrad's romantic

---

[2] John Daly Burk, *Bunker-Hill; or, The Death of General Warren* (1797), reprinted in *Dramas from the American Theatre, 1762–1909,* ed. Richard Moody (Cleveland: World Publishing Co., 1966), p. 80.
[3] Ibid., p. 85.

tragedy, *Jack Cade* (1841). Written by a Philadelphia lawyer and editor to suit the special talents of the great American actor Edwin Forrest, *Cade* was successfully performed for half a century and was a particular favorite with working-class audiences at New York's Bowery Theater. The plot centered on a historic occurrence: a rebellion of English serfs and yeomen against their overlords in 1450. But Judge Conrad turned his hero Cade—the leader of this medieval uprising—into an archetypal bourgeois rebel for whom property rights were sacred and legal procedures punctiliously enforced.

When, for example, the king sends representatives to negotiate a peace settlement with the rebels, Cade produces a written scroll containing a guarantee of freedom for all serfs. This document, he insists, must be signed and sealed with the great seal of the realm before he will disband his forces. While these formalities are being attended to, Cade is mortally wounded by his enemy Lord Say. As he sinks to the floor, excited shouts of "The charter! the charter!" are heard offstage, and his lieutenant Mowbray rushes in, bearing the charter unrolled, and exhibiting the seal. "The charter!" Mowbray cries. "Seal and all!" Whereupon, according to the stage directions, Cade "starts up with a wild burst of exultation, rushes to him, catches the charter, kisses it, and clasps it to his bosom." "Free! free!" he gasps. "The bondman is avenged, my country free!"[4] He then falls dead, as the curtain descends.

It requires little imagination to see some resemblance between Cade's decorous rebellion and the American Revolution, or to discern in his charter of liberties an ancestor of our national Bill of Rights. In other respects, too, the play affirms some fundamental tenets of republicanism. Cade, the son of a poor farmer, is presented as a born leader, a "natural aristocrat" in Jefferson's phrase, who rises from obscurity to power through talent alone. His baronial foes, on the other hand, owe their influence to inherited rank and privilege. The contrast between feudal and democratic claims to leadership is spelled out at several points in the play, as when Lord Say remarks defensively to an associate: "Some men are nobler than the mass, and should, by nature's order, shine above their brethren." To which his friend rejoins: "'Tis true, the *noble* should: but who is noble? Heaven and not heraldry makes noble men."[5]

One should not infer, however, that heaven (or nature) creates an

---

[4] Robert T. Conrad, *Jack Cade* (1841), reprinted in *Representative Plays by American Dramatists*, ed. Montrose J. Moses (New York: Benjamin Blom, 1964), 2:520.
[5] Ibid., p. 475.

abundance of such leaders. Despite an occasional reference to the majesty of the common people, the plays of liberation are quite elitist and class-conscious in outlook. The liberty they extol is a freedom to compete with others on equal terms for the prizes of life; but, as they make clear, the highest honors are reserved for a few individuals of exceptional merit. Most can look forward to improving their condition only within the limits set by class and occupational factors—a restatement in nineteenth-century terms of the Puritan doctrine of the "calling." The political message instilled by these dramas is that the masses will never outgrow their need for heroic national leaders, but that they are capable of selecting such leaders for themselves from the ranks of an educated and gentlemanly elite. Even Jack Cade appreciates the importance of intellectual attainments as a prerequisite for public service; he prepares himself for the responsibilities of power by scientific study during his years of exile in Italy. The persistence of the gentlemanly ideal in dramas of democratic revolt points to the survival of deferential attitudes toward authority inherited from the colonial age and to the efforts of playwrights to justify those attitudes in terms applicable to republican office-holders.

The major themes stated in *Jack Cade* reappeared in other forms of literature that dealt directly with the antebellum bar. Early legal biographers presented their subjects as republican heroes, self-made individuals who achieved success through hard work and talent. Many of these biographers were themselves lawyers. Through their contributions to such periodicals as the *Port Folio*, *Analectic Magazine*, *Monthly Anthology*, and *North American Review*, they helped to popularize an idealized view of bar leaders that persisted throughout the nineteenth century.

Two complementary images of the model lawyer are discernible in legal biographies: the neoclassic gentleman and the romantic genius. The gentlemanly stereotype represents a holdover from the eighteenth century, when lawyers as a class rose to power in a stratified colonial society. Aware of the deference paid to aristocratic English barristers, American practitioners prior to the Revolution held themselves out as a comparable elite. Law, they insisted, was an arduous intellectual discipline, to be mastered only after years of specialized training. One could not become a great lawyer without the proper social and educational credentials: affiliation with the ruling gentry through birth or marriage; a classical education of the sort required of

English gentlemen at home; some familiarity with the cosmopolitan culture of the Enlightenment; and a commitment to public service based on notions of *noblesse oblige*.

In the postrevolutionary decades biographers redefined the character of the lawyer-gentleman to suit the taste of republican audiences. Avoiding invidious class distinctions or references to English models of gentility, they now stressed competitiveness and individual merit as the keys to professional success. Yet they also reaffirmed the elitism of the bar in intellectual terms by pointng to the heroic mental exertions required of bar leaders. Typical was the record of Chief Justice William M. Richardson of the New Hampshire Superior Court, as reported in a sermon delivered on his death in 1838:

> Hour after hour, and frequently to the amount of twelve or fourteen hours in a day, has he applied his mind to his professional studies. And besides this, he extended his researches into almost every branch of learning. With the ancient and modern languages, and with the best English productions, he was exceedingly familiar. To these rigid habits of industry, he was indebted for the credit with which he so long performed the duties of Chief Justice.[6]

How many prospective lawyers would have the fortitude to emulate such an example? Although writers agreed that any man of intelligence and cnergy might succeed at the bar, the image of the learned professional was calculated to discourage recruits from less affluent social groups. Some nineteenth-century biographers therefore created an alternative legal stcreotype that appealed more strongly to the rising democratic temper of the age. In their hands the model lawyers remained gifted commoners, whose intuitive understanding of human nature enabled them to triumph over social and educational deficiencies.

The new stereotype received its classic formulation in William Wirt's *Sketches of the Life and Character of Patrick Henry* (1817), a rags-to-riches study that went through twenty-five editions by 1871. Born of yeoman stock on a frontier farm, young Henry was emphatically a man of the people:

> His person is represented as having been coarse, his manners uncommonly awkward, his dress slovenly, his conversation very plain, his

---

[6] *Life of William M. Richardson, LL.D.* (Concord, N.H.: Israel S. Boyd & William White, 1839), p. 59.

aversion to study invincible, and his faculties almost entirely benumbed by indolence. No persuasion could bring him either to read or to work. On the contrary, he ran wild in the forest, like one of the *aborigines* of the country, and divided his life between the dissipation and uproar of the chase and the languor of inaction. . . . He was, indeed, a mere child of nature, and nature seems to have been too proud and too jealous of her work, to permit it to be touched by the hand of art. She gave him Shakespeare's genius, and bade him, like Shakespeare, to depend on that alone.[7]

Henry failed at business and farming before taking up the study of law, at the relatively advanced age of twenty-four. He spent no more than six weeks in preparing for his bar examination and expected to make only a modest income from his legal practice. Yet, on his first courtroom appearance in a major case, he stunned his audience by the overwhelming emotional force of his oratory. Spectators reported that he "made their blood run cold, and their hair to rise on end." Such inspired pleading, his biographer emphasized, was something "entirely new" to the profession. While the aristocratic bar leaders of Virginia studied and imitated the measured rhetoric of ancient Greeks and Romans, Henry—the "orator of nature"—read people instead of books. His successful debut in the "parsons' cause" made him a folk hero, and he nurtured his populist image through a long and lucrative career in law and politics:

With regard to himself, he saw very distinctly, that all his hopes rested on the people's favour. He therefore adhered to them with unshaken fidelity. He retained their manners, their customs, all their modes of life, with religious caution. He dressed as plainly as the plainest of them; ate only the homely fare, and drank the simple beverage of the country; mixed with them on a footing of the most entire and perfect equality, and conversed with them, even in their own vicious and depraved pronunciation.[8]

Although Wirt cautioned that Henry's success could not be duplicated by less gifted individuals, the legend of the backwoods genius strongly influenced popular thinking about the antebellum bar and its opportunities. Henry became the foremost example of the

---

[7] William Wirt, *Sketches of the Life and Character of Patrick Henry*, 9th ed. (Philadelphia: Thomas, Cowperthwait & Co., 1841), pp. 24–25.
[8] Ibid., pp. 52–53.

self-made lawyer, and later biographers incorporated elements of the Henry myth into their treatment of other bar leaders. By the 1840s the process of fusion was complete: Henceforth the model lawyer had to combine, in a watered-down form, both "genius" and intellectuality. *Genius* implied a love of nature, emotional courtroom speeches, and a sympathetic identification with the people and their needs; intellectuality connoted a mastery of legal principles through systematic study, but not the herculean feats of learning once expected of lawyer-gentlemen. With these modifications legal biographies became almost indistinguishable from other kinds of self-help literature addressed to the general public. One success manual published in 1850 used Wirt's own career as an example of what might be accomplished by young men from lower-class backgrounds.[9]

Antebellum novelists borrowed freely from such biographical sources in constructing their romantic fictions of life at the bar. Seven novels provide detailed accounts of the training and early professional activities of model lawyers: Susan A. L. Sedgwick, *Allen Prescott; or, The Fortunes of a New-England Boy* (1834); Frederick W. Thomas, *Clinton Bradshaw; or, The Adventures of a Lawyer* (1835); William Price, *Clement Falconer; or, The Memoirs of a Young Whig* (1838); Thomas H. Shreve, *Drayton: A Story of American Life* (1851); George Lunt, *Eastford; or, Household Sketches* (1855); and E. D. E. N. Southworth, *Ishmael; or, In the Depths*, and its sequel, *Self-Raised; or, From the Depths* (1864). Through their standardized plots and shared concerns, these works clarify popular expectations about the function of lawyers in a republican society.

The model attorney in antebellum fiction tends to be a self-made man, whose youthful struggles against adversity appeal to the sympathy of readers. Raised on a farm or in a small country town, he imbibes the Protestant work ethic from his poor but virtuous parents. His genealogy is impeccably Anglo-Saxon: Generally his ancestors emigrated from England several generations earlier and the family tree contains at least one Revolutionary War hero. In such republican surroundings the future advocate soon learns to despise artificial class distinctions. "Every man counts one in our country," notes Allen Prescott's father, a Connecticut seaman, "and insignificant as you

[9] On the mythmaking aspects of Wirt's career, see William R. Taylor, *Cavalier and Yankee: The Old South and American National Character* (London: W. H. Allen, 1963), pp. 67–94.

now are, by-and-by you'll be somebody."[10] Convinced that intelligence and determination can level all barriers, the ambitious country lad eventually departs for the city, in search of greater opportunities for public usefulness.

After a series of menial jobs and encounters with snobbish parvenus, he meets a distinguished lawyer who becomes his friend and patron. Under the guidance of this old-fashioned lawyer-gentleman, he reads law, attends court, and is admitted to the bar. Descriptions of law-office apprenticeship, the prevailing method of legal training before the Civil War, vary from author to author. Some do little more than mention the study of a familiar text like Blackstone's *Commentaries*; others outline a systematic course of readings and comment on the unequal abilities of rival law clerks. Real-life practitioners, such as Price, Thomas, and Lunt, often include lengthy avuncular advice on all kinds of subjects of presumed interest to law students, from proper study habits to the latest issues of law reform.[11]

Once admitted to practice, the young attorney becomes the special protector of the poor and defenseless. He undertakes his first Big Case—an apparently hopeless one—solely to vindicate the legal rights of his client. In the hands of women novelists the Big Case turns out to be a child custody suit or inheritance claim involving women's rights; male authors prefer a prosecution for murder or some lesser crime, in which the accused is a penniless laborer. The attorney, in either situation, displays unmistakable signs of "genius." On the night before the trial he is likely to be found wandering around the woods or seashore, rehearsing his argument in the open air, and his courtroom performance bears more than a passing resemblance to that of Patrick Henry in the "parsons' cause."

---

[10] [Susan Anne L. Sedgwick], *Allen Prescott; or, The Fortunes of a New-England Boy* (New York: Harper & Bros., 1834), 1:54.

[11] In a typical passage Ephraim Crabbe, leader of the Maryland bar, describes the best method of law study to his clerk Clement Falconer: "Read six hours a day. . . . It is as much as your mind can profitably go through at one sitting, and let it be your study to understand, rather than to remember all you read. No man can remember when every sentence is a maxim, the hundreth part of what he reads. But you will naturally recollect the book in which any particular subject is treated. If, therefore, you understand the law, and remember where it is to be found, it is all you can expect; nor need you wish for more. After your legal studies are finished for the day, read history, poetry, romance, chemistry, botany, any thing and every thing. Change of occupation is the best relaxation for the mind, and a lawyer's mind should be full of every thing." [William Price], *Clement Falconer; or, The Memoirs of a Young Whig* (Baltimore: N. Hickman, 1838), 1:64.

Here, for example, is Frank Drayton, delivering his maiden speech to the jury in defense of a suspected murderer:

> Sentence after sentence flashed rapidly from his lips. His impassioned tones rang over the multitude pressing forward with anxious faces to see the speaker. A profound silence was maintained, and every eye was turned on the orator. His clear and distinct enunciation—his appropriate language—the fervor and vehemence of his manner—the felicity of his illustrations, and, above all, the nervous and on-sweeping eloquence, which dashed like an ocean-tide against the tower of argument which the prosecutor had so skillfully built up, washing away its foundations, and causing it to totter and reel on its base, excited and fixed all attention on him.[12]

Southworth used even more frenetic imagery to describe the impression made by her deeply religious hero, Ishmael Worth: "He spoke for two hours, warming, glowing, rising with his subject, until his very form seemed to dilate in grandeur, and his face grew radiant as the face of an archangel; and those who heard seemed to think that his lips, like those of the prophet of old, had been touched with fire from heaven!"[13]

After such an auspicious debut, the victorious attorney can count on retainers from wealthy clients but continues to represent the indigent without charge. The merit of a claim, not the size of a fee, determines his choice of clients. Anyone who seeks to take unfair advantage of a legal technicality must look elsewhere for assistance. "I can have nothing to do, sir, in this matter," Allen Prescott tells the delinquent party in a contract dispute. "No honest man wants a lawyer's advice in regard to the payment of a just debt."[14] By his careful screening of clients and his concern for disinterested justice, the fictional practitioner defines himself as a "gentleman" of the bar. (In real life, professional mores were developing along different lines. As legal historians have recently shown, antebellum lawyers and judges were in fact stripping away the paternalistic and protective features of a preindustrial jurisprudence.[15] Judge George

---

[12] [Thomas H. Shreve], *Drayton: A Story of American Life* (New York: Harper & Bros., 1851), p. 259.

[13] E. D. E. N. Southworth, *Ishmael; or, In the Depths,* reprint ed. (New York: Street & Smith, n.d.), p. 296.

[14] Sedgwick, *Allen Prescott,* 2:155.

[15] See, for example, Morton J. Horwitz, *The Transformation of American Law, 1780–1860* (Cambridge: Harvard University Press, 1977).

Sharswood's *Essay on Professional Ethics* [1854], the leading code of legal ethics, enjoined practitioners *not* to pass moral judgments on potential clients, but to rely on the legal process itself to determine the merits of their claims.)

Novelists do not linger over scenes of office counseling or describe more than one or two courtroom situations. For most model attorneys, a legal career leads inevitably to political office. Through his reputation as a "people's lawyer," a man suddenly finds himself nominated for Congress or a state legislature by the working-class wards of his city. He campaigns and wins on a democratic platform: equal opportunities for all, special privileges to none. In canvassing for votes he remains a symbol of self-help; he scorns political bosses and will not subscribe to narrow party creeds. "[N]o, my fellow-citizens, I am under no man's patronage or pupilage," declares Clinton Bradshaw;[16] and Allen Prescott rejects the overtures of political lobbyists with the same severity he once applied to unworthy clients. Nonpartisan politics—the politics of conscience—provides an appropriate analogue to a public interest practice and enables the lawyer-hero to crown his career as a budding republican statesman. Somewhere along the way he also marries a beautiful and wealthy woman, whose money will presumably help to finance his pro bono activities in the future.

Like the robber barons of the late nineteenth century, antebellum lawyers captured public attention because of the power they appeared to wield in social and political matters. Through their ability to make and interpret the laws, they controlled the workings of republican institutions. Self-made individuals themselves in popular thinking, they established professedly neutral rules under which others competed for wealth and status in a developing nation. Professionalism, as embodied in the model practitioner, implied disinterested public service: a willingness to defend the rights of the individual, regardless of class or income. In return, the public acknowledged the preeminence of lawyers in a nominally democratic society. No other occupational group so well expressed the aspirations of a striving but orderly people.

There was, however, a darker side to the mythology of professional life. In popular literature the mirror image of the model attorney was the pettifogger, who stirred up needless litigation

---

[16] Thomas, *Clinton Bradshaw*, 2:271.

and exploited his clients and the legal system for personal gain. Pettifoggers were the inevitable by-product of a competitive, and largely unregulated, recruitment process. Republican ideology, which required that the professions, like other employments, be open to talented individuals from every social class, discouraged the development of effective screening procedures. Rascally lawyers thus flourished as a kind of professional underclass, whose well-publicized chicanery added a new chapter to our national folklore.

The pettifogger stereotype dominated the treatment of lawyers in antebellum schoolbooks. Most textbook authors, while acknowledging the merits of a few "legal statesmen" such as John Marshall, took a dim view of the profession as a whole. Eight readers and spellers that were widely used in elementary schools referred to a game called "The Colonists," which ranked occupations according to their social value. Farming stood at the head of the list, followed by a variety of other "useful" trades and callings. Lawyers did not fit into any socially acceptable category; they were defined as a parasitic group, whose emigration would only bring trouble to a new colony. Or, as some fifth-grade students learned to recite:

> To fit up a village with tackle for tillage
> Jack Carter he took to the saw.
> To pluck and to pillage the same little village
> Tim Gordon he took to the law.[17]

Unlike the ethnic "shysters" of the late nineteenth century, fictional pettifoggers were mostly white, Anglo-Saxon Protestants. They came from the same cultural background as model attorneys, although they espoused none of the *noblesse oblige* attitudes that characterized elite bar leaders. Mere technicians of the law, they were content to manipulate legal rules for the benefit of wealthy wrongdoers and often engaged in criminal activities themselves. Generically, they fell into two categories: declassed gentlemen and lower-class rogues.

Typical of the fallen gentleman was Morcell, the protagonist of George Watterston's *The Lawyer; or, Man As He Ought Not to Be* (1808), the first full-length portrait of a pettifogger in American literature. The son of an avaricious Maryland landowner, Morcell grows up in material comfort but without any moral guidance.

---

[17] Quoted in Ruth Miller Elson, *Guardians of Tradition: American Schoolbooks of the Nineteenth Century* (Lincoln: University of Nebraska Press, 1964), p. 26.

Pleased by the boy's precocious cunning and taste for vandalism, his father hires an exlawyer—one "well acquainted with the *arcana* of legal villainy"—to train him for the bar. Under this man's direction Morcell becomes proficient in his knowledge of technical legal rules, but remains "wholly ignorant of the fundamental principles of justice." Through personal experience, he also discovers that the conditions of legal practice are likely in themselves to turn the most upright man into a pettifogger after a while: "A lawyer, from the first moment he enters into business, becomes habituated to scenes of injustice and oppresson; from which, if he possess the smallest particle of sensibility, he turns at first with disgust and abhorrence; but custom soon renders them familiar, and in process of time, he can view them with the utmost coolness and indifference. . . . It is evident, that a perpetual fellowship with villainy, will in time, destroy every tender emotion and sap by degrees the foundation of the most rigid virtue."[18]

In Morcell's case the process of ethical deterioration is accelerated, since his only reason for practicing law is to make money. He never agonizes, like a model attorney, over the justice of a cause; nor does he ever represent a client without charge. After losing a poor widow's suit through his own negligence, he seizes her meager possessions—down to her sickbed!—to satisfy his fee. On another occasion he accepts a bribe from a wealthy defendant to undermine the case of his own client, an "honest mechanic." Despite such unscrupulous behavior, he continues to attract clients by his impudence and ingratiating courtroom manner. He rises to a position of prominence at the Maryland bar, only to experience belated twinges of conscience. Eventually he retires to a distant part of the state, where he lives in obscurity, "endeavouring by charity and benevolence to expiate, in some degree, the crimes of which I have been guilty."[19]

The scruples that sometimes affect the gentleman-turned-pettifogger never trouble the lower-class rogue, who displays only contempt for his victims. In novels of urban life the lower-class practitioner generally appears as a hanger-on of the criminal courts who preys on vulnerable defendants and their families. Counsellor Grey in Theodore S. Fay's novel, *Norman Leslie: A Tale of the Present*

---

[18] [George Watterston], *The Lawyer; or, Man As He Ought Not to Be* (Pittsburgh: Zadok Cramer, 1808), pp. 55–56.
[19] Ibid., p. 234.

Times (1835), offers to get the hero acquitted of a murder charge for the sum of one hundred dollars, part of which will be used to buy the testimony of a pretended eyewitness. Still more unsavory is the pettifogger Scrags in *Clinton Bradshaw*: He extorts money from his clients to arrange jailbreaks, then betrays the escaped prisoners to the police for a second reward. For sheer audacity and inventiveness, however, urban pettifoggers could not compete with the favorite legal villains of the antebellum era: those semiliterate practitioners whose exploits were chronicled in the literature of the frontier.

Lawyers and judges made a distinctive contribution to this literary genre—the early western—by publishing what might be termed the "folklore of the circuit." Circuit riding was the standard means of bringing the law to scattered settlements in the years before the Civil War. Judges were required to ride long distances from town to town, accompanied by a group of lawyers who sought to attract clients on a catch-as-catch-can basis at each stopping place. In its heyday (which varied in duration from locality to locality), the frontier circuit bar operated as a close-knit legal fraternity that brought a touch of the theater and the revival tent to isolated hamlets. By the 1830s such men as Augustus Baldwin Longstreet of Georgia, Johnson J. Hooper of Alabama, and Judge James Hall of Cincinnati began to record the tall tales they had encountered on the circuit, along with impressions of backwoods practitioners and clients. They described frontier justice from an elitist perspective and used humor and satire to expose the frauds practiced by untrained attorneys on a gullible public.

A good example of such legal fiction is Joseph G. Baldwin's *The Flush Times of Alabama and Mississippi* (1853), which has survived as a minor humorous classic of the Old Southwest. Baldwin offered his readers a veritable rogues' gallery of assorted pettifoggers, from Ovid Bolus, Esq., the "natural liar," to the outrageous Simon Suggs, Jr., who wins his law license in a card game. Suggs' extralegal methods of winning cases typified the stratagems employed by other successful sharpers:

> Instead of waiting to create prejudices in the minds of the jury until they were in the box, or deferring until then the arts of persuasion, he waited upon them before they were empanelled; and he always succeeded better at that time, as they had not then received an improper bias from the testimony. In a case of any importance, he always managed to have his

friends in the court room, so that when any of the jurors were challenged, he might have their places filled by good men and true; and, although this increased his expenses considerably, by a large annual bill at the grocery, he never regretted any expense, either of time, labor or money, necessary to success in his business. Such was his zeal for his clients![20]

In the theater, too, the stereotype of the village pettifogger flourished. The quintessential stage villain of the nineteenth century was Lawyer Cribbs, a character in W. H. Smith's phenomenally successful temperance play, *The Drunkard* (1844). During the course of this turgid melodrama Cribbs, described by another character as a "black beetle," turns the hero into an alcoholic, attempts to seduce the heroine, drives another young woman to insanity, passes a counterfeit check, and forges a will. When his misdeeds are finally brought to light, he remains unrepentant. "I have lived a villain—a villain let me die," he sneers to the assembled onlookers, as he is led away by the police.

The range of Cribbs's criminality, which parallels that of other fictional pettifoggers, suggests the limits of deviant behavior as depicted by antebellum writers. In an individualistic age, fictional lawbreaking entailed either some violation of personal trust (e.g., embezzlement, fraud) or some act of personal violence. Although authors mentioned land companies, banks, and other corporations, they never analyzed corporate behavior nor acknowledged the principle of corporate guilt. Even outlaw gangs were treated as collections of individuals who were held together by the will of a single powerful leader. In *Richard Hurdis* (1838), one of his "border romances," William Gilmore Simms described the authority wielded by one man over the interstate criminal organization he had created:

> On all hands he found friends and followers—men ready to do his bidding—to follow him in all risks—to undertake all sorts of offences, and in every respect to be the instruments of his will, as docile and dependent as those of any Oriental despot known in story. His followers soon grew numerous, and having them scattered through all the slave states, and some of the free, he could enumerate more than fifteen hundred men ready at his summons and sworn to his allegiance.[21]

[20] Joseph G. Baldwin, *The Flush Times of Alabama and Mississippi* (New York: Sagamore Press, 1957), p. 99.
[21] W. Gilmore Simms, *Richard Hurdis: A Tale of Alabama*, rev. ed. (Chicago: Donohue, Henneberry & Co., 1890), p. 314.

The outlaw leader usually proved to be a fallen gentleman, since writers were reluctant to credit the common man with superior intelligence or initiative. In a few cases, as in Simms's *Guy Rivers* (1834) and Alfred W. Arrington's *The Rangers and Regulators of the Tanaha* (1856), a former lawyer directs the operations of a criminal band. The transition from lawyering to outlawry did not strain credibility; in popular thinking the gentleman pettifogger, who had renounced public service in favor of personal enrichment, had always seemed little better than a licensed robber.

Compared to practitioners, antebellum judges received only limited attention from creative writers. With some notable exceptions, such as Marmaduke Temple in James Fenimore Cooper's novel *The Pioneers* (1823), judges did not appear as major characters in fiction or drama. To the average reader the judicial function seemed lacking in dramatic potential. Although historians rightly regard the early nineteenth century as an era of extraordinary judicial creativity, judges at the time insisted that they were merely applying well-settled principles of natural law or statutory construction. "Judicial power, as contradistinguished from the power of the laws, has no existence," declared John Marshall in *Osborne v. Bank of the United States* (1824). "Courts are the mere instruments of the law, and can will nothing. When they are said to exercise a discretion it is a mere legal discretion, a discretion to be exercised in discerning the course prescribed by law. . . ."[22] Nineteenth-century Americans tended, on the whole, to accept such statements, whose negative and mechanistic overtones were not calculated to stir the imagination.

Most fictional judges accordingly functioned as little more than symbols of righteousness, whose behavior on and off the bench illustrated the moral certainties of the natural law. Judge Howard, who presides at Norman Leslie's murder trial, is austere and incorruptible, a man who could condemn his own son to death with "the sternness of a Roman." Mark Sutherland, a judge in E. D. E. N. Southworth's novel, *India; or, The Pearl of Pearl River* (1856), lives by an equally rigorous code of ethics. "Family considerations, personal pride, never have influenced my conduct, and never will do ' so," Sutherland warns a relative who seeks to avoid prosecution for

---

[22] Quoted in Robert Kenneth Faulkner, *The Jurisprudence of John Marshall* (Princeton, N.J.: Princeton University Press, 1968), p. 67.

his crimes. "In every question there is a right and a wrong. I obey the right."[23]

Apart from being virtuous and wise, the fictional judges seldom display any professional skills. In trial situations they rarely rule on a motion, instruct a jury, or look up a point of law. Since most authors knew little about courtroom procedure or substantive legal doctrines, the typical case turns on a disputed question of fact, which the jury decides. While the strategies of opposing counsel provide dramatic interest, the judge remains a benign, and largely inarticulate, presence in the background.

At the appellate court level the drama of the adversary system—which John McWilliams explores in his essay on fictionalized criminal trials—diminishes. There are no jurors to arouse, no witnesses to examine, no exciting new facts to uncover. The judge overshadows the advocate, and legal doctrines must be understood and explained to readers. One finds no significant fictional accounts of appellate proceedings until the twentieth century, when the public began to think of judicial power in more realistic terms than those suggested by John Marshall.

The prevailing idealization of the judiciary in antebellum literature did not go completely unchallenged, of course. An occasional writer introduced a corrupt or incompetent judge into his work, but these judicial villains invariably prove to be party hacks who operate at the lowest levels of the court system. As elective officeholders they lack the independence and dignity associated with long-term appointments to the bench, and their willingness to betray their public trust makes them the judicial equivalents of pettifogging attorneys.

John Treat Irving in *The Attorney; or, The Correspondence of John Quod* (1842) describes a police court magistrate who is as vicious as any of the criminals brought before him for examination, and the pseudonymous author of *Raising the Veil; or, Scenes in the Courts* (1856) observes that trial judges in New York City are often "second or third rate lawyer[s]" who "become accomplices of notorious thieves and murderers."[24] Although such writers describe the victimization of the poor by judges and other court officials, they refuse to impute any class bias to the law itself. The basic problem, as they present it, is one of individual integrity: If good men filled

---

[23] E. D. E. N. Southworth, *India; or, The Pearl of Pearl River*, reprint ed. (New York: Hurst & Co., n.d.), p. 207.
[24] Ball Fenner (pseud.), *Raising the Veil; or, Scenes in the Courts* (Boston: James French and Co., 1856), p. 128.

even the lowest judicial posts, no question of unequal justice could arise.

Theodore S. Fay's *Norman Leslie* well illustrates the limits of judicial criticism in popular fiction. During Leslie's trial for murder a partisan press accuses the court of showing favoritism to him because of his social position. As a result, his acquittal enrages the lower classes of New York City. "Upon the *poor* [the power of the law] would doubtless fall," cries one old woman; "but the rich can escape, no matter what *they* have done."[25] Although the details of Fay's plot effectively refute this charge, he considers it necessary to lecture his readers at length upon the beneficence of a republican legal system:

> We must remark here, that in no quarter of the globe are the laws more purely and properly administered than in the United States. The decisions are probably as equitable as it is in the nature of human laws to be. . . . If injustice occurs, it appears in those fantastic combinations of accidental circumstances—exceptions in the usual order of society— which the broad and immutable course of a general law cannot be turned aside to correct; but the law itself is acknowledged to be, as far as mortal institutions may be, broadly and beneficially adapted—without being warped by barbarous ages, or distorted into uncouth shapes to suit present individual interests—wisely and impartially to the whole body of the people. *No currents flow to favour particular persons or classes.*[26]

The image of a legal system that was open and responsive to all Americans had little meaning for one group in the population, however. Blacks, whether slave or free, could not expect even-handed treatment from white courts and legislatures. To dramatize the abuses of a racist society, antislavery writers developed a form of documentary fiction—the forerunner of the modern "problem novel." This literature, which exposed the gap between republican rhetoric and institutional realities, proved a potent weapon in the campaign to abolish the "peculiar institution."

Harriet Beecher Stowe's *Dred: A Tale of the Great Dismal Swamp* (1856) examined the legal foundations of slavery more skillfully than any other abolitionist novel. Edward Clayton, Stowe's hero, is a young North Carolina lawyer who tries to reform the slave system from within. Acting as counsel for a female slave, Clayton sues the white employer who beat and shot her. In an eloquent

---

[25] [Theodore S. Fay], *Norman Leslie: A Tale of the Present Time* (New York: Harper & Bros., 1835), 2:7.
[26] Ibid., pp. 9–10. Emphasis added.

courtroom argument he urges that a slave should be entitled to the same protection that the law affords to other dependents, such as children, wards, and servants. "The eyes of the world are fastened upon us," he warns. "Let us therefore show, by the spirit in which we administer our laws, by the impartiality with which we protect their rights, that the master of the helpless African is his best and truest friend."[27] Impressed by Clayton's moral fervor, the trial judge accepts his guardianship theory, and the jury renders a unanimous verdict for his client.

On appeal to the state supreme court, however, the decision is overruled. Judge Clayton, Edward's father, rejects any analogy between the status of a slave and that of a freeborn child or other dependent. In words that echo the ruling actually handed down in the landmark case of *State v. Mann* (1829),[28] the elder Clayton affirms the absolute dominion of a master or authorized employer over his slave. The law of domestic relations, which looks to the happiness and moral development of minors, has no application to the master-slave relationship, he remarks:

> The end [of slavery] is the profit of the master, his security, and the public safety; the subject, one doomed, in his own person and his posterity, to live without knowledge, and without the capacity to make anything his own, and to toil that another may reap the fruits. . . . Such services can only be expected from one who has no will of his own; who surrenders his will in implicit obedience to that of another. Such obedience is the consequence only of uncontrolled authority over the body. . . . THE POWER OF THE MASTER MUST BE ABSOLUTE, TO RENDER THE SUBMISSION OF THE SLAVE PERFECT. . . . The slave, to remain a slave, must be made sensible that there is no appeal from his master; that his power is, in no instance, usurped, but is conferred by the laws of man, at least, if not by the law of God. The danger would be great, indeed, if the tribunals of justice should be called on to graduate the punishment appropriate to every temper, and every dereliction of duty.[29]

The legislature, of course, may regulate or modify the duties of slaveholders, but courts are powerless to effect any changes in the law of slavery. Although personally a humane man, Judge Clayton

[27] Harriet Beecher Stowe, *Dred: A Tale of the Great Dismal Swamp* (Boston: Phillips, Sampson and Co., 1856), 2:42.
[28] 13 N. C. 263 (1829).
[29] Stowe, *Dred*, 2: pp. 103–104.

subscribes to the narrow Marshallian view of the judicial function: "I sit in my seat, not to make laws, nor to alter them, but simply to declare what they are."[30]

Unable to obtain redress through the courts, Edward Clayton abandons his legal practice to work for legislative reforms, including measures that will allow slaves to testify in judicial proceedings and sue for injuries. He seeks the help of churchmen and other civic leaders; appeals to the public conscience through speeches and newspaper articles; and drafts petitions to the legislature. For these efforts, which prove completely unavailing, he soon acquires a reputation as a crank and a troublemaker. "The holders of slaves are an aristocracy supported by special constitutional privileges," his father explains. "They are united against the spirit of the age by a common interest and danger, and the instinct of self-preservation is infallible."[31] As Southern fears of an abolitionist conspiracy multiply, postal officials open Clayton's mail in search of incendiary literature, masked vigilantes beat him severely for daring to speak in favor of gradual emancipation, and a mob attacks his plantation and burns the schoolhouse he had provided for the education of his slaves. Having exhausted every means of peaceful reform, he admits defeat and emigrates with his slaves to Canada.

A subplot explores the theme of slave rebellion within the context of the American revolutionary tradition. Dred, a son of the famous black rebel Denmark Vesey, is a visionary who preaches a holy war of extermination against the white oppressor. From his stronghold in the Great Dismal Swamp, he makes periodic forays into the outside world, gathering a band of loyal followers for the approaching struggle. In one of her most dramatic scenes, Stowe describes a midnight meeting in the swamp, at which Harry, an educated mulatto, encourages some new recruits by reading to them the Declaration of Independence. He concludes:

> Brothers, . . . you have heard the grievances which our masters thought sufficient to make it right for them to shed blood. . . . Now, the Lord judge between us and them, if the laws they put upon us be not worse than any that lay upon them. They complained that they could not get justice done to them in the courts. But how stands it with us, who cannot even come into a court to plead?[32]

---

[30] Ibid., pp. 99–100.
[31] Ibid., p. 151.
[32] Ibid., pp. 225–226.

While preparations for the projected uprising are still going forward, a white mob tracks Dred through the swamp and kills him. Leaderless and demoralized, the other fugitives abandon their hopes of deliverance through armed struggle. Stowe thus brings her tale to a grim conclusion, as the repressive power of the state triumphs over all forms of internal opposition.

Early black novelists presented a more positive view of slave resistance. Henry Blake, the hero of Martin R. Delany's *Blake; or, The Huts of America* (1859), travels throughout the South, organizing his fellow slaves into revolutionary cells. At a given signal these local groups will rise up in a general assault upon the slave system. William Wells Brown, in *Clotel; or, The President's Daughter* (1853), likewise surveyed slavery from an interstate perspective and described various modes of effective resistance. Both writers took note as well of the discriminatory laws that affected free blacks in the North, and compared the movement for racial justice in America to the republican revolutions that were taking place in Europe. "Had Clotel escaped from oppression in any other land . . . and reached the United States," Brown noted bitterly, "no honour within the gift of the American people would have been too good to have been heaped upon the heroic woman. But she was a slave, and therefore out of the pale of their sympathy. . . . They boast that America is the 'cradle of liberty;' if it is, I fear they have rocked the child to death."[33]

<hr>

II

Fictional Lawyers and the Rise of the Corporate State

*"What a tower of Babel—an industrial Babel, you are building, John—
you and your kith and kind. The last century gave us Schopenhauers
and Kants, all denying God, and this one gives us Railroad Kings and
Iron Kings and Wheat Kings, all by their works proclaiming that
Mammon has the power and the glory and the Kingdom. O ye workers
of iniquity!" she cried, and her voice lifted, "ye wicked and perverse—"*

William Allen White, *A Certain Rich Man* (1909)*

<hr>

[33] William Wells Brown, *Clotel; or, The President's Daughter*, reprint ed. (New York: Arno Press and The *New York Times*, 1969), p. 218.
* Excerpts from William Allen White, *A Certain Rich Man* (New York: Macmillan, 1909) are reprinted by permission of Mrs. William Lindsay White for the William Allen White Estate. I acknowledge with thanks her generous assistance.

Despite its covert racism, the republican creed served the nation well through the first half of the nineteenth century. Thereafter, accelerated urban and industrial growth threatened to overwhelm established values and institutions, including the law. With the completion of transcontinental rail and communications networks, giant corporations developed to serve and to exploit national markets, defying the competitive rules of classical economics. An unskilled immigrant work force, drawn increasingly from unfamiliar regions of southern and eastern Europe, provoked middle-class fears of alien domination and class war. Some observers warned that America was sinking into a "new feudalism," complete with robber barons and rebellious serfs; and the great labor upheavals of the late nineteenth century seemed to confirm such predictions. After 1890 the idcology of laissez-faire republicanism came under increasing attack from both scholarly critics and muckraking journalists, who called for active governmental interference in the economy to protect workers, consumers, and other disadvantaged groups. Politicians who favored such an expanded role for government called themselves "Progressives"—a term now used to describe the era of frenetic reform activity that occurred between the turn of the century and World War I.

The power of big business both fascinated and frightened a public accustomed to thinking of life in Darwinian terms as a harsh competitive struggle that destroyed the unfit. Between 1865 and 1914 businessmen appeared as major characters in 158 Broadway plays, almost three-fourths of which were produced after the passage of the Sherman Antitrust Act in 1890.[34] In the cheap new magazines of the 1890s, such as *Munsey's, McClure's,* and *Cosmopolitan,* businessmen replaced lawyers, judges, and politicians as the favored subjects of laudatory or apprehensive biographical articles.[35] Newspaper cartoonists, serving the mass market created by Pulitzer, Hearst, and other publishing impresarios, mirrored popular fears of an uncontrollable plutocracy in drawings that even a child could understand.

Homer Davenport pictured "The Trust"as a huge barbarian with an Assyrian-style beard, who looked as though he might have

[34] Jeremiah Dromey, "The Businessman in the American Drama, 1865–1914" (M. A. thesis, Dept. of English, Catholic University of America, 1949).
[35] Theodore P. Greene, *America's Heroes: The Changing Models of Success in American Magazines* (New York: Oxford University Press, 1970).

stepped from the facade of some ancient temple; in contrast, Frederick Burr Opper's symbol of "The Common People" was an insignificant little man who peered out at the world through big glasses with an anxious and puzzled look. Representatives of the law appeared equally diminutive in the presence of a bloated and predatory Capitalism. Art Young, the most trenchant political cartoonist of the Progressive period, featured a cowed or subservient bench and bar in many of his best drawings. In a typical courtroom scene an impatient judge, dressed like Uncle Sam, waits for a "malefactor of great wealth" to be brought before him, while outside in the corridor a burly emblem of the "Money Power" applies a stranglehold to the neck of a scrawny "Public Prosecutor." Young's caption read:

JUDGE: "Bring in the Prisoner."
PUBLIC PROSECUTOR: "He won't let me."[36]

Although novelists and playwrights were equally impressed by the power of the "soulless corporation," they tended to be more ambivalent in their criticism. Some turn-of-the-century writers romanticized the exploits of fictional businessmen and stressed the benefits that economic concentration would eventually bring to the public. "Roger Drake, Captain of Industry," the hero of a novel by Henry Kitchell Webster, schemes to create a copper trust for utilitarian reasons that have little to do with personal enrichment:

What I wanted to do was incorporate that industry throughout the entire district, into an economical, efficient system; to bring it up to the level of its highest capability. I planned the district just as an architect plans a building, or better, as a mechanic designs a locomotive, to develop as much power as possible out of as little fuel, and to waste as little as possible in noise and friction; and that I was to live in the building, or ride behind the engine, had nothing to do with it.[37]

Even more public-spirited is "John Dorn, Promoter," an ardent conservationist who organizes a great lumber combine to illustrate

---

[36] The cartoons of Davenport, Opper, and Young are reproduced in Stephen Hess and Milton Kaplan, *The Ungentlemanly Art: A History of American Political Cartoons,* rev. ed. (New York: Macmillan, 1975).
[37] Henry Kitchell Webster, *Roger Drake, Captain of Industry* (New York: Macmillan, 1902), p. 188.

the merits of scientific forest management. Dorn explains to a business associate:

> If something isn't done to protect the timber lands, this country will be lumberless in half a century, and the dead forest will get even with us by letting the rains run away unchecked. We shall have a series of floods and droughts. We'll be landless, as well as timberless. We must stop this ignorant slaughter of the trees, and work along natural lines. I'm going to form a combination to stop a crime, and I'll make money in doing it.[38]

Through a "preservation annex" included in the corporate charter, Dorn commits his new organization to a policy of selective cutting and reforestation.

Most authors took a less optimistic view of corporate planning. Influenced by the literary realism of William Dean Howells and the legal realism of Roscoe Pound and others, these writers created a new form of legal fiction that dramatized corporate abuses and their effect on democratic institutions. Such novels as Frank Norris's *The Octopus* (1901) and Francis Lynde's *The Grafters* (1904) detailed the unsavory methods—including stock market manipulations, legislative deals, and phony receivership proceedings—by which certain railroads gained monopolistic control of their rivals. Playwrights, drawn increasingly to economic problems, found made-to-order themes in the exposés of crusading journalists. Owen Davis's play, *The Power of Money* (1906), described the efforts of a ruthless tycoon to crush a small manufacturer and introduced President Theodore Roosevelt as a trust-busting *deus ex machina*. William J. Hurlbut likewise dipped into current headlines for *The Writing on the Wall* (1909), which capitalized on journalistic revelations concerning the ownership of New York tenements by the "respectable classes" of Wall Street and Trinity Church. Between 1900 and 1914 twenty-nine plays condemned various aspects of corporate behavior, from lobbying to labor relations.[39]

Few works attacked capitalism itself, however, or proposed fundamental changes in political or economic institutions. While

[38] Charles Eugene Banks, *John Dorn, Promoter* (Chicago: Monarch Book Co., 1906), p. 79.
[39] Dromey, "Businessman in the American Drama," pp. 63–95. For a more detailed account of the relationship between muckraking journalism and drama, see Maxwell Bloomfield, "Muckraking and the American Stage: The Emergence of Realism, 1905–1917," *South Atlantic Quarterly* 66 (Spring 1967): 165–178.

approving government regulation of harmful business practices, writers looked primarily to an enlightened public opinion to remedy the evils they had uncovered. A new social ethic was emerging, they maintained, that would alter the thinking of businessmen as well as laborers, consumers, and lawmakers. Once persuaded that the growth of corporate power entailed commensurate obligations to society, even a robber baron would be led to modify his antisocial practices. The image of the business titan as a product of cultural lag permeated the legal fiction of the Progressive years, and gave rise to innumerable conversion scenes of the sort found in William Allen White's *A Certain Rich Man* (1909).

John Barclay, White's protagonist, is a midwestern grain tycoon who has built his empire through the use of sundry extralegal methods that were tolerated by the society of his youth. Although he controls the politics of his home state, he cannot prevent the passage of federal antitrust legislation. One day an honest inspector from the Bureau of Corporations arrives to look over the company books; shortly thereafter, to his amazement, Barclay finds himself facing multiple lawsuits:

> Here are five suits in county courts in Texas against me; a suit in Kansas by the attorney-general, five or ten in the Dakotas, three in Nebraska, one or two in each of the Lake states, and the juries always finding against me. I haven't changed my methods. I'm doing just what I've done for fifteen years. I've had lots of lawsuits before, with stockholders and rival companies and partners, and millers and all that—but this standing in front of the mob and fighting them off—why? Why? What have I done? . . . What's got into the people?[40]

The answer, White emphasizes, is that "the people" have experienced a moral awakening and will no longer submit to the rule of a privileged economic elite. Under the tutelage of muckraking journalists, Americans are reasserting the democratic ideals of the Declaration of Independence against the forces of corporate tyranny. The reform impulse is nonviolent but irresistible: "When this public opinion rises sure and firm and strong, no material force on this earth can stop it. . . . For it is God moving among men."[41]

Barclay himself succumbs to the new ethic in the course of a midnight vision. He wakes from a fitful sleep to find his room flooded

---

[40] William Allen White, *A Certain Rich Man* (New York: Macmillan, 1909), p. 331.
[41] Ibid., p. 326.

with light, and sees inscribed across the family organ the motto, "Righteousness exalteth a Nation, but sin is a reproach to any people":

> ... As he gazed at the text its meaning came rushing through his brain. It came so quickly that he could not will it back nor reason it in. Righteousness, he knew, was not piety—not wearing your Sunday clothes to church and praying and singing psalms; it was living honestly and kindly and charitably and dealing decently with every one in every transaction; and sin—that, he knew—was the cheating, the deceiving, and the malicious greed that had built up his company and scores of others like it all over the land. That, he knew—that bribery and corruption and vicarious stealing which he had learned to know as business—that was a reproach to any people, and as it came to him that he was a miserable offender and that the other life, the decent life, was the right life, he was filled with a joy that he could not express, and he let the light fail about him unheeded, and lay for a time in a transport of happiness. He had found the secret.[42]

In proof of his moral regeneration, Barclay voluntarily liquidates his grain trust and turns over to the White House his comprehensive card file on the corporate connections of every politician in the country. He retires to the small Kansas town where he was born, to reestablish his solidarity with "the people" through acts of disinterested benevolence. His altruism eventually costs him his life, as he drowns while trying to rescue the town prostitute from flood waters. "Some one said that as the skiff shot over the dam, John, still standing up, had a smile on his face, and that he waved his hand to the crowd with a touch of his old bravado."[43]

If Barclay's redemption seems about as convincing to a modern reader as that of Ebenezer Scrooge, it nevertheless satisfied the demands of Progressive audiences. In scores of popular novels and plays "the people" won bloodless victories over "the interests" through the use of moral suasion. (Middle-class journalists likewise called for a revitalized ethic of public service to subdue the "selfish" tendencies of capital and labor.) Few hard-bitten financiers in popular fiction could withstand even the most simple-minded appeals for class harmony and a return to the Golden Rule in business

---

[42] Ibid., p. 403.
[43] Ibid., p. 432.

operations. "Ready Money Ryder," the autocrat of Charles Klein's record-breaking stage hit, *The Lion and the Mouse* (1905), embraces the cause of economic democracy after a few edifying discussions of this sort with his secretary, Shirley Rossmore:

SHIRLEY: So you think your life is a good example to follow.
RYDER: Isn't it?
SHIRLEY: Suppose we all wanted to follow it, suppose we all wanted to be the richest, the most powerful personage in the world—
RYDER: Well?
SHIRLEY: I think it would postpone the Era of the Brotherhood of Man, indefinitely—don't you?
RYDER: I never looked at it from that point of view. . . . [44]

Historians have demonstrated that ethical considerations influenced business mores far less than did the pragmatic needs of the business community. By the early twentieth century the major American corporations desired some form of government regulation as a means of standardizing industrial production, eliminating less efficient competitors, and gaining access to foreign markets. Instead of capitulating to a triumphant citizenry, big business shaped the terms of much "reform" legislation and established a close working relationship with the new regulatory agencies of the federal government.[45] Although few contemporary observers were aware of this corporate strategy, at least one novelist—Stewart Edward White—accurately perceived the trend toward government-business collaboration in the lumber industry.

Bob Orde, the hero of White's superior western *The Rules of the Game* (1910), is the son of a lumber magnate. After learning the logging business from the ground up, young Orde becomes a convert to the ecology movement and joins the United States Forest Service. The rangers, he finds, are becoming professionalized and business-minded. In earlier years their job was primarily defensive: Like lonely "knights-errant," they patrolled vast stretches of the public domain and repelled the incursions of sheep ranchers, lumber companies and other trespassers. Now, under the direction of experts

[44] Charles Klein, *The Lion and the Mouse* (New York: Samuel French, 1906), p. 49.
[45] James Weinstein, *The Corporate Ideal in the Liberal State: 1900–1918* (Boston: Beacon Press, 1968).

from the Bureau of Forestry, they are learning the techniques of scientific management and coordinated group activity.

"We no longer speak of Forest Reserves, but of National Forests," explains Ashley Thorne, a supervisor of Forest Service operations in California.

> We've saved them; now . . . we are going to use these forests for the benefit of the people. We're going to cut the ripe trees and sell them to the lumber manufacturer; we're going to develop the water power; we're going to improve the grazing; we're going to study what we have here, so that by and by from our forests we will be getting the income the lumberman now gets, and will not be injuring the estate. Each Forest is going to be a big and complicated business, like railroading or wholesaling. . . . There's sure to come a time when it will not be too much off balance to *require* private firms to do things according to our methods.[46]

Up to this point the plot has followed the familiar outline of the muckraking novel: A materialistic businessman, confronted with evidence of corporate wrongdoing, renounces self-interest in favor of public service. Significantly, however, Orde does not remain with Thorne and his bureaucratic rangers. At the invitation of his father, the lumber tycoon, he returns to private industry to demonstrate that scientific logging practices can be made economically profitable. "You can't lead a commercial class by ideals that absolutely conflict with commercial motives," Orde informs a government official. "In order to educate them you must fix it so your ideals don't actually spell *loss*! Rearrange the scheme of taxation, for one thing. Get your ideas of fire protection and conservation on a practical basis. . . . We've got to make it so easy to do things right that anybody at all decent will be ashamed not to."[47]

White leaves little doubt that Bob Orde's venture will succeed. With tax concessions and watered-down governmental directives, the corporation can well afford to modernize its procedures. The emphasis on corporate pragmatism and resiliency in *The Rules of the Game*

[46] Stewart Edward White, *The Rules of the Game* (New York: Doubleday, Page and Co., 1910), pp. 326, 381.
[47] Ibid., pp. 380–381.

offers a welcome contrast to the sentimentality of the average business novel in the early twentieth century. As one veteran lumberman notes at the end of the book: "Things change; and a man is foolish to act as though they didn't. He's just got to keep playing along according to the rules of the game. And they keep changing, too."[48]

Business fiction created as one of its by-products a new legal stereotype, the corporation lawyer, whose evolution is most thoroughly explored in Winston Churchill's novel *A Far Country* (1915). Hugh Paret, the protagonist, is the son of an urban attorney, an old-style "model lawyer" with an inflexible Calvinist conscience, an aristocratic manner, a taste for the classics and for modern English literature, and a general reputation for competence and fair dealing. Hugh rejects the paternal example, however, as unsuited to the get-rich-quick opportunism of the Gilded Age. From his schooling in the 1870s he learns that enlightened self-interest is the highest good and that established institutions and values must be preserved inviolate. These lessons are confirmed for him during his years at the Harvard Law School, which he enters in 1881. At Harvard, he later recalls,

> were instilled into me without difficulty the dictums that the law was the most important of all professions, that those who entered it were a priestly class set aside to guard from profanation that Ark of the Covenant, the Constitution of the United States. In short, I was taught law precisely as I had been taught religion,—scriptural infallibility over again,—a static law and a static theology,—a set of concepts that were supposed to be equal to any problems civilization would have to meet until the millennium.[49]

Equipped with this reassuring intellectual baggage, Hugh returns home to enter the law firm of Theodore Watling, a prominent corporation lawyer. Through Watling he meets the handful of bankers, industrialists, and railroad executives who control local and state politics by purchasing the services of venal bosses and office-holders. Hungry for wealth and status, Hugh joins the ranks of the

---

[48] Ibid., p. 644.
[49] Winston Churchill, *A Far Country* (New York: Macmillan, 1915), pp. 113–114. Permission to reprint material from Winston Churchill, *A Far Country* (New York: Macmillan, 1915) was granted by Mr. Creighton Churchill. I acknowledge with thanks his generous assistance.

ruling elite and uses his legal skills to promote corporate exploitation and privilege. His professional reputation expands beyond the limits of his state, and he is eventually summoned to New York City to advise a powerful and unnamed "Personality" (clearly modeled on J. P. Morgan) about ways to circumvent the Sherman Antitrust Act.

Hugh rationalizes his sellout to the corporations by appealing to a crude version of Social Darwinism, as expounded by his mentor Watling:

> I hadn't practised law very long [Watling observes] before I began to realize that conditions were changing, that the new forces at work in our industrial life made the older legal ideals impracticable. It was a case of choosing between efficiency and inefficiency, and I chose efficiency. . . .
> We are a nation divided against ourselves; democracy—Jacksonian democracy, at all events, is a flat failure, and we may as well acknowledge it. We have a political system we have outgrown, and which, therefore, we have had to nullify. There are certain needs, certain tendencies of development in nations as well as in individuals,—needs stronger than the state, stronger than the law or constitution. In order to make our resources effective, combinations of capital are more and more necessary, and no more to be denied than a chemical process, given the proper ingredients, can be thwarted. The men who control capital must have a free hand, or the structure will be destroyed. This compels us to do many things which we would rather not do, which we might accomplish openly and unopposed if conditions were frankly recognized, and met by wise statesmanship which sought to bring about harmony by the reshaping of laws and policies.[50]

But professional success, achieved through compliance with these economic imperatives, leaves Hugh lonely and dissatisfied. As muckraking journalists expose the social costs of a regime of business efficiency his conscience twinges; and his conservative values are finally shattered through a series of confrontations with Hermann Krebs, a former Harvard classmate and a modern example of the "people's lawyer." Krebs, the son of a German emigrant who fought on the liberal side in the Revolutions of 1848, is a self-made man who has worked his way through college and law school. A champion of labor, he views law as a purposive instrument for the attainment of broadly democratic reforms, including, presumably, trust-busting

---

[50] Ibid., pp. 224–225.

and workmen's compensation. He recognizes, however, that specific programs for the disadvantaged will accomplish little so long as society's archaic values remain unchanged. The laissez-faire mentality of the nineteenth century must be replaced by a more social ethic, and this can only be accomplished through a massive program of "reeducation," or what, in today's jargon, would be termed "consciousness-raising."

"Go away from all this and get straightened out," Krebs urges Hugh Paret.

> Make yourself acquainted with the modern trend in literature and criticism, with modern history, find out what's being done in the field of education, read the modern sciences, especially biology, and psychology and sociology, and try to get a glimpse of the fundamental human needs underlying such phenomena as the labour and woman's movements. . . . I don't mean to say we can ever see the whole, but we can get a clew, an idea, and pass it on to our children."[51]

Convinced, Hugh drops out of the corporate rat race and rejoins his estranged wife, resolved to give his children the kind of scientific and socialistic upbringing they will need to cope with life in twentieth-century America.

Other novelists and playwrights added little to the Paret stereotype. The principal traits of the corporation lawyer remained constant from work to work: an old-stock WASP background; extensive formal education, including college and law school; affiliation with one of the new corporate law firms; a narrowly technical and manipulative view of the law; and a cynical acceptance of socially harmful business practices. Some authors did probe more deeply into the institutional aspects of the great Wall Street firms that arose at the end of the nineteenth century to serve the needs of a corporate clientele. By focusing upon the structural changes and personal conflicts that took place *within* these "law factories," Albion W. Tourgée, Arthur Train, and others cast further light upon the modernization of legal practice.[52]

---

[51] Ibid., pp. 483–484.
[52] See, especially, Albion W. Tourgée, *With Gauge and Swallow, Attorneys* (Philadelphia: Lippincott, 1889) and Arthur Train, *Ambition* (New York: Grosset & Dunlap, 1928). For a picture of life in a Wall Street firm today, see Louis Auchincloss, *The Partners* (Boston: Houghton Mifflin, 1974) and John Jay Osborn, Jr., *The Associates* (Boston: Houghton Mifflin, 1979).

Although a restrictive stereotype of the corporation lawyer became standard, novelists and playwrights showed some flexibility in creating updated versions of the "people's lawyer." To offset the alleged commercialism and class-consciousness of the metropolitan bar, they offered their readers an idealized image of the rural practitioner. Often the butt of humor or satire in antebellum literature, small-town attorneys now became effective symbols of professional integrity and resistance to the dehumanizing tendencies of the corporate state. As community leaders who represented all types of clients, they preserved the *noblesse oblige* attitude of the antebellum elite and found their greatest satisfaction in public service.

"Frankly, I would not exchange my particular lot in this life with any man," observes a practitioner from a small midwestern town in Arthur M. Harris's *Letters to a Young Lawyer* (1912):

> Most of the old settlers, as you know, refer their disputes to me, and my opinion is accepted by them as unquestioningly as if it were a mandate of the Supreme Court of the United States. This is well, and as it should be. The true lawyer is a pacifier, not a provoker. His efforts are more than commercial, higher and nobler than merely mercenary. On his integrity and good sense depend the well-being, not only of individuals in their petty differences, but also of the community as a whole, which prospers when time is saved by a peaceable settlement of disputes, and money goes into the land, instead of into the county treasury for costs, or into the pockets of ravenous lawyers for fees.[53]

Despite their nostalgia for a more stable agrarian society, few small-town lawyers can escape the inroads of corporate growth. Sam Randolph, the hero of Henry A. Shute's *The Country Lawyer* (1911), spends much of his time fighting the efforts of a New York corporation to establish a racetrack in the Edenic countryside of New Hampshire; another New Hampshire practitioner, "T. Thorndyke, Attorney-at-Law," battles unsuccessfully in the state courts against a large paper mill that refuses to pay damages to an injured employee;

[53] Arthur M. Harris, *Letters to a Young Lawyer* (St. Paul: West Publishing Co., 1912), pp. 58–59.

and in "Heart's Desire," New Mexico, attorney Dan Anderson must thwart the land-grabbing schemes of an Eastern railroad.[54]

Professional migration from country to city occurs as often in Progressive fiction as it did in antebellum literature. Judge Isaac Furman, a character in Arthur Train's novel *Ambition* (1928), is but one of a long line of small-town crusaders who bring their democratic sympathies and passion for social justice to the centers of corporate power. The best known of these old-fashioned idealists in the early twentieth century was Ephraim Tutt, another of Train's creations and the homespun hero of innumerable stories in the *Saturday Evening Post*. Described as "a combination of Robin Hood, Abraham Lincoln, Puck and Uncle Sam,"[55] Mr. Tutt successfully defended the rights of the little man for a quarter of a century and was the most popular lawyer in American fiction prior to Perry Mason.

In addition to such country types, who represented old-stock Americanism, the ranks of fictional "people's lawyers" broadened around the turn of the century to include a few women and minority practitioners. Novelists began to give serious consideration to women's capacity for legal practice as early as 1886, when Maurice Thompson published his semiautobiographical *A Banker of Bankersville*. Marian Wilton, the heroine of this work, is the daughter of a small-town college president and an advocate of women's rights. Under the direction of a young male attorney, she pursues a course of intensive reading for the bar, and Thompson leaves no doubt that she is intellectually qualified to enter the profession. She succumbs, however, to prevailing Victorian conceptions of sex roles and abandons her career aspirations for the delights of marriage and housekeeping.

Gender prejudices also figure strongly in Leroy Scott's *Counsel for the Defense* (1912), the first significant treatment of a woman lawyer in American fiction. Katherine West, a Vassar graduate and licensed attorney, returns, to her home town to defend her father, a local doctor, against a false criminal charge. She soon finds herself the object of community censure for presuming to engage in an occupation traditionally reserved for men. "No self-respecting wom-

---

[54] Herbert I. Goss, *T. Thorndyke, Attorney-at-Law* (Boston: C. M. Clark Publishing Co., 1907); Emerson Hough, *Heart's Desire* (New York: Macmillan, 1905).
[55] Arthur Train, *Yankee Lawyer: The Autobiography of Ephraim Tutt* (Chicago: Consolidated Book Publishers, 1944), p. x.

anly woman would ever think of wanting to be a lawyer," complain the housewives of the town. "Everybody knows her reason for being a lawyer is only that it gives her a greater chance to be with the men."[56]

Undaunted, Katherine continues her search for evidence that will clear her father's name. Acting more like a detective than a lawyer, she uncovers and defeats a sinister plot by a big-city corporation to take over the municipally owned water works, of which her father is superintendent. In the process she disarms local prejudice and vindicates her right to an independent career. The most stubborn resistance to changing gender roles comes from her future husband, newspaper editor Arnold Bruce, with whom she argues the claims of the "new woman":

> "I demand for myself the right that all men possess as a matter of course—the right to work!"
>
> "If you must work," he cried, a little exasperated, "why, of course, you can help in the housework."
>
> "But I also demand the right to choose my work. Why should I do work which I do not like, for which I have no aptitude, and which I should do poorly, and give up work which interests me, for which I have been trained, and for which I believe I have an aptitude? . . . Try to understand me—please do, please do. Work is a necessity of life to you. It is also a necessity of life to me. I'm fighting with you for the right to work. I'm fighting with you for my life!"[57]

Sex discrimination gives way to racial prejudice as a dominant theme in the literature of minority practitioners. Paul Laurence Dunbar's powerful story, "One Man's Fortunes," traces the abortive efforts of a talented young black to enter the legal profession in turn-of-the-century Ohio. After graduating from the state university, Bertram Halliday returns to his home town of Broughton (Dayton), resolved to become a lawyer. He applies unsuccessfully for work in the office of H. G. Featherton, a white attorney, who seeks to dissuade him from thoughts of a legal career: "I say the law is a hard profession to get on in, and as a friend I say that it will be harder for

---

[56] Leroy Scott, *Counsel for the Defense* (New York: A. L. Burt Co., 1912), p. 82
[57] Ibid., pp. 284–286.

you. Your people have not the money to spend in litigation of any kind, . . . [and] the time has not come when a white person will employ a colored attorney."[58]

Unable to find any job commensurate with his abilities, Halliday becomes a janitor at a local factory and continues to study law at home in the evenings. As an important election approaches, he receives an unexpected summons from Featherton, who has decided to run for judicial office and now invites him to become his law clerk. Convinced that he will be judged hereafter on his merits, Halliday accepts the position and works tirelessly on Featherton's behalf among the black voters. Once Featherton wins the election, he dismisses Halliday and hires a white law student in his place. With his old job at the factory no longer available, an embittered Halliday prepares to seek employment as a schoolteacher in some Southern state:

> Nothing so breaks a man's spirit as defeat, constant, unaltering, hopeless defeat. That's what I've experienced. I am still studying law in a half-hearted way for I don't know what I am going to do with it when I have been admitted. Diplomas don't draw clients. We have been taught that merit wins. But I have learned that the adages, as well as the books and the formulas were made by and for others than us of the black race.[59]

In sharp contrast to the educated Halliday is Lawyer Carmichael, a minor character in Clement Wood's *Nigger* (1922), who operates out of a musty office above the Magic City Billiard Parlors in Birmingham, Alabama. A self-styled "hustler" with no formal schooling, Carmichael learned his letters and his law from "ol' Judge Head, uv Tuscumbia," whose office he swept out every day. The judge's instruction enabled him to pass the state bar examination and launched him on a long and continuing career as an advocate for the black community. "I began as a cawn-fiel' nigger," he tells a group of admiring youngsters; "now I'm a successful practitioner in all the cou'ts uv law 'n' equity, includin' the Soopreme Cou't. An' w'ut I's done, you kin do." Yet he discourages other blacks on pragmatic grounds from taking up the study of law: "Thar's nothin' in it, for a black man. I pays my rent; that's about all. Niggers ain' got no

---

[58] Paul Laurence Dunbar, *The Strength of Gideon and Other Stories* (New York: Arno Press and *The New York Times*, 1969), p. 144.
[59] Ibid., p. 160.

sense nohow; they takes all their cases to white lawyers. W'ut with a white judge 'n' a white jury, they ain' got much chance nohow."[60]

An occasional writer presented a more positive view of the black practitioner, but only at the expense of some special pleading. Otis M. Shackelford's *Lillian Simmons; or, The Conflict of Sections* (1915) features a middle-aged black attorney whose career in an unidentified Northern city at first follows a familiar course. Frank Maxwell, an "educated man," had "completed a course in law in a Northern college and had at one time belonged to the Bar Association. But on account of a lack of practice, he was forced to abandon the profession, and at fifty without the care of a family, he was custodian of one of the large down town bank buildings." Improvement lies ahead, however, as Shackelford's book turns into a brief for black separatism and racial solidarity in the face of white repression. Once these principles are accepted by the black community, a new era of prosperity dawns for minority business people and professionals. Frank Maxwell returns to his law practice, assured this time of a supportive black clientele. "His people are patronizing him," Shackelford concludes. "He often lectures to them, and is now advocating the doctrine of unity, and patronage of one's own enterprises."[61]

If the black lawyer was usually depicted as a champion of racial justice, the Jewish lawyer appeared as a civil libertarian in much Progressive fiction. Paul Stollberg, a character in Robert Herrick's *Waste* (1924), is a typical example of the breed. An immigrant from Europe, Stollberg is a self-made man who, like Hermann Krebs, has worked his way through "a large eastern law school" and established a good practice at the Chicago bar. "Like many others who had come to America as to a heaven," Herrick observes, "he cared more for the basic principles of his adopted land than did Americans of older blood."[62] During the Red Scare of 1919 Stollberg proves to be one of the few lawyers in Chicago who is willing to defend the rights of radical clients.

These variant types of "people's lawyers"—women, blacks, Jews—represented only minor deviations from a still dominant Anglo-Saxon norm. Until World War I, legal heroes in fiction and

---

[60] Clement Wood, *Nigger* (New York: Dutton & Co., 1922), pp. 100, 101.
[61] Otis M. Shackelford, *Lillian Simmons; or, The Conflict of Sections* (11th ed.; Kansas City, Mo.: McNerney & Corrigan, 1927), pp. 53–54, 203.
[62] Robert Herrick, *Waste* (London: Jonathan Cape, 1924), p. 365.

drama remained overwhelmingly WASP, reflecting the limited influence that women and minority professionals in fact enjoyed within the bar and in the public consciousness. Indeed, the basic components of the "people's lawyer" stereotype remained substantially unchanged from antebellum days, except for the addition of formal law school training. The prototypical "people's lawyer" continued to come from an old WASP family, and from a Western or rural background in which a Lincolnesque concern for the common people still prevailed. Typically, too, he remained a solo practitioner, although he might sometimes be found in government service—in the Justice Department, as in David Graham Phillips' *The Fashionable Adventures of Joshua Craig* (1909), or as a state or local prosecutor, as in William Sage's *The District Attorney* (1906).

Although ethnicity played only a minor role in shaping the image of the "people's lawyer," it was crucial in defining a new professional underclass of "shysters." According to Richard Rovere, the term "shyster" derived from a New York attorney named Scheuster, whose offensive courtroom manners so infuriated the justices of the Essex Market Police Court in the 1840s that they took to rebuking other lawyers for "Scheuster practices."[63] By the end of the century the old "pettifogger" label, with its Anglo-Saxon connotations, had largely dropped out of use and the modern "shysters" tended overwhelmingly to be Irish Catholics or Jews from eastern Europe. In one of his "Mr. Tutt" stories, Arthur Train provides a revealing glimpse of the stereotyping process at work, as Mr. Tutt ponders the implications of shysterism with his partner and managing clerk:

> "A shyster," said Mr. Tutt, reading from the Century Dictionary, "is defined as 'one who does business trickily; a person without professional honor; used chiefly of lawyers.'"
> "I nominate for the first pedestal in our Hall of Legal Ill Fame—Raphael B. Hogan," announced Tutt [George Tutt, Mr. Tutt's partner].
> "But he's a very elegant and gentlemanly person," objected Miss Wiggin as she warmed the cups. "My idea of a shyster is a down-at-the-heels, unshaved and generally disreputable-looking police-court lawyer—preferably with a red nose—who murders the English language—and who makes his living by preying upon the ignorant and helpless."
> "Like Finklestein?" suggested Tutt.

[63] Richard H. Rovere, *Howe & Hummel* (New York: Farrar, Straus, 1947), p. 30.

"Exactly!" agreed Miss Wiggin. "Like Finklestein."

"He's one of the most honorable men I know!" protested Mr. Tutt. "My dear Minerva, you are making the great mistake—common, I confess, to a large number of people—of associating dirt and crime. Now dirt may breed crime, but crime doesn't necessarily breed dirt."

"You don't have to be shabby to prey upon the ignorant and helpless," argued Tutt. "Some of our most prosperous brethren are the worst sharks out of Sing Sing."[64]

The notorious firm of Howe & Hummel, which flourished in New York City between 1869 and 1907, provided a real-life model for writers interested in the seamier side of professional life. Arthur Train drew directly upon his knowledge of Howe & Hummel's practices in writing *The Confessions of Artemas Quibble* (1911), an amusing account of a pair of professional rogues whose bag of tricks includes blackmail, fraud, and perjury. Less derivative was Samuel B. Ornitz's *Haunch Paunch and Jowl* (1923), the finest fictional treatment of a turn-of-the-century shyster and the society that sustained him.

Meyer Hirsch, Ornitz's protagonist and narrator, is a Russian Jew who grows up in poverty on New York's East Side. A clever and ambitious youngster, he manages to make good grades in school while directing the operations of a teen-age Jewish gang on the side. Prodded by his Uncle Philip, a ruthless sweatshop operator, he attends classes at City College and later goes to law school. After his admission to the bar he forms a partnership with his friend Maxie Freund, and settles down to exploit his immigrant neighbors.

Hirsch and Freund establish their offices in a store across from the Essex Market Courthouse, beneath a garish swinging sign that advertises the word "Lawyer" in three languages: English, Yiddish, and Russian. Clients swarm down upon them almost at once, and the partners soon develop an effective working relationship:

I keep the political irons hot, fix the cops, do all the backing and filling in connection with the criminal cases. I split fees with court clerks, attendants, keepers, detectives, policemen, their superiors, saloon-keepers—anybody who will bring us cases. I take care of the boys all the

---

[64] Arthur Train, "The Shyster," in *By Advice of Counsel* (New York: Scribner's, 1925), pp. 9–10.

way down the line from the judge on the bench to the bootblack in the criminal courts' hallway. Maxie' s province is the civil courts, and his skill and subtlety as a cross-examiner along new lines have already earned him a reputation. But Maxie knows that legal knowledge only, on the part of a lawyer, even plus cleverness and preparation—entitles a lawyer to starve in New York courts. So he keeps his hand in the political grab-bag and is a note broker; only judges' notes. . . . Maxie's system was simple. All he wanted was the good will of the jurist. He did not ask any outright preference from the finicky and the fourflushers, just wanted the shade on his side. Soon the judges found it was safe to rule in his favor. . . . So, the notes bore fruits of perennial bloom. Judges became our steerers.[65]

Business continues to prosper, as Hirsch organizes the pushcart peddlers into a "Protective Association," helps to introduce gang warfare into labor disputes, and becomes the attorney for the pimps and prostitutes of the ghetto. He cultivates the orthodox Jews as well through regular attendance at the synagogue, and builds up a strong political machine on the East Side: "I am a lawyer, politician, champion of Jewry and member of a dozen Jewish lodges, societies and charity organizations. I became a Professional Jew in emulation of the successful Irish politician whose principal capital is being a Professional Irishman."[66] When a personal scandal threatens to end his political career, he negotiates with the leaders of the opposition party for an appointment to the bench of the Superior Criminal Court, offering in return to suppress an explosive sex case involving his client, a janitor's daughter, and a millionaire reformer. The newspapers, ignorant of the true state of affairs, hail his appointment as a triumph for the principle of a nonpartisan judiciary.

As Hirsch's career suggests, the muckraking impulse did not spare judges and courts. To antebellum writers the judicial system had seemed the embodiment of republican virtue and neutrality; now it was commonly perceived as an instrument of corporate oppression and class rule. Clarence Darrow's series of short stories titled *Easy Lessons in Law*, which appeared in Hearst's Chicago *Evening American* in 1902, attacked the bases of laissez-faire jurisprudence by focusing on the legal rules that governed liability for industrial

---

[65] [Samuel B. Ornitz], *Haunch Paunch and Jowl: An Anonymous Autobiography* (New York: Boni & Liveright, 1923), pp. 206–207.
[66] Ibid., p. 183.

accidents. Through dramatized case histories Darrow exposed the brutal exploitation of workers and their families that resulted from such judicially created employer defenses as the Fellow Servant Rule and the Doctrine of Assumed Risk.[67] Theodore Dreiser described the operation of the criminal justice system from a similar legal realist perspective in *An American Tragedy* (1925).

Other authors muckraked the courts by applying the insights of early behavioral psychology to the careers of fictitious judges. William Allen White's novel *In the Heart of a Fool* (1918) provided an exhaustive account of the personal and environmental influences that shaped the character of a corrupt Kansas judge; in *The Federal Judge* (1899) Charles K. Lush examined the ways in which appointment to the lower federal bench might alter a simple man's attitudes toward wealth and status.

Even the United States Supreme Court came under sharp attack from Progressive critics as the result of a series of controversial decisions. During the first five months of 1895, the Court refused to apply the Sherman Act against the notorious Sugar Trust, invalidated a popular and well-publicized federal income tax law, and approved the issuance by federal judges of sweeping injunctions against workers in labor disputes. [68] The cumulative impact these decisions had on the public mind was great and lasting. Thereafter, few writers overlooked the political power of the Court, or depicted the Justices as dispassionate Olympians. Twentieth-century authors have rather emphasized the all-too-human motives and stratagems at work in judicial deliberations, finding excitement and intrigue where the Victorians sensed only gentle intellectual discourse.

The image of a politicized Court, which dominated the fiction of the Progressive era, found its earliest expression in several Utopian novels that were written in direct response to the conservative decisions of 1895. Each of these thinly disguised tracts followed a

---

[67] For a thorough summary and analysis of Darrow's newspaper stories, which have not been republished, see Abe C. Ravitz, *Clarence Darrow and the American Literary Tradition* (Cleveland: The Press of Western Reserve University, 1962), pp. 43–69. According to the Fellow Servant Rule, an employee could not recover damages from an employer for on-the-job injuries sustained through the negligence of a fellow employee; the Doctrine of Assumed Risk held that "dangers normally and necessarily incident to the occupation" of a given individual are undertaken at his or her risk, not at the risk of the employer.

[68] The decisions referred to are *United States v. E. C. Knight & Co.*, 156 U.S. 1 (1895); *Pollock v. Farmers' Loan & Trust Co.*, 158 U.S. 601 (1895); and *In re Debs*, 158 U.S. 564 (1895).

similar plot line, and each called for a "peaceful" or "legal" revolution to restore political power to the people. Since, according to the authors, every branch of the government was controlled by powerful corporate interests, fundamental change could only be brought about through the assembling of a "people's convention" to rewrite the Constitution. The new charter invariably granted to the federal government regulatory powers that had been denied by the Supreme Court. Its ratification by a nationwide popular referendum signaled the beginning of a golden age of political justice.

Henry O. Morris, whose *Waiting for the Signal* (1897) went through several printings, dramatized the people's case against the Court more effectively than other Utopian novelists. Morris did not balk at introducing living persons into his story and rather appropriately permitted labor organizer Eugene Debs to deliver the principal attack on the high bench:

> The money power now dominates every department of justice, even to the Supreme bench [Debs asserts]. It is not possible for a poor man to get into the Supreme Court. It is omnipotent and answerable to nobody. A short time ago Congress passed a law taxing the rich of the country, and this court adjudged it unconstitutional. If this law had been a tax on the poor, it would have been all right. Under the laws of the land the rich are always right, the poor are always wrong.[69]

Through its subservience to corporate wealth the Court unwittingly starts a revolution. Under pressure from the "multimillionaires," the Justices declare that all labor organizations are proscribed by the Sherman Act. Thereupon the workers go underground, form secret revolutionary lodges, ally with other discontented social groups, and prepare to take over the government. On May 1, successful, and generally bloodless, coups occur across the country. Only in New York City—the cesspool of corporate America, in Utopian thinking—does widespread violence and destruction result, as the plutocrats hire an army of criminals to resist the people's forces. Once order is restored, the commanding general calls for the election of delegates to a constitutional convention. This body, which meets in Chicago on July 4, drafts a people's constitution that guarantees employment to every person, revives the income tax,

---

[69] Henry O. Morris, *Waiting for the Signal* (Chicago: Schulte Publishing Co., 1897), p. 228.

toughens the antitrust laws, and nationalizes the railroads and telegraph companies.

Morris provided his readers with the complete text of the new constitution, whose stipulations concerning the judiciary are instructive. Except for limiting judicial tenure to a single term of eight years, the framers left the basic powers of the Supreme Court intact. They did, however, add several sections that were aimed at curbing some recent abuses of the judicial function. Article III, section 4, declared:

> Injunction[s] shall not be granted for light or trivial causes. No court shall have power to issue an injunction restraining a citizen or citizens from leaving the employment of any individual or corporation or from assembling on the public highways.[70]

And section 5 drastically curtailed the power of federal judges to punish for contempt.

More radical assaults upon judicial independence appeared in the model constitution proposed by Frederick Upham Adams in his novel *President John Smith* (1897). Adams advocated a majoritarian democratic state in which the popular will could not be overridden by any governmental agency. Accordingly, his constitution denied the Supreme Court jurisdiction over all "laws passed by the people of the United States."[71] Since every major piece of legislation had to be referred to the people for approval or rejection, Adams's system left the Justices with relatively little to do. They were required to furnish Congress with advisory opinions on the constitutionality of pending measures, but their advice might be ignored. If, despite these restrictions, they ever proved troublesome, they might be removed from office by a majority vote of the people.

While the Utopian novelists fitted the Court into cosmic visions, other writers of the early twentieth century probed more deeply into judicial values by concentrating on particular decisions. In *The Radical* (1907), a Socialist novel, Isaac Kahn Friedman showed how one Justice had been inexorably conditioned by his socioeconomic background to vote against the constitutionality of a child labor law. "And of those others [on the Court]," Friedman added, "shall it not be said that they were human, therefore fallible too, swayed by the

---

[70] Ibid., p. 350.
[71] Frederick Upham Adams, *President John Smith,* reprint ed. (New York: Arno Press and The *New York Times*, 1971). p. 242.

prejudgments and the class consciousness of those to whom they owe birth, education and power, as unable to represent abstract justice as democracy to phrase it!"[72]

Liberal novelists, although less deterministic, were equally outraged at the Court's penchant for upholding property rights at the expense of social welfare. They suggested, however, that the conditions of professional training might be primarily responsible for judicial callousness. Robert Herrick's *A Life for a Life* (1910) portrayed the Justices as ancient logic machines, programmed to respond only to the legal formulae of a preindustrial age. When a government lawyer in an important antitrust case urges public policy considerations upon the Court, one Justice inquires irritably: "Is it law or equity you are discussing?"[73] The defendant corporation wins the case, because its counsel avoids all mention of justice or morality, and argues instead from "irreproachable logic." Herrick's scene imaginatively captures the formalism of American jurisprudence at the turn of the century. Until the ideas of the legal realists became dominant in the 1920s and 1930s, law was commonly regarded as an objective science whose progress depended upon a strict adherence to established precedents, regardless of their social consequences.

But reformers might also wield precedents effectively, as demonstrated by David Graham Phillips in *The Fashionable Adventures of Joshua Craig* (1909). Josh Craig, the hero of this novel of manners, is a Lincolnian type, a crude but crafty Westerner who comes to Washington to serve as Deputy Attorney General. Handed an almost hopeless case to argue on his first appearance before the Court, Craig confounds all expectations by winning a victory for the government. The key to his success, Phillips makes clear, lay in his style of advocacy, not in the fairmindedness of the Justices:

> Never was there a better court manner; the Justices, who had been anticipating an opportunity to demonstrate, at his expense, the exceeding dignity of the Supreme Court, could only admire and approve. As for his speech, it was a straightway argument; not a superfluous or a sophomoric word, not an attempt at rhetoric. . . . There is the logic that is potent but answerable; there is the logic that is unanswerable, that gives no opportunity to any sane mind, however prejudiced by association with dispensers of luxurious hospitality, of vintage wines and dollar cigars,

[72] I. K. Friedman, *The Radical* (New York: Appleton, 1907), p. 337.
[73] Robert Herrick, *A Life for a Life* (New York: Macmillan, 1910), p. 222.

however enamored of fog-fighting and hair-splitting, to refuse the unqualified assent of conviction absolute. That was the kind of argument Josh Craig made. And the faces of the opposing lawyers, the questions the Justices asked him plainly showed that he had won.[74]

Despite their occasional insights into judicial behavior, the novelists and playwrights of the early twentieth century did not succeed in creating a believable picture of the Court at work. They found it difficult to translate their political and economic concerns, such as trust busting, into dramatic courtroom material; they knew little about appellate procedure and nothing of the Court's internal administration; and they were singularly inept at drawing flesh-and-blood judicial characters. The Justices of Phillips and Herrick are as abstract and stereotyped as those of any antebellum writer: They continue to be aged, passionless creatures whose sole function is to protect from democratic contamination a body of obsolete legal precepts.

Nonfiction writers offered the public a more impressive revisionist view of the Court during these same years. Charles Warren's *The Supreme Court in United States History* (1922) and Gustavus Myers's *History of the Supreme Court of the United States* (1912) broke important new ground in their treatment of the high bench and humanized the work of the Justices far better than any contemporary fiction. Warren explored in rich detail the political dimensions of decision making, including the public's response to major Court pronouncements. "The reaction of the people to judicially declared law has been an especially important factor in the development of the country," he reminded his readers; "for while the Judges' decision makes law, it is often the people's view of the decision which makes history."[75] Warren's sympathetic, but not uncritical, appraisal of the Court's past record relied heavily on newspaper, periodical, and manuscript sources that provided future commentators with a fund of colorful anecdote.

Myers's work, on the other hand, was a vigorous Socialist critique that combed the public records for evidence of the Justices' corporate connections and financial dealings. This information Myers used to

---

[74] David Graham Phillips, *The Fashionable Adventures of Joshua Craig* (New York: Grosset & Dunlap, 1909), p. 75.
[75] Charles Warren, *The Supreme Court in United States History*, rev. ed. (Boston: Little, Brown, 1926), 1: 3.

support his thesis that the Court had always represented the interests of a dominant capitalist class, whose actions it legitimized through its decisions. In analyzing the Court as a capitalist institution, however, Myers was careful not to impute any personal wrongdoing to the Justices. "The influences so consistently operating upon the minds and acts of the incumbents were not venal, but class, influences," he noted, "and were all the more effective for the very reason that the Justices in question were not open to pecuniarily dishonest practices."[76] Muckraking novelists might have profited greatly from a reading of this book, but it produced no significant literary reverberations. Not until the 1960s would writers achieve a credible portrayal of the Court in American fiction.[77]

III

Epilogue: Into the Space Age

"Let me quote from the Interplanetary Charter, Article One, Section Two. 'The jurisdiction of the aforesaid Commission shall extend to all members of the Solar System and its component bodies, planets, moons, satellites, asteroids, meteors, comets, flotsam and jetsam; and the space surrounding them.' But Comet X is not a member or body of the Solar System. It came from another System, or perhaps another Universe."

"I knowed it! I knowed it!" chortled Jem. "Leave it ta Kerry Dale ta think up some doodad."

Nat Schachner, *Space Lawyer* (1953)

Momentous changes have taken place in American life since the Progressive period ended in the cynical aftermath of World War I. New forms of mass communication, such as radio and television, have arisen. American society has grown more pluralistic, as organized ethnic minorities have won greater political and economic power. The continuing struggle for social justice—from the New Deal initiatives of the 1930s to the antipoverty programs of today—has added enormously to the store of popular material on law and lawyers. Yet the terms of public discourse have changed relatively

---

[76] Gustavus Myers, *History of the Supreme Court of the United States* (Chicago: Charles H. Kerr & Co., 1918), p. 8.
[77] See, for example, Andrew Tully, *Supreme Court* (New York: Simon and Schuster, 1963); William Woolfolk, *Opinion of the Court* (Garden City, N.Y.: Doubleday, 1966).

little since the Progressive era, and the unresolved problems of that time still provide basic themes for discussion in our contemporary mass media. Some modifications have occurred, of course. The domestic trust has been replaced in the scale of villainy by the multinational corporation; administrative government, once hailed as a panacea, is now perceived as an additional source of oppression; and "people's lawyers" these days tend to be largely female, black, or ethnic and spend much of their time combating the abuses of a WASP-dominated legal system.[78]

Those who interpret the law to popular audiences continue to perform a valuable service to society by encouraging their fellow citizens to reflect on contemporary social problems. In today's impersonal and computerized world this humanistic function—translating legal abstractions into meaningful human terms—takes on even greater significance. With the decline of juries and the fragmentation of community life, popular checks on the law through appeals to community mores have weakened. The media help to maintain a balance between mass behavior and legal rules, and to keep open the avenues to peaceful change. As Hugo Black once justly observed, "The right to think, speak, and write freely . . . is the most precious privilege of citizens vested with power to select public policies and public officials."[79]

[78] On the abuses of the multinational corporation, see Jonathan Ryder, *Trevayne* (New York: Delacorte Press, 1973) and Brian Garfield, *The Villiers Touch* (New York: Delacorte Press, 1970). Malfunctioning programs of the welfare state receive attention in R. J. Meaddough, *The Retarded Genius* (New York: Troisième Canadian Publishers, 1978) and Oliver Cote, *Going Down* (San Pedro: Singlejack Books, 1979). Contemporary "people's lawyers" appear in A. L. Conroy, *Storefront Lawyers* (New York: Bantam Books, 1970); Albert Gerber, *The Lawyer* (New York: World Publishing Co., 1972); John Nicholas Iannuzzi, *Courthouse* (Garden City, N.Y.: Doubleday, 1975); and Richard Kluger, *Star Witness* (Garden City, N.Y.: Doubleday, 1979).

[79] Hugo LaFayette Black, *A Constitutional Faith* (New York: Knopf, 1968), p. 43.

Bibliographical Essay

Historians have barely begun to study the complex ways in which law and popular literature interact. Patricia Kane's pioneering dissertation, "Legal Fictions: The Lawyer in the American Novel" (Ph.D. dissertation, Dept. of Modern Language and Literature, University of Minnesota, 1961), surveys changing professional mores as reflected in one important literary genre, but concentrates almost exclusively on the works of major authors from Cooper to Cozzens. Kane has also published a valuable essay on the legal fiction of Louis Auchincloss: "Lawyers at the Top: The Fiction of Louis Auchincloss," *Critique* 7 (1964–1965):36–45.

Other literary surveys that touch on legal topics in a useful way include: Gordon Milne, *The American Political Novel* (Norman: University of Oklahoma Press, 1966); Joseph Blotner, *The Modern American Political Novel, 1900–1960* (Austin: University of Texas Press, 1966); Walter B. Rideout, *The Radical Novel in the United States, 1900–1954* (Cambridge: Harvard University Press, 1956); Arthur Hobson Quinn, *A History of the American Drama from the Beginning to the Civil War* (2d ed.; New York: F. S. Crofts & Co., 1943), and Quinn, *A History of the American Drama from the Civil War to the Present Day* (New York: F. S. Crofts & Co., 1945); Ima Honaker Herron, *The Small Town in American Drama* (Dallas: Southern Methodist University Press, 1969); Caspar H. Nannes, *Politics in the American Drama* (Washington, D.C.: Catholic University of America Press, 1960); Malcolm Goldstein, *The Political Stage: American Drama and Theater of the Great Depression* (New York: Oxford University Press, 1974); Doris E. Abramson, *Negro Playwrights in the American*

174

Theatre, 1925–1959 (New York: Columbia University Press, 1967); Frank Luther Mott, *Golden Multitudes: The Story of Best Sellers in the United States* (New York: Macmillan, 1947); and James D. Hart, *The Popular Book: A History of America's Literary Taste* (New York: Oxford University Press, 1950). For annotated bibliographies of legal fiction, see John Henry Wigmore, "A List of One Hundred Legal Novels," *Illinois Law Review* 17 (1922):26, and Karen L. Kretschman, *Legal Novels: An Annotated Bibliography* (Austin: University of Texas Law School Foundation, 1976).

Several specialized studies explore the creative interplay between law and literature in antebellum America. David Brion Davis's *Homicide in American Fiction, 1798–1860* (Ithaca, N.Y.: Cornell University Press, 1957) combines research in psychology, criminal law, and popular literature to produce a fascinating account of changing concepts of responsibility for intentional killing in the early nineteenth century. Maxwell Bloomfield, in *American Lawyers in a Changing Society, 1776–1876* (Cambridge: Harvard University Press, 1976), analyzes a broad range of legal and literary materials in evaluating popular perceptions of lawyers and their work. For an insightful discussion of the legal influences that helped to shape the work of a major writer, see Jill Louise McKinney, "Herman Melville and the Law" (Ph.D. dissertation, Dept. of English, University of Pennsylvania, 1975). Two recent path-breaking books provide essential information on the evolution of legal institutions and values: Morton J. Horwitz, *The Transformation of American Law, 1780–1860* (Cambridge: Harvard University Press, 1977) and William E. Nelson, *Americanization of the Common Law: The Impact of Legal Change on Massachusetts Society, 1760–1830* (Cambridge: Harvard University Press, 1975).

The legal and literary trends of the late nineteenth century both found expression in the career of attorney Clarence Darrow. Abe C. Ravitz's *Clarence Darrow and the American Literary Tradition* (Cleveland: Press of Western Reserve University, 1962) skillfully relates Darrow's fiction to his philosophy of law reform. Changing legal and social values, as reflected in magazine articles and fiction, are discussed in Maxwell H. Bloomfield, *Alarms and Diversions: The American Mind through American Magazines, 1900–1914* (The Hague: Mouton & Co., 1967). Theodore P. Greene's *America's Heroes: The Changing Models of Success in American Magazines* (New York: Oxford University Press, 1970) explores the waning attractiveness of lawyers as role models in turn-of-the-century America. Donald G. Baker, in "The Lawyer in Popular Fiction," *Journal of Popular Culture* 3 (Winter 1969):493–516, examines the image of the lawyer in selected best sellers from 1900 to 1960.

Valuable studies of law and social change in modern America include Robert H. Wiebe, *The Search for Order, 1877–1920* (New York: Hill and

Wang, 1967); James Weinstein, *The Corporate Ideal in the Liberal State,
1900–1918* (Boston: Beacon Press, 1968); Jerold S. Auerbach, *Unequal
Justice: Lawyers and Social Change in Modern America* (New York: Oxford
University Press, 1976); and John W. Johnson, *American Legal Culture,
1908–1940* (Westport, Conn.: Greenwood Press, 1981). For informative
general surveys of American legal history, see Lawrence M. Friedman, *A
History of American Law* (New York: Simon and Schuster, 1973); James
Willard Hurst, *The Growth of American Law: The Law Makers* (Boston:
Little, Brown, 1950); and Grant Gilmore, *The Ages of American Law* (New
Haven: Yale University Press, 1977).

Finally, the legal fiction of other countries should not be ignored. Besides
illustrating unfamiliar doctrines and procedures, it offers many points of
comparison and contrast with our own system. Some representative legal
novels from England and France are discussed in John Marshall Gest, *The
Lawyer in Literature* (Boston: Boston Book Co., 1913); William S. Holdsworth, *Charles Dickens as a Legal Historian* (New Haven: Yale University
Press, 1929); Coral Lansbury, *The Reasonable Man: Trollope's Legal Fiction*
(Princeton, N. J.: Princeton University Press, 1981); Thomas Carbonneau,
"Balzacian Legality," *Rutgers Law Review* 32 (1979):719; and Jean
Marquiset, *Les Gens de Justice dans la Littérature* (Paris: R. Pichon et R.
Durand-Auzias, 1967).

STUDY QUESTIONS

1. How did professional life, as depicted in early novels and plays, reflect the idealism of a republican society?

2. Why did writers so often ridicule or condemn the country lawyer in antebellum literature?

3. Should lawyers be identified with their clients? Consider the case of the corporation lawyer. What arguments might be made in his or her defense?

4. Why did judicial power become a subject of serious popular concern by the end of the nineteenth century?

5. How can popular novels or films about the law contribute to the process of social change in a democratic society?

177

About the Authors

Carl S. Smith earned a B.A. in English and American Literature from Brown University and an M. Phil and Ph.D. in American Studies from Yale University. He is a member of the English department of Northwestern University, where he has been associated since 1979 with the Center for Urban Affairs and Policy Research. He helped found the Program in American Culture at Northwestern, and from 1979 to 1982 served as director. During the academic year 1977–1978, he was a fellow at the National Humanities Institute at the University of Chicago. He has received grants from Northwestern University and from the National Endowment for the Humanities. He has written on Dreiser, James, popular fiction, the painter Thomas Eakins, and, most recently, the literature of Chicago at the turn of the century.

John McWilliams received his B.A. from Princeton University and his M.A. and Ph.D. from Harvard University. He taught at the University of California, Berkeley, and the University of Illinois, Chicago Circle, before becoming Professor of American Literature at Middlebury College. He has received a Woodrow Wilson Fellowship, a Humanities Research Fellowship, and a National Endowment for the Humanities Fellowship. The author of many articles on American literary and historical subjects, he has published *Political Justice in a Republic: Fenimore Cooper's America* (1972) and has recently completed a book-length study of Hawthorne and Melville.

Maxwell Bloomfield received his B.A. from Rice University, an LL.B. from Harvard Law School (1957), and a Ph.D. in history from Tulane University in 1962. He is currently Professor of History at The Catholic University of America, where he has taught courses in American legal and constitutional history since 1966. From 1977 to 1980 he served as chairman of the History Department, and was Visiting Professor of American Legal History at the University of Virginia in 1973. A recipient of fellowships from the American Bar Foundation and Project '87, he is now completing a book on constitutional issues in modern American fiction. His previous publications include *American Lawyers in a Changing Society, 1776–1876* (1976), and he was recently appointed to the Committee on the History and Traditions of the Bar of the State Bar of Texas.

A Note on the Type

The text of this book was set in a computer version of Times Roman, designed by Stanley Morison for *The Times* (London) and first introduced by that newspaper in 1932.

Among typographers and designers of the twentieth century, Stanley Morison has been a strong forming influence as typographical adviser to the English Monotype Corporation, as a director of two distinguished English publishing houses, and as a writer of sensibility, erudition, and keen practical sense.

Typography by Barbara Sturman. Cover design by Maria Epes. Composition by The Saybrook Press, Inc., Old Saybrook, Connecticut. Printed and bound by Banta Company, Menasha, Wisconsin.

BORZOI BOOKS
IN LAW AND AMERICAN SOCIETY

Law and American History

EARLY AMERICAN LAW AND SOCIETY
Stephen Botein, *Michigan State University*

This volume consists of an essay dealing with the nature of law and early American socioeconomic development from the first settlements to 1776. The author shows how many legal traditions sprang both from English experience and from the influence of the New World. He explores the development of transatlantic legal structures in order to show how they helped rationalize intercolonial affairs. Mr. Botein also emphasizes the relationship between law and religion. The volume includes a pertinent group of documents for classroom discussion, and a bibliographic essay.

LAW IN THE NEW REPUBLIC: *Private Law and the Public Estate*
George Dargo, *Brookline, Massachusetts*

Though the American Revolution had an immediate and abiding impact on American public law (e.g., the formation of the federal and state constitutions), its effect on private law (e.g., the law of contracts, tort law) was less direct but of equal importance. Through essay and documents, Mr. Dargo examines post-Revolutionary public and private reform impulses and finds a shifting emphasis from public to private law which he terms "privatization." To further illustrate the tension between public and private law, the author develops a case study (the Batture land controversy in New Orleans) in early nineteenth century legal, economic, and political history. The volume includes a wide selection of documents and a bibliographic essay.

LAW IN ANTEBELLUM SOCIETY: *Legal Change and Economic Expansion*
Jamil Zainaldin, *Washington, D.C.*

This book examines legal change and economic expansion in the first half of the nineteenth century, integrating major themes in the development of law with key historical themes. Through a series of topical essays and the use of primary source materials, it describes how political, social, and economic interests and values influence law making. The book's focus is on legislation and the common law.

LAW AND THE NATION, 1865–1912
Jonathan Lurie, *Rutgers University*

Using the Fourteenth Amendment as the starting point for his essay, Mr. Lurie examines the ramifications of this landmark constitutional provision on the economic and social development of America in the years following the Civil War. He also explores important late nineteenth-century developments in legal education, and concludes his narrative with some insights on law and social change in the first decade of the twentieth century. The volume is highlighted by a documents section containing statutes, judicial opinions, and legal briefs, with appropriate questions for classroom discussion. Mr. Lurie's bibliographic essay provides information to stimulate further investigation of this period.

ORDERED LIBERTY: *Legal Reform in the Twentieth Century*
Gerald L. Fetner, *University of Chicago*

In an interpretive essay, the author examines the relationship between several major twentieth-century reform movements (e.g., Progressivism, New Deal, and the Great Society) and the law. He shows how policy makers turned increasingly to the legal community for assistance in accommodating economic and social conflict, and how the legal profession responded by formulating statutes, administrative agencies, and private arrangements. Mr. Fetner also discusses how the organization and character of the legal profession were affected by these social changes. Excerpts from relevant documents illustrate issues discussed in the essay. A bibliographic essay is included.

Law and Philosophy

DISCRIMINATION AND REVERSE DISCRIMINATION
Kent Greenawalt, *Columbia Law School*

Using discrimination and reverse discrimination as a model, Mr. Greenawalt examines the relationship between law and ethics. He finds that the proper role of law cannot be limited to grand theory concerning individual liberty and social restraint, but must address what law can effectively discover and accomplish. Such concepts as distributive and compensatory justice and utility are examined in the context of preferential treatment for blacks and other minorities. The analysis draws heavily on the Supreme Court's Bakke decision. The essay is followed by related documents, primarily judicial opinions, with notes and questions, and a bibliography.

THE LEGAL ENFORCEMENT OF MORALITY
Thomas Grey, *Stanford Law School*

This book deals with the traditional issue of whether morality can be legislated and enforced. It consists of an introductory essay and legal texts on three issues: the enforcement of sexual morality, the treatment of human remains, and the duties of potential rescuers. The author shows how philosophical problems differ from classroom hypotheticals when they are confronted in a legal setting. He illustrates this point using material from statutes, regulations, judicial opinions, and law review commentaries. Mr. Grey reviews the celebrated Hart-Devlin debate over the legitimacy of prohibiting homosexual acts. He places the challenging problem of how to treat dead bodies, arising out of developments in the technology of organ transplantation, in the context of the debate over morals enforcement, and discusses the Good Samaritan as an issue concerning the propriety of the legal enforcement of moral duties.

LEGAL REASONING
Martin Golding, *Duke University*

This volume is a blend of text and readings. The author explores the many sides to legal reasoning—as a study in judicial psychology and, in a more narrow sense, as an inquiry into the "logic" of judicial decision making. He shows how judges justify their rulings, and gives examples of the kinds of arguments they use. He challenges the notion that judicial reasoning is rationalization; instead, he argues that judges are guided by a deep concern for consistency and by a strong need to have their decisions stand as a measure for the future conduct of individuals. *(Forthcoming in 1984)*

Law and American Literature

LAW AND AMERICAN LITERATURE
A one-volume collection of the following three essays:

Law as Form and Theme in American Letters
Carl S. Smith, *Northwestern University*

The author explores the interrelationships between law aned literature generally and between American law and American literature in particular. He explores first the literary qualities of legal writing and then the attitudes of major American writers toward the law. Throughout, he studies the links between the legal and literary imaginations. He finds that legal writing has many literary qualities that are essential to its function, and he points out that American writers have long been wary of the power of the law and its special language, speaking out as a compensating voice for the ideal of justice.

Innocent Criminal or Criminal Innocence: The Trial in American Fiction
John McWilliams, *Middlebury College*

Mr. McWilliams explores how law functions as a standard for conduct in a number of major works of American literature, including Cooper's *The Pioneers,* Melville's *Billy Budd,* Dreiser's *An American Tragedy,* and Wright's *Native Son.* Each of these books ends in a criminal trial, in which the reader is asked to choose between his emotional sympathy for the victim and his rational understanding of society's need for criminal sanctions. The author compares these books with James Gould Cozzens' *The Just and the Unjust,* a study of a small town legal system, in which the people's sense of justice contravenes traditional authority.

Law and Lawyers in American Popular Culture
Maxwell Bloomfield, *Catholic University of America*

Melding law, literature, and the American historical experience into a single essay, Mr. Bloomfield discusses popular images of the lawyer. The author shows how contemporary values and attitudes toward the law are reflected in fiction. He concentrates on two historical periods: antebellum America and the Progressive era. He examines fictional works which were not always literary classics, but which exposed particular legal mores. An example of such a book is Winston Churchill's *A Far Country* (1915), a story of a successful corporation lawyer who abandons his practice to dedicate his life to what he believes are more socially desirable objectives.